T4-AJS-426

Trotsky and Djilas

Recent Titles in
Contributions in Political Science

TROTSKY AND DJILAS

Critics of Communist Bureaucracy

Michael M. Lustig

Contributions in Political Science, Number 234

GREENWOOD PRESS
New York • Westport, Connecticut • London

Library of Congress Cataloging-in-Publication Data

Lustig, Michael M.
    Trotsky and Djilas : critics of communist bureaucracy / Michael M.
Lustig.
        p.   cm. — (Contributions in political science, ISSN 0147-1066
    : no. 234)
    Bibliography: p.
    Includes index.
    ISBN: 0-313-24777-3 (lib. bdg. : alk. paper)
    1. Trotsky, Leon, 1879-1940.   2. Djilas, Milovan, 1911-   .
    3. Communism—Soviet Union.   4. Communism—Yugoslavia.
    5. Bureaucracy—Soviet Union.   6. Bureaucracy—Yugoslavia.
    I. Title.   II. Series.
    HX313.8.T76L87   1989
    335.43'7—dc19   89-1885

British Library Cataloguing in Publication Data is available.

Copyright ©1989 by Michael M. Lustig

All rights reserved. No portion of this book may be reproduced, by any process or
technique, without the express written consent of the publisher.

Library of Congress Catalog Card Number: 89-1885
ISBN: 0-313-24777-3
ISSN: 0147-1066

First published in 1989

Greenwood Press, Inc.
88 Post Road West, Westport, Connecticut 06881

Printed in the United States of America

The paper used in this book complies with the Permanent Paper Standard issued by
the National Information Standards Organization (Z39.48-1984).

10 9 8 7 6 5 4 3 2 1

LIBRARY
ALMA COLLEGE
ALMA, MICHIGAN

Copyright Acknowledgments

The author and publisher are grateful to the following for granting permission to use materials:

From *The Revolution Betrayed* by Leon Trotsky. Copyright ©1972 by Pathfinder Press, Inc. Reprinted by permission of Pathfinder Press.

From *In Defense of Marxism* by Leon Trotsky. Copyright ©1973 by Pathfinder Press, Inc. Reprinted by permission of Pathfinder Press.

From *The Struggle for the New Course* by Leon Trotsky. Copyright ©1965 by the University of Michigan Press. Reprinted by permission.

From *Land Without Justice* by Milovan Djilas. Copyright ©1958 by Harcourt Brace Jovanovich, Inc. Reprinted by permission of the publisher.

From *The Leper and Other Stories* by Milovan Djilas. Copyright ©1973 by Harcourt Brace Jovanovich, Inc. Reprinted by permission of the publisher.

From *Montenegro* by Milovan Djilas. Copyright ©1963 by Harcourt Brace Jovanovich, Inc. Reprinted by permission of the publisher.

From *Memoir of a Revolutionary* by Milovan Djilas. Copyright ©1973 by Harcourt Brace Jovanovich, Inc. Reprinted by permission of the publisher.

From *The New Class* by Milovan Djilas. Copyright ©1957 by Harcourt Brace Jovanovich, Inc. Reprinted by permission of the publisher.

Contents

Preface

This is a book about communist bureaucracy and about two of its most significant revolutionary figures and critics, Leon Trotsky and Milovan Djilas.

First and foremost, the book is not an intellectual biography although key biographical details about Trotsky and Djilas important to the discussion of communist bureaucracy are analyzed. Several excellent intellectual biographies of Trotsky are already available since for more than three decades his career was central to the Bolshevik Revolution and to the Soviet Union. There is perhaps a need for a full-dress biography of Djilas and the problem of political dissent in Yugoslavia in which Djilas continues to play such a vital role. My work explores Trotsky's and Djilas's perceptions of communist bureaucracy, how it functioned and how it was maintained under Lenin, Stalin and Tito, and what the consequences of its excesses signify for the revolutionary Marxist ideals. The active roles of Trotsky and Djilas in bureaucratic power politics after successful revolutions in the Soviet Union in 1917 and in Yugoslavia during World War II are critically evaluated. Their analysis of party leadership and its growing bureaucracy are as significant while they were in office as well as after they were unceremoniously removed from political power by Stalin and Tito. As co-leaders and chief architects of Soviet and Yugoslav party policies, both men realized early in their political careers that ruler-dominated communist bureaucracies evolve into personal instruments of the leader, who utilizes the party organization, hierarchy and discipline to project his own power. This book traces and interprets Trotsky's and Djilas's analysis and it places it within the larger context of Soviet and Yugoslav society.

I should first like to thank my mother, Anna, for her deepest kindness and patience. Unfortunately, my father's untimely death prevented him from seeing this work to fruition but I believe that it would have made him smile. The book is dedicated to his memory and to my mother. I owe my initial enthusiasm for intellectual history, politics and culture to William D. Irvine, Don Pilgrim and Michiel Horn of Toronto, who took extraordinary pains in my work when I was an undisciplined undergraduate. Professor Tom Gleason of Brown University directed the doctoral thesis upon which this book is based and gave constant guidance and encouragement. Although I often despaired of Trotsky and Djilas, Tom Gleason had the patience and kindness to provide support and never to despair of me. He taught me to be scholarly and critically minded, and he has repeatedly taken time from his own work to comment on Trotsky and Djilas. Professors John L. Thomas and Mary Gluck of Brown University have read all, or large parts, of the manuscript. Both have advised and corrected me in many ways, and whenever necessary tolerated my stubborn inability to change my mind or to do better. I should also like to thank the following colleagues at the College of Basic Studies of Boston University for their many suggestions, sound advice and constructive criticism: Helen Berger, Jay Corrin, Michael Kort and John Zawacki.

The preparation of this book has also been assisted by the financial support of Beneficial Grants of Brown University. I am happy to acknowledge my gratitude to Beneficial Grants because it made my research possible at several libraries in Yugoslavia. I am very grateful to the personnel of the libraries at University of Belgrade and University of Zagreb. I also owe special thanks to the staff at the Russian Research Center of Harvard University who supplied me with many necessary articles, books and other essential materials.

Most of all, my wife, Jackie, deserves a special paragraph of thanks for enduring and helping this work along at every stage. Without her inspiration, encouragement, good humor and support, the book would not have been written. I am indeed grateful for my good fortune.

1

The Role and Nature of
Communist Bureaucracy

The emergence of modern bureaucracy has raised an immense number of problems. Bureaucracy as a malignant growth, escaping popular control, usurping democratic processes, and stifling the initiative of citizens and administrators alike, has preoccupied critics in both capitalist and communist societies. In the communist countries of the Soviet Union and Eastern Europe, the administrative machinery has assumed unparalleled comprehensiveness. Based upon long traditions of executive absolutism, administration has become a leviathan dominating the entire body politic. In the economy, the state, and especially in the Communist Party, it is the bureaucracy that makes key decisions.

First the term bureaucracy must be defined. What is a bureaucracy? There are significant differences between the popular and the scientific definitions of bureaucracy. In common parlance, the term implies the insolence of office, administrative delays, red tape, and the fear of making decisions. Scientific explanations, on the other hand, attempt to examine the relationship of the administrative and managerial apparatus to the specific social context in which it arose and to define that relationship in terms of a larger conceptual framework. I shall start from the premise that a bureaucracy does not merely consist of incompetent and blundering officials but reflects a broader set of substantive relations to which certain types of political, economic and cultural administration give rise.

Bureaucracies may be characterized in a variety of ways, and the type of classification an analyst adopts will depend on what aspects of bureaucratic behavior he wants to examine and compare. One model used in our analysis is the ruler-dominated bureaucracy.[1] I hope to demonstrate that bureau-cracies in such systems are highly personal instruments of a political leader who exercises total control and who utilizes his bureaucratic and exclusive clientele to project his authority and post his goals on the subjects he rules. Loyal members of such bureaucracies may obtain and exert considerable in-fluence because of their personal qualities and the confidence the leader may have in them and in their abilities; in fact, the existence of political favorites simply underscores the subservient nature and style of the bu-reaucracy's institutional role. The political strength and dynamism derives chiefly from the leader and then proceeds down the hierarchy of his admin-istrative machinery. A leader pursuing change will search for bureaucratic instruments suited to his political ends, but the character of the underlying relationship remains such that bureaucratic innovation will not be likely to develop into a spontaneous phenomenon.

Historians and sociologists have also categorized bureaucracies by the types of functions they perform.[2] Here the range of functions may run from tax collection and national defense to comprehensive planning and man-agement of the whole society. Alfred Meyer, for example, views the complex Soviet bureaucracy in terms of numerous "bureaucratic combinations"[3] in-volving different degrees of emphasis on the political, economic and social sector of the nation.

Another possible way of categorizing bureaucracies points to the internal configuration of party leadership and the degree of rationality which it em-ploys to rule. Here the important and relevant question is the extent to which professional training is needed in order to qualify for entrance into state service. How are appointments and promotions made? How signifi-cant are such factors as merit, favoritism and venality? How does the system allocate and distribute power? Does the bureaucracy perform its functions on a "rational basis"?[4] Are the processes of decision-making regulated by general and well-known rules of conduct or are they determined by the ar-bitrary consideration of the ruler?

The belief in the "legal-rational" system has drawn considerable attention and support form Max Weber's classic theory of bureaucracy.[5] Weber con-cluded that along with the construction of a "legal-rational" system, a rationalized administrative structure was also formed. The impact of his study has had significant influence upon the character and nature of bureaucracy. One political analyst summed up Weber's findings in this manner:

It is one of the characteristics of industrialized societies, irrespective of their own form of government, to develop a civil service recruited on the basis of specific re-quirements. "Bureaucratic administration means fundamentally the exercise of con-trol on the basis of knowledge," observed Max Weber. It is above all a rational organization characterized by: (a) a clearly defined sphere of competence subjected to impersonal rules: (b) a hierarchy which determines in an orderly fashion relations of superiors and subordinates; (c) a regular system of appointments and promotions on the basis of free contract; (d) recruitment on the basis of skills, knowledge, or technical training; and (e) fixed salaries.[6]

According to Weber, no government can rule effectively without a clearly defined and organized bureaucracy. In the modern state especially, a crucial position is occupied by "officials working in offices,"[7] whose task is to carry out the politics decided by those in power. Receiving instructions from above and giving orders to those below, the administrators or civil servants constitute a hierarchy of command, or in Weber's expressive words, a system of "imperative coordination."[8] Normally operating within a framework of legal norms, the administrators' function is to apply these abstract rules to a particular set of cases, and to compel the citizens to obey them.

Such criteria may be utilized in an attempt to define the place and order of each bureaucratic structure on a rational-irrational scale.[9] There is danger, however, of accepting Weber's model too quickly. No bureaucracy can be completely separated from its political, cultural and economic systems of values. As we shall see in our study of Trotsky's and Djilas' formulations on bureaucracy, when Weber's theory is superimposed on the Soviet and Yugoslav political context, the results more often than not lead to frustration rather than clarification. A less rational framework with a more flexible structure and organization, but one capable of sustaining a living connection with the political, cultural and social forces, may be much more revealing. The point is that large administrative organizations can be governed and managed by structures that do not exactly adhere to Weber's classical model of bureaucracy. Examples and patterns of administrative rule provided by Trotsky and Djilas have developed in the Soviet Union and Eastern Europe that attest to this. Our knowledge of governmental personnel and some public controlled industry there challenges the notion that complex systems need particular structures in order to function well. The Soviet and Yugoslav situations demonstrate that public administration can be managed through the complete domination of a political party that is normally outside the governmental service. To call the party an effective part of the Soviet and Yugoslav bureaucracy may help to explain what occurs, but it also clearly damages the elegance of Weber's analysis.

The task in the pages that follow then will be to investigate, describe and analyze the nature of communist bureaucracy through the works and personal experience of Leon Trotsky and Milovan Djilas. What were their views of bureaucracy when they were in and when they were out of power? Can modern bureaucracy more generally be comprehended within their frame of reference? What were the origins of Soviet and Yugoslav bureaucratism? Finally, do they suggest any possibilities for the reform or amelioration of this development?

The basis for a thorough comparison of the two critics was chiefly provided by their key works on bureaucracy—Trotsky's *The Revolution Betrayed*
and Djilas' *The New Class*. I hope to show clearly that their views did not remain static, but developed and changed throughout their political careers
and years out of power, in exile or in prison. Even after Trotsky's political
demise in 1927, he, unlike Djilas, remained completely committed to the
classical Marxist interpretation of bureaucracy: the view that the bureaucracy does not and cannot constitute an independent power, but is an instrument in the hands of broader social and political interests.[10] We shall observe how and why Trotsky adapted such Marxist axioms in order to
describe and widen his interpretation of the nature of the Soviet Union's
development.

Which term best describes bureaucracy? While best known for his critique of the new class, Milovan Djilas early in 1953 advanced the notion of a
privileged caste. His preference of one classification over the other presupposes a distinction between ownership and control and a choice as to which
of these should receive greater emphasis. Also, as we follow through his
political struggles with Tito and the party, the term "bureaucratic" emerges
and becomes less vague and confusing. The initial narrow definition of the
bureaucratic phenomenon expands into a full blown analysis of Soviet and
Yugoslav bureaucratic power. In other words, the critique eventually includes the analysis of the government and its hierarchy, and finally the
analysis of political rule and ownership.

Both Trotsky and Djilas pointed to the historical, social and cultural backwardness as the source of the extravagant quality of bureaucratic development in the Soviet Union and Yugoslavia. I hope to illustrate how they
analyzed the consequences of the problem. Was the burden of backwardness, together with the post-revolutionary exhaustion, chiefly responsible
for Stalinist and Titoist bureaucracy? If historical and social backwardness
were largely incompatible with socialism, how did Trotsky intend to confront the issue? Was there really an alternative to Stalinist development?
Contradictions in this area of Trotsky's analysis appear to recur again and
again in *The Revolution Betrayed* and in his other writings in the 1930s.

Trotsky's work also reflects the incredible difficulty of describing and
analyzing the bureaucratic phenomenon from a revolutionary point of view.
For Dijilas, the incompatibility of backwardness—viewed both in its economic and socio-cultural senses—and socialism was a persistent theme in his
prerevolutionary writing. He abandoned it after his expulsion in 1954 from
the Communist Party of Yugoslavia. During his revolutionary period, as
with Trotsky throughout his career, Djilas took for granted that socialism
was dependent on the highest development of productive forces. In his
view, social and economic backwardness were never the principal roots of
Soviet bureaucracy. He placed much more emphasis on the nature of the
revolutionary party and its leadership.

Revolutionaries since 1789 have been traumatized by the possibility of "Thermidor"—that major reversal along the revolutionary path which plucks the fruits of victory from the hands of those in whose name the battle was fought. It is interesting that Djilas, unlike Trotsky has never employed the term "Thermidor," but he is profoundly concerned that "his" (Yugoslav) revolution makes those mid-course corrections necessary to keep it headed toward its true destination, and equally disturbed when this does not happen.

The predicament is, of course, bureaucratism, which Djilas in time refined into the concept of the new class. As we shall see, the origins of his new class will send us back to the roots of some of Marx's own most perplexing doctrines. In short (and to be examined in great detail in the chapters on Djilas) how is Marx's division of labor to be abolished and, in particular, the division between manual and mental "labor"—so that one can "hunt in the morning, fish in the afternoon, rear cattle in the evening, criticize after dinner, in accordance with one's inclination?" Furthermore, "all work in which many individuals cooperate, necessarily requires for the coordination and unity of the process of a directing will ... " How can this "labor of superintendence and management" be made nonantagonistic?[11]

An earlier thinker who confronted these problems head on was Waclaw Machajski.[12] He drew such a total distinction between manual and intellectual workers that no permanent congruence of interests was possible for the two groups. The revolutionary intelligentsia might on occasions lend support to workers' and peasants' demands, but their actions were only tactical moves in their personal struggle for power. Similar to other groups in society, the intellectuals possessed interests of their own. As Max Nomad has noted:

In Machajski's conception, the socialist radicals of the nineteenth century expressed the interests of the intellectual workers—not those of the ordinary working class, in which he placed the manual workers only. The mental workers, he argued, were a rising privileged class, fighting for a place in the sun against the old privileged classes, the landowners and capitalists. Higher education was their specific "capital"—the source of their actual or potential higher incomes. . . . The socialism which the radical intelligentsia really aspired to was nothing but State Capitalism: a system of government ownership, under which private capitalists would have yielded place to office holders, managers, engineers.[13]

Machajski has a broad conception of "bourgeois" society, which includes not only capitalists but also the noncapitalist owners of education and skill. Consequently, expropriation of the capitalist class alone by no means signifies an expropriation of the entire bourgeois society.

The latter after elimination of the capitalists, remains the same ruling society as it was before, the educated master, the world of the "white hands." It remains the owner of the national surplus value which is distributed in the form of higher salaries to intellectual workers.[14]

And none other than Marx, comments Machajski, applied an elaborate analysis supporting this inequality which amounts to concealed parasitism. According to Marx's analysis, this labor, "of a higher and more complicated character than average labor," is "labor power whose production has cost more time and labor, and which therefore has a higher value" entitled to greater income.[15] By concentrating on the factory owner, therefore, socialism would leave intact the superior rewards of the mental workers, who, if left to themselves, would prefer nothing more than to perpetuate the slavery of the manual workers. Simply put, economic demands were the most that the proletariat could fight for: complete equality in educational possibilities,[16] and provisions for the unemployed if necessary. In other words, a "workers" government is an impossibility, for whether composed of intellectuals or self-instructed workers:

The new incumbents of political power, even assuming that originally they harbored the most altruistic feelings with regard to the horny-handed underdog, once in the possession of power, would inevitably assert their own class interests of educated organizers of a socialist state, or in their own words: they would yield to their natural urge to establish themselves as a ruling class enjoying the concomitant advantages expressed in higher incomes and the opportunities for higher education to their offspring only.[17]

Clearly opposition and pressure against this sort of development could only come from below.

Machajski's *Intellectual Worker* also theorized that the European socialist movement of the 1880s and 1890s had mainly expressed the ideology of disgruntled and largely dissatisfied intellectual elite.[18] He concluded that socialism could not result in a classless society but in the formation of a new ruling class of intellectuals, allied with the middle class, in a type of society he referred to as "state capitalism."[19] Yet he was not completely pessimistic about the future of socialism, and in essence he believed that through gradual improvement of state education the predominance of the intellectual class might be diminished and a classless society eventually established.

The concern of historians and sociologists with the creation of an intellectual bureaucratic elite originated not only with Machajski's *Intellectual Worker* at the end of the nineteenth century but it can also be observed in the works of Robert Michels, Gaetano Mosca and Max Weber.[20] The original and main aim of their theories was either to comment on Marx's formulations or to refute Marxist socialism. For example, Weber's opposition to socialism was inspired by the fear that Marxism would result in the loss of individual freedom and in the more or less complete regimentation of society.[21] Where Marx observed in the history of modern societies a concentration of the means of production in the hands of a tiny capitalist class, Weber, Michels and Mosca viewed a process of concentration of the means of a bureaucratic elite which would reach its apogee in socialism, with serious consequences for the individual. As Weber noted:

The modern state is initiated through the action of the prince. He paves the way for the expropriation of the autonomous and private bearers of executive power who stand beside him, of those who in their own right possess the means of administration, warfare and financial organization ... The whole process is a complete parallel to the development of the capitalist enterprise through gradual expropriation of the independent producers. In the end, the modern state controls the total means of political organization.

Robert Michels, a close personal friend of Weber, used a similar model to explain the bureaucratic organization of the German Social Democratic Party in his *Political Parties*. Like Weber, Michels was deeply concerned with political parties, trade unions and other large organizations that tended to develop highly rational and hierarchial bureaucracies. In his analysis of the German Social Democratic Party, he pointed out the sheer problem of its administration. As he stated: "Every party organization which has attained to a considerable degree of complication demands that there should be a certain number of persons who devote all their activities to the work of the party."[23] And although he agreed with Weber that democratic social action is possible only through bureaucratic organization, he nevertheless concluded that rational bureaucratic structure was destructive of human and democratic values:

Bureaucracy is the sworn enemy of individual liberty, and of all bold initiative in matters of internal policy. The dependence upon superior authorities characteristic of the average employee suppresses individuality and gives to the society in which employees predominate a narrow petty-bourgeois and philistine stamp. The bureaucratic spirit corrupts character and engenders moral poverty. In every bureaucracy we may observe place-hunting, mania for promotion and obsequiousness towards those upon whom promotion depends; there is arrogance towards inferiors and servility towards superiors.[24]

Michels concluded in *Political Parties* that socialism was not only an economic but an administrative problem. He predicted that socialist leaders would eventually become conservative bureaucrats who would adhere to their political self-interest rather than follow their original revolutionary ideology. His conclusions were validated only three years after the publication of *Political Parties* in 1915 when the German Social Democratic Party, instead of declaring a general strike against the German government, voted for war credits and supported the Kaiser's war effort.[25]

According to Michels, this abrupt volte-face of the German Social

Democratic Party was a natural consequence of their social and political power position. As he shrewdly observed in the second edition of *Political Parties*: "the life ... must not be endangered. ... The party gives way, hastily sells its internationalist soul, and impelled by the instinct of self-preservation, undergoes a transformation into a patriotic party."[26] He correctly envisioned that World War I socialists would put the needs of their party unity, organization and survival well ahead of their revolutionary dogma and ideology. The 1917 revolution in Russia presented an even more dramatic example of his other hypothesis that a successful socialist upheaval would not result in the victory of the working class democracy but in the removal of one group of autocratic rulers by another.[27]

No evidence exists that Djilas ever heard of Machajski. In writing and in conversation with journalists and when specifically asked about the Polish theoretician,[28] he has maintained that his analysis of the Soviet and Yugoslav bureaucratic phenomenon was reached independently. He has repeatedly asserted that he has also had no prior knowledge of such theories as that of Weber, Mosca and Michels. Whether he was aware of it or not, the bureaucratic themes he discussed were apparent well before 1917. Weber and Michels before World War I recognized and wrote about the increasing growth of bureaucratic elites and government functionaries. Weber, for instance, questioned whether the power of the bureaucracy could be adequately checked by political authorities even in a parliamentary system:

The power position of a fully developed bureaucracy is always overwhelming. The "political master" finds himself in the position of the "dilettante" who stands opposite the "expert," facing the trained official who stands within the management of administration. This holds whether the "master" whom the bureaucracy serves is a "people," equipped with the weapons of "legislative initiative," the "referendum," and the right to remove officials, or a parliament, elected on a more aristocratic or more democratic basis and equipped with the right to vote a lack of confidence.[29]

Weber's interpretation was unduly influenced by the example of the blundering Prussian bureaucracy, and of the ineffectiveness of liberal politicians in Germany.[30] Nevertheless, his theory of the increasing power of bureaucracy soon gained support from the experiences of the Russian Revolution and from the consequences of the more extensive control of economic activity by the state in both the democratic and socialist countries of Europe. It is interesting that Djilas arrives at a viewpoint similar to that of Weber, Machajski and even Michels. Whether he realized it or not, he largely employed many of their concepts and ideas in order to explore the Soviet and Yugoslav bureaucratic system.

Leon Trotsky, unlike Djilas, was familiar with Machajski's and Weber's views and positions. Although "impressed at first by these theories," he was "mainly shocked"—but not led to any self-doubt that we may discern. He was not the kind of man ever to submit, ever to surrender. His pride and his intelligence forbade it; and in addition to his personal pride there was the more exalted kind of pride, with which he viewed himself as a significant historical figure. In *The Revolution Betrayed*, he intended to demonstrate with mathematical precision exactly how the corruption of the world's first socialist state took place, not because there were any flaws in the Marxist argument but because an overwhelming bureaucracy took command and set about deliberately to "betray" socialist principles. As he observed in 1927 at the time of his demise and expulsion from the Communist Party of the Soviet Union: "We have a worker's state with bureaucratic distortions," adding that "the swollen privileged administrative apparatus devours a very considerable part of our surplus value." Or as he put it in his full-scale attack, the Soviet Union "has very privileged commanding strata of the population, who appropriate the lion's share in the sphere of consumption."[31]

"The conquest of power changes not only the relations of the proletariat to other classes, but also its own inner structure. The wielding of power becomes the specialty of a definite social group, which is the more impatient to solve its own social problem, the higher its opinion of its own mission."[32] So governing, or in this case ruling, is a specialized function, but this is only the broadest of Trotsky's generalizations. Clearly the Soviet bureaucracy's specific character was a direct consequence of two significant and underlying forces: The Russian Revolution occurred in an economically underdeveloped country, which even Marx did not foresee. Subsequently, Russia suffered a period of prolonged international isolation, which even Lenin had not anticipated. Hence the need for the application of socialist methods to solve presocialist economic problems. Economic underdevelopment and cultural backwardness demanded that accommodations be made to those privileged groups in the new regime whose existence was absolutely necessary for defense, industry and science. And material poverty, the revolutionary change of power notwithstanding, meant a continuing struggle of each against all. As Trotsky commented in 1935: "When the lines are very long, it is necessary to appoint a policeman to keep order. Such is the starting point of the Soviet bureaucracy."[33]

Why must economic backwardness lead to a swollen bureaucracy? Although Trotsky tended to exaggerate the extent to which economic and social forces had made change inevitable before the social upheaval in 1917, he did warn Lenin and the rest of the Bolshevik leadership after the revolution of the "vengeance" of underdevelopment. In order to survive, or make progress according to Trotsky, the new regime needed to solve poverty, improve its primitive industrial and agricultural techniques, educate the masses, and also obtain aid from the rest of the European proletariat. In his final analysis, he seems to imply that it was the post-revolutionary failure that helped to foster bureaucratic development. He saw the origins of the bureaucracy in very simple and candid terms: "The basis of bureaucratic rule is the poverty of society in objects of consumption, with the resulting struggle of each against all. When there are few foods, the purchasers are compelled to stand in line."[34] Trotsky thus adhered to the orthodox Marxist view of bureaucracy. Like previous nineteenth-century socialists in Russia, Trotsky was deeply influenced by Marx's utopian and highly abstract notions of the future. Like Marx, Trotsky's view had consisted of the belief that once economic depravity was brought under control and affluence achieved, problems of distribution would disappear, and with them the necessity for specialists, bureaucrats and even military personnel. Although he took over this position completely, he also noted and later experienced the problems of an underdeveloped society—something Marx failed to take into account. Even Lenin did not recognize the serious nature of the problem until the end of the revolution. According to Trotsky:

A development of the productive forces is an absolutely necessary practical premise of Communism, because without it want is generalized, 'and with want the struggle for necessities begins again, and that means that all the old crap must revive.' This thought Marx never directly developed, and for no accidental reason: he never foresaw a proletarian revolution in a backward country. Lenin also never dwelt upon it, and this too was not accidental. He did not foresee so prolonged an isolation of the Soviet state.[35]

Trotsky is here recalling Lenin's *State and Revolution*, in which Lenin viewed bureaucratism as merely a reflection of the masses unfamiliarity with the new administration and its potential to alleviate economic backwardness. For Lenin, the problem of bureaucratic development could and would be solved by "political measures."[36] For Trotsky, the issue and problem of bureaucratic distortion was not really political, not even administrative, but one of social and economic underdevelopment. In Trotsky's view, these were the absolute evils that combined to create the conditions for the ultimate triumph of the "Thermidor":

It is for this very reason, that a proletariat still backward in many respects achieved in a space of a few months the unprecedented leap from a semi-feudal monarchy to a socialist dictatorship, that the reaction had developed in a series of consecutive waves. External conditions and events have vied with each other in nourishing it. Intervention followed intervention. The Revolution got no direct help from the West. Instead of the expected prosperity of the country, an ominous destitution reigned for long. Moreover, the outstanding representatives of the working class either died in the civil war, or rose a few steps higher and broke away from the masses. And then after an unexpected tension of forces, hopes and illusions, there came a long period of weariness, decline, and sheer disappointment in the results of the Revolution. The ebb of "plebian pride" made room for a flood of pusillanimity and careerism. The new commanding caste rose to its place upon this wave.[37]

Was the Thermidorian bureaucracy therefore inevitable, the necessary result of the social upheaval of 1917? By constantly pointing to the post-revolutionary exhaustion and scarcity as the source of bureaucratism this is clearly what Trotsky seemed to imply. Yet, he strongly believed that an alternative course was possible. *The Revolution Betrayed* and his other post-1935 articles on the Thermidorian bureaucracy remain contradictory and incomplete. As we shall have time to observe, Trotsky's deep contempt for Stalin and his "caste will provide us with some clues for the obvious contradictions. His meanings and definitions of Thermidor, as well as his criticism of the extent and of its penetration into the Soviet regime were frequently revised and reformulated. Inconsistencies prevailed in this area of his work as well but he was more willing to admit and even clarify his own contradictions. As we trace and closely observe his analysis of the rise of the Thermidor, we shall see that his explanations of the victory of the bureaucracy was not simply the result of "backwardness," "isolation," and the "degeneration" of the October Revolution, a ridiculously superficial explanation. It clearly omits the political function of Lenin's and his own view of the socialist revolution and the bureaucratic-authoritarian character of the Bolshevik Party. Trotsky's theory of the "objective conditions,"[38] especially the low development of the productive forces, lack of education and culture after the Russian Revolution, do not fully explain either the breeding ground of bureaucratism or its growth and consolidation of power under Stalin.

Trotsky's socialism of austerity at best constitutes Marx's "lower stage" in which economic distribution according to work appears inescapable.[39] He suggests that this is his view, claiming that the workers' state has a "dual" character: the state is partly socialist because it defends social property in the means of production; but the state is also partly bourgeois, strangely without the bourgeoisie, because the distribution of its goods is carried out with a capitalist measure of value and all the ensuing consequences, particularly socialist inequality.[40] To follow Trotsky one step further, from these essentially economic problems arises political reality. "The bourgeois organ of the workers's state" quickly develops and asserts a logic and rational interests of its own. It becomes, according to Trotsky, a "caste of specialists in distribution," and nobody, "who has wealth to distribute ever omits himself."[41] The upshot of the whole argument, and for Trotsky it could not be explained away as a remnant of the past, was a new tendency to personal gain and accumulation.

After his political downfall in 1927–28, Trotsky naturally became pessimistic about the Soviet Union's future under Stalin. Still, he did not render a totally negative judgment on the Soviet state. Remaining true to his revolutionary faith, he even entitled an article "The Question of the Character of the Soviet Union not yet Decided."[42] The basis for this hope—and the factor making the regime a reality—remained the "partly socialist" aspect of the "workers' state." As he explained:

The Soviet bureaucracy has expropriated the proletariat politically in order by methods of its own to defend the social conquest. By the very fact of its appropriation of political power in a country where the principal means of production are in the hands of the state, creates a new and hitherto unknown relation between the bureaucracy and the riches of the nation. The means of production belong to the state. But the state, so to speak, "belongs to the bureaucracy." . . . It is compelled to defend state property as the source of its power and its income. In this aspect of its activity it still remains a weapon of proletarial dictatorship.[43]

The state, in spite of everything, remains the repository of the property relations which resulted directly from the Russian Revolution. Although Stalin and the cult of his cadres might be an obstacle to Trotsky's own utopian vision of permanent revolution, the present regime at least represents a stopgap measure preserving the principles of planned economy and precluding a return to capitalist modes of production.

The validity of Trotsky's definition of the workers' state rested on the rather dubious assumption that the workers' state must eventually evolve away from its "dual" character and towards socialism. Trotsky could never quite make up his mind as to how to describe the nature and character of the Soviet society created by the "caste bureaucracy." In principle, he did not accept the conventional analysis that the Soviet Union was a "dictatorship of the proletariat" and, as such, it was a "preparatory regime transitional from capitalism to socialism."[44] Trotsky, implies therefore, that the Soviet regime is in an unusual temporary stage.

But the rapid growth rather than diminution of the bureaucracy, the increase in the power of the state organs, and the intensification of Stalin's rule in the 1930s, suggested that the ultimate nature and character of Soviet regime could move in a non-socialist direction. In Trotsky's view only two ultimate alternatives existed, capitalism or socialism. A third possibility, that the bureaucrats could maintain their hold on power and keep the Soviet Union as a sort of "intermediate society" did not seem likely to Trotsky.

Like Herzen in the nineteenth century, Trotsky frequently made historical comparisons. In particular, earlier revolutionary experience was for Trotsky, and as we shall see for Djilas as well, the basis for understanding the present and the future, especially after their fall from power. The key event for Trotsky was of course the French Revolution, which provided him with a constant source of analogies, models and social and political precedents. Especially in the years following Lenin's death in 1924 and during Trotsky's political struggle with Stalin, he in fact became obsessed with the French experience. The final fate of the French Revolution, especially the development from Jacobinism, to Thermidor, to Napoleon's dictatorship he believed was to be repeated in the Soviet Union under Stalin. Ironically, however, when late in the 1920s the character of the Russian Revolution began to be debated in terms of the French experience, it was Trotsky who strictly defended the Bolshevik-Jacobin tradition.

Directly related to Trotsky's comparison and discussion of Thermidor is his interpretation of Soviet bureaucratic developments through the personality of Stalin. Stalin was the Napoleon of the Russian Revolution. Trotsky could find no other way of understanding how Stalin consolidated his rule:

In the former case (i.e., Napoleon I), the question involved was the consolidation of the bourgeois revolution through the liquidation of its principles and political institutions. In the latter case, (i.e., Stalin), the question involved is the consolidation of the worker-peasant revolution through the smashing of its international program, its leading party, its soviets. Developing the policies of the Thermidor, Napoleon waged a struggle not only against the democratic circles of the petty and middle bourgeoisie; in this way he concentrated the fruits of the regime born out of the revolution in the hands of new bourgeois aristocracy. Stalin guards the conquest of the October Revolution not only against the feudal-bourgeois counter-revolution but also against the claims of the toilers, their impatience and their dissatisfaction; he crushes the left-wing which expresses the ordered historical and progressive tendencies of the unprivileged working classes; he creates a new aristocracy by means of an extreme differentiation of wages, privileges, ranks, etc. Leaning for support against the lowest—sometimes vice versa—Stalin has attained the complete concentration of power in his own hands. What else should this regime be called if not Soviet Bonapartism.[45]

The mainspring, claimed Trotsky, of both Stalin's and Napoleon's careers was the usurpation and monopolization of political power. In Trotsky's view, Stalin actually imitated Napoleon's methods of rule. The personalization of Stalin's dictatorship, or the "charisma of his leadership"[46] served a number of very significant functions; in the first place, observed Trotsky, it created a national symbol for the bureaucracy which provided the regime with a form of national identification; second, it became an alternative to what Trotsky thought should have been the focus of the socialist revolutionary content of the regime; and third, the goal of the "super-arbiter" of the entrenched bureaucracy was to rule firmly and to provide a semblance of political stability. It is here that Trotsky focuses on Stalin's total preoccupation with absolute control and power. Trotsky pointed out the importance of Stalin to the bureaucracy in the following trenchant terms:

The increasingly insistent deification of Stalin is, with all its elements of caricature, a necessary element of the regime. The bureaucracy has need of an inviolable superarbiter, a first consul if not an emperor, and it reins upon its shoulders him who best responds to its claim for lordship. That "strength of character" of the leader which so enraptures the literary dilettantes of the West, is in reality the sum total of the collective pressure of a caste which will stop at nothing in defence of its position. Each one of them at his post is thinking: *l'etat, c'est moi*. In Stalin each one easily finds himself. But Stalin also finds in each one a small part of his own spirit. Stalin is the personification of the bureaucracy. That is the substance of his political personality.[47]

Stalinist bureaucracy, Trotsky believed, in all its different forms, centered around Stalin. Like Stalin, it rose to political power against a background of the disintegration of post-revolutionary society. Political institutions, the Bolshevik Party, workers organizations, and local soviets had to be virtually liquidated or suppressed. Although Trotsky himself was one of the Bolshevik leaders who in fact approved and participated in the suppression from 1917 to 1922, he subsequently refuted the idea that he was at all responsible for the rise of the bureaucratic strata under Lenin or Stalin.[48]

These were some of the main themes Trotsky formulated about Soviet bureaucracy from 1920 to 1940. I have already noted that he was greatly influenced by Marx's analysis of modern bureaucracy. Like Marx, he believed that a bureaucracy cannot constitute an independent power, that it does not rule, but that it is an important instrument in the hands of broader socioeconomic class interests. These concepts and ideas will be explored in considerable detail in the chapters about Trotsky. Trotsky repeated, reformulated and broadened Marxist axioms in order to explain the special nature of the Soviet Union. Unlike Antonio Gramsci, whose critique of Soviet bureaucracy was written in Mussolini's prison, and whose criticism was chiefly directed against Leninist forms of communism,[49] Trotsky believed that Leninism had nothing to do with the "degenerated state" but was the result of Stalin's political trickery and the socioeconomic backwardness which he inherited from the tsarist regime. As we shall see, he was determined to illustrate that Stalin's bureaucratic character arose and developed in this milieu. This is a significant theme in Trotsky's overall critique and, therefore, we shall pay special attention to the way in which he puts it forward.

Trotsky's and Djilas' theoretical critiques of bureaucracy have a biographical dimension. Since both thinkers remain significant political actors, their views of Soviet and Yugoslav bureaucracy frequently reflect personal revolutionary experience. My study examines the bureaucratic characteristics of their respective regimes when they were in and when they were out of power. Chapters 2 and 3 focus on Trotsky's formulations on bureaucratic development from the great upheaval in 1917 to his murder in Mexico in 1940. His early work, *The New Course*, (1923) signifies Trotsky's emergence both as a critic of bureaucracy and of repressive tendencies of Stalinism. Here I hope to demonstrate his failure to comprehend the real nature of Stalin's bureaucratic power. Trotsky's thesis of a "degenerated workers' state" under Stalin, as argued in *The Revolution Betrayed* in 1936, lacked political reality and common sense. Chapter 4 explores the variety of Marxist bureaucratic theories of the 1930s that Trotsky's dogmatic cast of mind rejected. In the process of doing so, he not only lost many political followers but also greatly weakened his own theory of bureaucratic development in the Soviet Union.

Djilas' concept of the "new class" may be viewed as a corrective to Trotsky's classical Marxist interpretation of bureaucracy. Chapter 5 examines Djilas' revolutionary background and his long standing preoccupation with political, social and economic change. Evidence indicates that his earliest values are crucial to Djilas' political career. Chapter 6 traces the nature of the Yugoslav political system from 1945 to 1954 at the time of his expulsion from the Communist Party of Yugoslavia, with the emphasis here on his increasing objections to the bureaucratization of the Yugoslav Communist Party and to the growing political power of Tito. Chapter 7 provides examples of the character of the "new class" rulers and explores the all-important consequences of their political power.

The final chapter attempts to locate Trotsky and Djilas in the tradition of modern political thought. While Trotsky wrote about bureaucratic "degeneration" or "betrayal of socialism," he nevertheless remained faithful to revolutionary socialist goals. Djilas rebelled against the communist world of unqualified bureaucratic rationality bent on efficiency and purposiveness at the expense of such values as nature, beauty and political freedom. Unlike Trotsky, he became disillusioned with his inability to endure the moral ambiguities and un-freedom of revolutionary politics.

NOTES

1. Scholars have increasingly turned to various concepts of bureaucracy since the publication of Trotsky's and Djilas' works in order to comprehend the nature of Soviet and Yugoslav political system. Such models as "administered" and "organizational" society have been advanced by several authors. Theoretical models and views of the following writers will be referred to in our study. Allen Kassof, "The Administered Society: Totalitarianism without Terror," *World Politics* 16 (July 1964), pp. 558-575; Merle Fainsod, *Smolensk Under Soviet Rule*, (Cambridge, Massachusetts, 1958). Even though it covers only one province, this is an extremely significant book. All aspects of Soviet life in the 1920s and 1930s are examined, and revelations about the bureaucratic apparatus are especially important; Barrington Moore, Jr., *Political and Social Theory*, (Cambridge, Massachusetts, 1958); John A. Armstrong, *The Soviet Bureaucratic Elite*,(New York, 1959). This is essentially a case study of the party officials in the Ukraine; Alfred G. Meyer, *The Soviet Political System*, (New York, 1965); Alfred G. Meyer, "The Comparative Study of Communist Political Systems," (*Slavic Review* 26 (March 1967),p. 11; Zbigniew Brzezinsky, "The Soviet Political System:

Transformation or Degeneration?" *Problems of Communism* 15 (January-February 1966), p. 10; T.H. Rigby, "Traditional, Market, and Organizational Societies and the USSR," *World Politics* 16 (July 1964), pp. 539-557; George Zaninovich, ed., *Comparitive Political Leadership*, (New York, 1973); Samuel P. Huntington and Zbigniew Brzezinski, *Political Power* USA/USSR, (New York, 1964); Reinhard Bendix, "Socialism and the Theory of Bureaucracy," *The Canadian Journal of Economics and Politics* 16 (1950), pp. 501-514; Marx F. Morstein, "Bureaucracy and Dictatorship," *Review of Politics* 3 (1941), pp. 110-117; Philip Selznik, "The Iron Law of Bureaucracy," "Modern Review 3 (1949), pp. 157-165.

2. For the classical statement see, Max Weber, *The Theory of Economic and Social Organization*, translated by A. M. Henderson and T. Parsons (New York, 1947), p. 335. Historians and sociologists since Max Weber's study have further analyzed and contributed to the role of functions. See the following excellent studies: Michel Crozier, *The Bureaucratic Phenomenon*, (Chicago, 1964); Robert K. Merton, *Social Theory and Social Structure*, (New York, 1968); Peter M. Blau and M. W. Meyer, *Bureaucracy in Modern Society*, (New York, 1971); Anthony Downs, *Inside Bureaucracy*, (Boston, 1967).

3. Alfred G. Meyer, *The Soviet Political System*, p. 469.

4. For a detailed sociological analysis of this problem see the excellent article by Robert K. Merton, "Bureaucratic Structure and Personality," in Eric and Mary Josephson, eds., *Man Alone: Alienation in Modern Society*, (New York, 1962), pp. 123-133; also see Merton, "The Role of the Intellectual in Bureaucracy," in *Social Theory and Social Structure*, pp. 261-278.

5. Max Weber, *The Theory of Economic and Social Organization*,p. 334; also see S. N. Eisenstadt's commentary on Weber in the author's *Max Weber on Charisma and Institution Building*, (Chicago, 1968),pp. 9-41.

6. Talcott Parsons, "Some Principal Characteristics of Industrial Societies" in Cyril E. Black, ed., *The Transformation of Russian Society*, (Cambridge, Massachusetts, 1960), pp. 13-42.

7. Weber, *The Theory of Economic and Social Organization*, p. 331.

8. Ibid., p. 332.

9. For another view of this idea see, Alvin W. Gouldner, "On Weber's Analysis of Bureaucratic Rules," *The American Sociological Review*, Vol. XIII, (1948), pp. 396-400.

10. A handy compendium is Lewis S. Feuer, ed., *Marx and Engels: Basic Writings on Politics and Philosophy*, (New York, 1959), pp. 349-392. See also Robert C. Tucker, ed., *The Marx-Engels Reader*, (New York, 1972), p. 521.

11. Karl Marx, *The German Ideology*, (New York, 1939), pp. 68-70.

12. Waclaw Machajski published two books at the end of the nineteenth century and both still remain to be translated into English. However, *The Evolution of Social Democracy* (1899) and *The Intellectual Worker* (1905) are available in Russian and Polish.

13. Max Nomad, *Rebels and Renegades*, (New York, 1932), p. 206. That "mental workers" might include philosopher-theorists as well as the specialist technical intelligentsia is a further distinction apparently not ascertained by Machajski. Their roles in the socialist movement are not necessarily the same, but the point is beyond our concern here.

14. Machajski, excerpted in V. F. Calverton, *The Making of Society: An Outline of Sociology*, (New York, 1937), p. 428.

15. Marx, *The German Ideology*, p. 69.

16. Nomad, *Rebels and Renegades*, p. 435.

17. Nomad, "White Collars and Horny Hands," *The Modern Quarterly*, VI, 3 (Autumn 1932), pp. 71-72.

18. A. D'Agostino, "Intelligentsia Socialism and the 'Workers' Revolution: The Views of J. W. Machajski," *International Review of Social History*, XIV/1 (1969), p. 56.

19. Ibid., pp. 55-89.

20. See Robert Michels, *Political Parties: A Sociological Study of the Oligarchical Tendencies of Modern Democracy*, (New York, 1962); and Gaetano Mosca, *The Ruling Class*, (New York, 1939). On Weber also consult H. H. Gerth and C. Wright Mills, eds., *From Max Weber: Essays in Sociology*,(New York, 1946).

21. Weber, "Politics as a Vocation," in Gerth and Mills, *From Max Weber*.

22. Weber, "Bureaucracy," in Eisenstadt, ed., *Max Weber on Charisma and Building*, pp. 66-69. For some interesting perspectives and criticisms of Weber's views see, Carl J. Friedrich, "Some Observations on Weber's Analysis of Bureaucracy," and Frederic S. Burin, "Bureaucracy and National Socialism: A Reconsideration of Weberian Theory," in Gerth and Mills, *From Max Weber*.

23. Michels, *Political Parties*, p. 61.

24. Ibid., p. 191. For criticism of Michel's view and his exaggerated restrictive analysis of bureaucracy see, Alvin Gouldner, "The Metaphysical Pathos and the Theory of Bureaucracy," in S. M. Lipset and N. W. Smelser, eds., *Sociology: the Progress of a Decade*, (Englewood Cliffs, 1961), pp. 61-65.

25. Carl Schorske, *German Social Democracy 1905-1917*, (Cambridge, Massachusetts, 1955), pp. 45-78.

26. Michels, *Political Parties*, p. 6.

27. Ibid., p. 202.

28. Interview with Paul Foot of the British Broadcasting Corporation (BBC), 1972.

29. Weber, "Bureaucracy," in Eisenstadt, ed., *Max Weber on Charisma and Institution Building*, pp. 68-73.

30. Ibid., pp. 22-35.

31. Leon Trotsky, *The Revolution Betrayed*, (New York, 1965), pp. 19, 102.

32. Ibid., p. 57, "The application of *socialist* methods for the solution of *pre-socialist* problems—that is the very essence of the present economic and cultural work in the Soviet Union." For Trotsky, as we shall see later, socialists methods remain identical— an equation many non-Soviet socialists would have certainly rejected.

33. Ibid., p. 112.

34. See note 33 above.

35. Ibid., p. 56.

36. V. I. Lenin, *State and Revolution*, (New York, 1972), pp. 27-28.

37. Trotsky, *The Revolution Betrayed*, p. 89. For an earlier (1929-1930) but very similar definition of Trotsky of the relationship between bureaucratism and backwardness see his "Problemy razvitiia SSSR," p. 10.

38. Ibid., p. 9.

39. Ibid., p. 54.
40. Ibid., p. 59.
41. Ibid., p. 113.
42. Ibid., pp. 252-256.
43. Ibid., p. 249.
44. Ibid., p. 255.
45. Trotsky, *Rabochoe Gosudarstvo, Termidor I Bonapartizm*, p. 12.
46. Ibid., p. 11.
47. Trotsky, *The Revolution Betrayed*, pp. 249-250.
48. For Trotsky's participation in the suppression of the Kronstadt revolt of 1921, see especially Paul Avrich, *Kronstadt 1921*, (Princeton, 1970), pp. 134-137.
49. Antonio Gramsci, *The Modern Prince and Other Writings*, (New York: International Publishers 1957).

In the bureaucratic state not all the executive functions need to be concentrated in the bureaucracy and exercised by it. One might even declare that so far in history that has never been the case. The main characteristic of this type of social organization lies, we believe, in the fact that, wherever it exists, the central power conscripts a considerable portion of the social wealth by taxation and uses it first to maintain a military establishment and then to support a more extensive number of public services. The greater the number of officials who perform public duties and receive their salaries from the central government or from its local agencies, the more bureaucratic a society becomes.

Gaetano Mosca, *The Ruling Class*

2

Trotsky, Stalin and the Rise of Soviet Bureaucracy

In December 1923, Trotsky wrote a series of political articles in *Pravda*, which were subsequently published in book form under the title *Novyi Kurs* (*The New Course*). With Lenin on his deathbed, and the struggle for the succession already underway, Trotsky's articles raised a number of significant social issues over which he would finally become estranged from the party leadership in the aftermath of Lenin's death. Trotsky's title, *The New Course*, was a direct reference to the so-called party discussion in 1922–23, aimed at bringing about further democratization of various party institutions.

Stalin's already organized clientele regarded Trotsky's *New Course* with suspicion.[1] Trotsky understood their ploy was a tactical maneuver against him and that the initiators never took *The New Course* seriously but in fact intended to bring about the opposite of democratization. Although years were to pass between the publication of *The New Course*, and Trotsky's more complete analysis of the Soviet bureaucracy in *The Revolution Betrayed*, the former is still a very important work, not only because of its grasp of emerging dangers to the revolution but also because it clearly anticipated many subsequently institutionalized components of the new Soviet political system. A brief summary of *The New Course* will provide an appropriate introduction to Trotsky's later critique of Soviet bureaucracy.

The role of the revolutionary party and its organizational structure, the influence of the party ideology upon key precepts and ideals, the need, on the one hand, for a firm, select leadership and, on the other, for worker and peasant participation—all these issues had deeply concerned Trotsky from his earliest days as a revolutionary in Russia and Europe. He had not always agreed with Lenin on tactics and plans. In 1903 he was suspicious of Lenin's attitudes towards discipline, democracy and the organization of the party. For several years, along with Rosa Luxemburg, he tenaciously fought and challenged Lenin's Bolshevik principles.[2] In 1917, however, he abruptly changed his political position, and as long as Lenin remained alive, these disagreements hardly recurred. In fact, he permitted himself to be so carried away by his enthusiasm and passion for Bolshevism that he appeared to shut his eyes to numerous developments that he had earlier envisioned in his anti-Bolshevik period. He had become, in essence, the most ardent defender, if not apologist, of a political system which was quickly in the early twenties becoming authoritarian and repressive.

It was not until the middle of the agricultural crisis of 1921-23 that he became aware of the inherent dangers in these developments, though significantly it was not the rule of the Bolshevik party as such but its internal configuration and nature that aroused his concern. He realized during the debate on the economy of the country that the nature and character of the party was undergoing important changes. These political alterations, of course, had begun before Lenin's illness but with Lenin incapacitated in 1924, and organizational matters completely in Stalin's hands, the process was being accelerated.[3]

It is in this political context that Trotsky formulated *The New Course*. Nothing could be farther from the truth than to present Trotsky in the subsequent political controversy as the voice of freedom and democracy—as some Trotsky apologists and even such respectable historians as E. H. Carr and Isaac Deutscher have done. Deutscher, in the last chapter of *The Prophet Armed*, shows Trotsky "stumbling" into tragedy and eventually abandoning the hope of "proletarian democracy." And Trotsky's personal tragedy is equated with the tragedy of Bolshevism:

At the very pinnacle of power Trotsky, like the protagonist of a classical tragedy, stumbled. He acted against his own principle and in disregard of a most solemn moral commitment. Circumstances, the preservation of the revolution, and his own pride drove him into this predicament. Placed as he was he could hardly have avoided it. His steps followed almost inevitably from all that he had done before; and only one step now separated the sublime from the sinister—even his denial of principle was still dictated by principle. Yet in acting as he did he shattered the ground on which he stood.[4]

Trotsky, indeed, "shattered the ground" by propounding militarization of labor and of trade unions as a permanent policy. He advocated labor camps and he was sincerely disappointed when Lenin and Bukharin rebuffed his proposal.[5] As a military commander, he was always ready to use force to persuade people and to defend the "principles of proletarian democracy."[6] For Trotsky, the issues were not democratization or liberalization of the system, not the legitimacy of the one-party rule, not even the extent of the political authority of the Bolshevik party. If anything, he strove for a return to the type of regime created by himself and Lenin: this meant highly disciplined, organized and strict military rule. For him, that form of government was far more egalitarian and enlightened than Stalinism but it could hardly be described as democratic. In addition, he was no more interested in party unity than were his opponents, and he was no less intolerant than the men he criticized. The principal of "centralism" and the dictatorship of the party remained for him key foundations of the Soviet political apparatus.

The central problem, therefore, was the internal configuration of the party and ultimately the distribution of political power in it; to some extent on certain issues Trotsky was closer to the democratic principles than the rest of the Bolshevik leadership.[7] As a result, one of the key demands which he formulated in *The New Course* was a policy which would widen the mass basis of the party, increase membership from among the workers, stimulate mass participation, and force party functionaries by rules and codes to be open to the influence of the rank-and-file.[8] Besides, it was the new generation of Bolshevik youth, imbued with revolutionary spirit and duty, that he hoped not simply to win over to his ideas but also to mold and influence in new directions. Although he belonged to the generation of the "Old Guard," *The New Course* was clearly written as a warning against the dangers of permitting veterans to dominate the party.[9]

Accustomed to persuade people by force of argument and reason, Trotsky pleaded in *The New Course* for freedom of expression, for values attached to criticism, independence of thought, and the possibility of open debate.[10] Unlike most influential party members, he denounced the whole concept of bureaucratic "yes-men," and others that he referred to as "empty well-wishers who know what side their bread is buttered on."[11] He completely rejected all tendencies that lead to one-man rule; he believed that the central principle of Bolshevik "democracy" was always the rule of "collectivity,"[12] and that this principle had to be restored immediately. Of course, he never defined it as meaning the elimination of hierarchy, and the substitution for it of some sort of organizational equality; he was after all a military administrator who enforced hierarchy and discipline. In his opinion the decision making process should represent the "collective will" at each party level, including the participation of provincial organizations and not that of a single individual or "secretary" strategically located by virtue of his function.[13]

However intense Trotsky's appeal to the party leadership in 1923–24 for democratization of party organs may have sounded, the central theme of *The New Course*, again repeated at the Thirteenth Party Congress on 24 May 1924, remained the preservation of the revolutionary spirit. At a crucial period when the socio-economic revolution in the Soviet Union, not to mention the political revolution in Western Europe, had hardly begun, it appeared to him that the Bolshevik party was already turning into an institutionalized, conservative force. It was too concerned, according to Trotsky, with protecting the little that had been gained rather than pursuing the much that remained to be achieved through the revolutionary process.

Younger members, newer ideas, more discussions, and constant appeal to the masses—all these, he insisted, would not only democratize the party but, more importantly, help to keep its revolutionary character. He was obsessed with the party's revolutionary successes, and as military commander he was deeply inspired by its concrete achievements. In *The New Course*, he expressed concern about the loss of revolutionary spirit and the party's sense of duty to the society. Replacing the party, he claimed, was a new driving force completely different in its character and implications. This new force, he asserted, was "bureaucratism," the very antithesis of revolutionary spirit.

Trotsky made some trenchant observations about bureaucratic rule in *The New Course*, but as we shall see it was not until the 1930s that his more original critique of bureaucracy emerged. Nevertheless, in *The New Course* his understanding and implications of bureaucratic rule by a small Soviet elite was profound. He had no doubt that the bureaucracy was a powerful new force. He envisioned that its rule would provide stability, order and security from foreign powers and other needs that had to be met in order to ensure the survival of postrevolutionary Russian society. He recognized its potential, especially when it was backed by unlimited power and coercion. He believed that the bureaucratic system would automatically exclude the fulfillment of those very goals and ideals which the revolution had originally set out to realize; therefore, whatever initial advantages might arise from bureaucratic government would be lost by the damage it would cause to the whole state.[14] In Trotsky's opinion, the bureaucracy was simply incompatible with socialism—as Marx had shown in his classic, *The Eighteenth Brumaire*. Like Marx, he claimed that the sources of bureaucratism were always opposed to socialist aims: bureaucratism was merely a substitute and according to both men, an artificial one at that, for that sort of social harmony which still remained unrealized. This is how Marx described the French bureaucracy:

Every common interest was straightaway severed from society, and counterposed to it as a higher, general interest, snatched from the activity of society's members themselves and made an object of government activity, from a bridge, a school-house and the communal property of a village community to the railways, the national wealth and the national university of France ... It was the instrument of the *ruling class*, however much it strove for power of its own.[15]

Trotsky commented on a similar development in the Soviet Union:

Bureaucratism is a social phenomenon in that it is a definite system of administration of men and things. Its profound causes lie in the heterogeneity of society, the difference between the daily and the fundamental interests of various groups of the population. Bureaucratism is complicated by the fact of the lack of culture of the broad masses. With us, the essential source of bureaucratism resides in the necessity of creating and sustaining a state apparatus that unites the interests of the proletariat and those of the peasantry in a perfect harmony, from which we are still far removed. The necessity of maintaining a permanent army is likewise another important source of bureaucratism.[16]

Throughout *The New Course* and his other newspaper articles and pamphlets, it is not so much the sources as the nature and consequences of bureaucratism that worried Trotsky. Like Marx, he in 1924 recognized the bureaucracy as a system in which the administrative apparatus becomes the dominant organ of rule; instead of implementing decisions and policies, which is its proper function, it makes them. Functionaries and specialists are either appointed to the political posts, or political questions are referred to the administrative structure they control. In addition, decisions are reached in accordance with administrative considerations which now become the supreme criteria. Discussion of the problems of issues involved is therefore primarily technical and involves only those party members who are supposedly competent to deal with such matters. Trotsky does not realize or purposely ignores the fact that economic and social reconstruction confronting postrevolutionary society demanded a substantial increase in governmental offices and functions. As an impatient and supreme military administrator, it is difficult to believe that Trotsky did not recognize the significance of some kind of an efficient bureaucracy being clearly inevitable and necessary to respond to the growing list of problems after the Revolution and the Civil War. And it was precisely the expert with administrative skills and abilities who was both drawn by and ultimately welcomed into the new state institutions.[17] The peasant and the uneducated worker obviously found themselves excluded in this process. As a result, "the state and various party organizations became the virtual monopoly of a new type of "revolutionary," the bureaucrat, whose response to all political and social problems remained business-like and down-to-earth."[18]

In Trotsky's opinion, the seclusion of the idealistic members in the new generation was compounded by the fact that "Old Guard" factions,[19] formerly moved by idealistic motives, also developed in the aftermath of revolutionary successes a deep desire for successful careers, material rewards and social privileges. To Trotsky, these were the initial steps that led to the bureaucratization of the Revolution. Many party members were simply motivated by their hope of retaining power and control.[20]

In 1917–1918 approximately one million people were employed in the administrative offices of the Soviet Union; by 1921–22 this number had already increased to almost three million.[21] Of course, many bureaucratic functions had been assumed by those active in the revolutionary underground, in the Revolution itself, but the most official positions remained under the influence of specialists of the old regime. In one of his last statements to the Central Committee in 1923, Lenin reported that although Bolsheviks had not obtained the most significant administrative positions, they were actually still being controlled by the old bureaucratic system. He remarked that just as victorious nations had in the past often been assimilated into the culture of the defeated country, the Bolsheviks seemed to be undergoing a similar transformation—although the culture by which they were being devoured was a miserable one.[22] He emphasized the same point at the Comintern meeting on 4 December 1922, [23] lamenting to the Comintern officials that the takeover by the Bolsheviks of the tsarist administrative apparatus was in reality a serious misfortune. Deep down below the surface there were thousands upon thousands of old-time bureaucrats inherited from the hated autocratic system and from bourgeois society. Just before Lenin was removed from his political office in 1924 by a stroke, he characterized the new government as being largely a remnant of the old one with a slightly repainted surface.

Portraying the same historic period of the Revolution as Lenin, political analyst and historian Lev Kritzmann gave an account of the process which contributed to the rapid growth of the bureaucracy.[24] According to Kritzmann, the Revolution brought the whole administrative machine to a standstill and "released spontaneous forces to an extent which had hardly been anticipated."[25] The expectations for the future called forth by the overthrow of the autocracy and the widespread trend toward self-sufficiency generated high enthusiasm in those individuals and groups unexpectedly called upon to participate in running the government. This enthusiasm led Lenin and Trotsky to think in terms of completely new ways of organizing society, or at least to identify themselves with this belief. The workers' and soldiers' soviets which sprang up everywhere in the country and which took charge of social planning obviously replaced the "dead" tsarist bureaucracy.[26] But as Kritzmann accurately points out, it was extremely difficult to provide for a country in which production depended on innumerable small businesses and whose normally inadequate transportation system was barely able to function. The already famine-struck land was subjected to growing numbers of new and stricter regulations to assure the delivery and distribution of agricultural products.[27]

For a short period during the war for communism, in 1918 and 1919, the workers did control the nation but the reserve of competent manpower and personnel was much too small and the general level of education too low to stem the rising tide of bureaucratic power. Cadres of thousands of workers were sent by the party to the provinces and into the countryside to take control and assume administrative duties.[28] Instead of being able to analyze governmental policy or the violation of democratic and human rights, they suddenly found themselves appointed presidents of collective farms, directors of state farms, or as organizers of different nationalities of cultural groups of which they had little or no knowledge. In this manner the political energy of the "working class" was exhausted.[29]

At this same time, which was one of the extreme economic scarcity, Trotsky and the rest of the Bolshevik leadership lost patience with manifestations of local willfulness. Praise of decentralized local government was replaced by the demand for discipline and subordination. Bukharin had been one of the first, in April 1918, to warn against "bureaucratic centralization," and the danger of the "enslavement of the working class."[30] But shortly after that he argued that the nationalization of unions and the political nationalization of all other proletarian mass organizations resulted from the internal logic of the change itself. He believed that the smallest nuclei of the workers' apparatus had to become the basic transmission units of a universal process of organization, systematically planned and controlled by what he regarded as the collective judgment of the working class. The latter would find its material embodiment in the highest and all-encompassing organization, its governmental machine.[31]

Bureaucratization could also be viewed as a consequence of utter exhaustion and of years of revolutionary underground activity, resulting in the wish to reap immediate benefits rather than wait for long-term promises. Rosa Luxemburg recognized this aspect of the Bolshevik movement as early as 1918:

In the place of representative bodies elected by general plebiscite, Lenin and Trotsky have proclaimed the soviets as the only true representatives of the proletariat. However, as the country's political activities are progressively suppressed, the soviets, too, must grow weaker. But unless general elections are held, unless there is freedom of the press and of assembly, as well as freedom of expression, life dies out in every public institution. What is left is a sham existence, in which only bureaucracy remains as the active element.[32]

Luxemburg envisioned a revolutionary party trained on centralist principles to form a dictatorial state. When Trotsky's "Old Guard" revolutionaries finally came to power they forced out all other parties. Contrary to all of Marx's theories, because they were convinced that the party, in its role as the organized repository of the spirit of history, could dictate the course of historical events, the Bolsheviks expected to create a socialist system in a country whose conditions of productivity were completely underdeveloped. According to Trotsky, however, these same "Old Guard" revolutionaries became greedy and opportunistic. Early in the post-Lenin period and especially during his personal struggle with Stalin in 1925–26, Trotsky realized and worried about this "degenerated" clique. He wrote:

But no less great is the danger, at the other pole, of the regime that has lasted too long and become synonymous in the party with bureaucratism ... Does bureaucratism bear within it a danger of degeneration, or does it not? He would be blind who denied it. In its prolonged development, bureaucratization threatens to detach the leaders from the masses, to bring them to concentrate their attention solely upon questions of administration, of appointments and transfers, of narrowing their horizon, of weakening their revolutionary spirit, that is, of provoking a more or less opportunistic degeneration of the Old Guard, or at the very least of a considerable part of it. Such processes develop slowly and almost imperceptibly, but reveal themselves abruptly.[33]

In any case, the political harm, according to Trotsky, was not simply that all power would become centralized and concentrated in the hands of few "secretaries" who controlled the party organizations, but that the dictatorship of the party would inevitably "sap the basis of the revolution."[34] For him, bureaucratization fostered and thrived on conservatism. It enshrined the past and the present at the expense of the future. It "killed initiative," discouraged inventiveness, and negated in principle all that seemed in the least experimental, new, untried and original. Bureaucracy, then, preserved a static tradition, supplying formally but fanatically methods and thinking which, though perhaps successful in the past, could prove unsuitable in new and different contexts.[35] And under the rule of bureaucracy tradition had no chance of developing since individuals who inherited it had no prospect of being enriched by it; tradition, as he explained, simply became a body of absolute criteria instead of a source of inspiration and guidance:

The fairly great bureaucratization of the party apparatus is inevitably accompanied by the development of conservative traditionalism with all its effects. It is better to exaggerate this danger than to underrate it. The indubitable fact that the most conservative elements of the apparatus are inclined to identify their opinions, their methods and their mistakes with "old Bolshevism," and seek to identify the criticism of bureaucratism with the destruction of tradition, this fact, I say, is already by itself the incontestable expression of a certain ideological petrification.[36]

In another comment to the Central Committee at the Thirteenth Party Congress, Trotsky reasserted that "this is not to say, that our party is completely free of certain conservative traditionalism: a mass party cannot have such an ideal liberty." But he concluded that "its strength and potency have manifested themselves in the fact that inertia, traditionalism, routinism, were reduced to a minimum by a far-sighted, profoundly tactical initiative, at once audacious and realistic."[37]

Whom did Trotsky have in mind? In his attempt to illustrate the exact opposite of conservatism and tradition, Trotsky referred to Leninism. He identified it with true revolutionary spirit and duty and by inference included himself in the connection. As he summed it up in *The New Course*:

Leninism cannot be conceived of without theoretical breadth, without a critical analysis of the material bases of the political process ... Leninism is, first of all, realism, the highest qualitative and quantitative appreciation of reality, from the standpoint of revolutionary action ... Leninism is genuine freedom from formalistic prejudices, from moralizing doctrinalism, from all forms of intellectual conservatism attempting to bind the will of revolutionary action. ... Leninism includes the morality, not formal but genuinely revolutionary, of mass action and the mass party. Nothing is so alien to it as functionary-arrogance and bureaucratic cynicism ... Leninism is orthodox, obdurate, irreducible, but it does not contain so much as a hint of formalism, canon, nor bureaucratism. In the struggle, it takes the bull by the horns. To make out of the traditions of Leninism a supratheoretical guarantee of the infallibility of all the words and thoughts of the interpreters of these traditions, is to scoff at genuine revolutionary tradition and transform it into official bureaucratism.[38]

Like all Communists of his generation, Trotsky conceded that obedience, party discipline, morality and unity were indispensable components of action. These were the ultimate characteristics of a "Leninist" party. But he refused to identify these characteristics with the type of regimentation which was a function of obvious dictatorial methods, based on "orders from above," divorced from all sense of collective responsibility, and functioning in accordance with bureaucratic regulations. In his view, party unity and effective discipline could only be achieved through criticism, debate, free airing of opinions, and a collective form of decision making. Like Lenin, whom he criticized in the prerevolutionary period but from whom he learned much during the revolutionary upheaval in 1917–18, Trotsky stressed that once a decision was made it was the duty of each party member to abide by it faithfully. But the party official would best carry it out if he knew that the decision had been reached in open discussion in which the official's views, even if in opposition, was permitted a hearing. So Trotsky lauded what he called Leninist principle of uniting "the indestructable alliance of revolutionary initiative, of critical, bold elaboration of questions, with iron discipline in action."[39] He insisted throughout *The New Course* that the regimentation of the bureaucracy would simply result in the suppression of the "collective will" of the party, in "passive obedience," in "careerism" and in "factionalism".[40] As he explains further in another comment:

Out of the party with passive obedience, with mechanical levelling by the authorities, with suppression of personality, with servility, with careerism! A Bolshevik is not merely a disciplined man; he is a man who in each case and on each question forges a firm opinion of his own and defends it courageously and independently, not only against his enemies, but inside his own party. Today, perhaps, he will be in the minority in his organization. He will submit because it is his party. But this does not always signify that he is in the wrong. Perhaps he saw or understood before the others did a new task or the necessity of turn. He will persistently raise the question a second, a third, a tenth time, if need be. Thereby he will render his party a service, helping it meet the new task fully armed or carry out the necessary turn without organic upheavals, without factional convulsions.[41]

In the above statement and in other passages in *The New Course*, Trotsky's position on discipline indicates the character and limits of his commitment to democracy within the party. Although he continued to debate this point with his admirers and political enemies throughout his career,[42] he nevertheless remained opposed to any activity that aimed at providing minority opinions with an organization base. So *The New Course* articles and numerous newspaper editorials constantly warned the party against any type of faction.[43] The tendency towards "groupings" or "factionalism" was, he later realized, inevitable in a one-party system, since the party had to be sufficiently broad to encompass such a wide variety of views and interests. This was especially true in the case of the Bolshevik party, since, its key concern was to close the gap between the workers and peasants. Factionalism had to be severely resisted and even "crushed" if necessary, because, he believed, every "grouping" created internal dissension and was potentially the source of party division. Like Lenin, he argued that in the party of the proletariat, the rise of "factional formations" would mean the rise of opposition to the proletarian society. In other words, it was not simply the threat of rival "groupings" within Bolshevik organizations which factionalism made possible but the fear of some prospect of transforming the party into an arena of class divisions.

If this were really the case, how then did Trotsky explain his own personal position? Had he not inspired and in fact became associated with "factions"? Did he not, on the other hand, contribute to the establishment of the bureaucratic regime? He never conceded this, constantly reiterating that neither factions nor the present bureaucracy had anything in common with his own and Lenin's rule. He argued that it was those who supported bureaucratism who were deviating from the correct revolutionary policy by introducing methods which would alienate the masses and paralyze their ability to take part in revolutionary policy. As he wrote in another article, "Groups and Factional Formations," in *The New Course*:

We are witness, on the contrary to a new offensive at the present time by the latter, who reject every criticism of the "old course," formally condemned but not yet liquidated, by treating it as a manifestation of factional spirit. If factionalism is dangerous, and it is—it is criminal to shut your eyes to the danger represented by *conservative bureaucratic factionalism.*[44]

According to Trotsky then, the non-bureaucratic position belonged to him, which of course represented the correct road, the road to socialist proletarian society, while the bureaucratic "groupings and factions" threatened to "sap the basis of the revolution."[45] As we shall see, this was to become in the 1930s the central theme of his critique of Stalinism. In 1923–24, at the time of his "new course" formulations, he could not imagine the depths to which the bureaucratic "degeneration" could reach. Throughout the 1920s he continued to believe that these developments were only "deviations" which the Bolshevik leadership could correct were it to renew its ties and faith with the workers and peasants. As he explained, the leadership had to reassert and follow the original Leninist principles:

Every unit of the party must return to collective initiative, to the right of free and comradely criticism—without fear and without turning back—the right of organizational self-determination. It is necessary to regenerate and renovate the party apparatus and to make it feel that it is nothing but the executive mechanism of the collective will . . . And before anything else, the leading posts must be cleared out of those who, at the first word of criticism, of objection, or of protest, brandish the thunderbolts of penalties before the critic. The "new course" must begin by making everyone feel that from now on nobody will dare terrorize the party . . . The renovation of the party apparatus—naturally within the clear-cut framework of the statutes—must aim at replacing the mummified bureaucrats with fresh elements closely linked with the life of the collectivity, or capable of assuring such a line.[46]

Even though Trotsky was convinced that he was on the side of "truth," and obviously the party bureaucrats were the "betrayers" of its gospel, we still need to know why Trotsky continued to adhere to Leninism. Why did he continue his faith in Bolshevism? Why he did not attack the post-Lenin leadership with action instead of words, why he did not try to usurp power as he did during the revolutionary upheavals in 1905 and 1917? Among many historians this continues to be the central enigma of Trotsky's personality and of his personal judgment to this day.[47] This is a tactical and political issue which cannot be considered here but will be examined in the next chapter along with his views of Stalinism.

It is evident that Trotsky placed supreme importance on loyalty to the party and especially on party unity. Looked at from this angle, it is not surprising that he was so reticent in his quest for political power. Throughout *The New Course* articles, he emphasized that the Bolshevik who was of the minority opinion in the party had nevertheless to "submit because it is his Party." At the Thirteenth Party Congress in May 1924, he once again appealed to the principle of obedience in a style which clearly illustrated his sense of loyalty, but at the same time betrayed the contradiction of his own position as well as that of the Leninist conception of the party on which it was based. Responding to charges by the Stalinist "triumvirate" at the conference—he said little of importance in his last speech to the members of the party. Isaac Deutscher's seminal but extremely sympathetic treatment of Trotsky focused on his inactivity. Deutscher viewed the tragedy of his hero in the following passage:

None of us wishes to be right or can be right against his party. Ultimately, the party is always right because it is a unique historical instrument given to the proletariat for the realization of its fundamental tasks. I have already said that nothing would be easier than to say before the party: "All this criticism, all these declarations, warnings and protests were simply mistaken in their entirety. I cannot, however, say so, comrades, because I do not think that it is so. I know that one cannot be right against the party. One can be right only with the party and through the party since history has not created any other paths for the realization of that which is right. The English have a saying: "My country, right or wrong." With far greater historical justification we can say: "Right or wrong—wrong on certain specific, concrete questions—but it is my party" . . . It would be ridiculous perhaps, almost indecent, to express personal statements here, but I hope that should the need arise I shall not prove to be the lowest soldier on the lowest Bolshevik barricades.[48]

Trotsky's comments above fully expressed his rather uncomfortable position in the party. His pride and often arrogant self-assurance did not permit him to admit that he was wrong; instead he continued to argue that the party must remain united even when serious errors were committed. When the final conflict arose between his own opinions and those of the party, he bowed to the latter. In this manner, he decided to defend and preserve the principles of Leninism and obedience. As we shall see shortly in his analysis of Stalinism in *The Revolution Betrayed*, it was a principle he continued to support until the end of his political career.

After Lenin's death on 21 January 1924, Trotsky and other members of the Communist Party of the Soviet Union continued to struggle against the increasing bureaucratization of the party in particular and the Soviet state in general. The "Left Opposition," as this loosely constituted group was known, launched an attack on the nature of the political system. In a letter to the Central Committee of 7 October 1923, Trotsky publicly complained that Stalin, Zinoviev and Kamenev were responsible for the fact that:

The bureaucratization of the party apparatus has developed to unheard of proportions by means of the method of secretarial selection . . . Appointment of the secretaries of provincial committees is now the rule. That creates for the secretary a position essentially independent of the local organization . . . There has been created a very broad stratum of party workers, entering into the apparatus of the government of the party, who completely renounce their own opinion, at least the open expression of it, as though assuming that the secretarial hierarchy is the apparatus which creates party opinion and party decisions.[49]

One week later, on 15 October 1923, Trotsky and several members of the "Left Opposition," including such well-known and highly respected members as Christian Rakovsky and Evgenii Preobrazhensky, presented another statement to the Politburo. Known as the *Platform of Forty-Six*, the authors of the document explicitly argued that the secretarial hierarchy of the party must be slowly brought to a stop. Preobrazhensky and his committee called for stricter membership procedures and recruitment policies and requested immediate party action. The essential thesis of their document was that "the secretarial hierarchy of the party to an ever greater extent recruits the membership of conferences and congresses, which are becoming to an ever greater extend the executive assemblies of this hierarchy."[50] *The Platform of Forty-Six*, like Trotsky's *New Course*, in which he passionately argued for a thorough-going renovation, also came too late. The party leadership was already firmly in Stalin's hands.

In 1926, when his political demise was no longer in doubt, Trotsky began to view bureaucratic development and his internal party struggle in much broader terms than expressed either in *The New Course* or in the *Platform*. For the first time, he recognized the effects of the postrevolutionary economic crises. In his diary, he admitted that the revolution had not fulfilled the high hopes and expectations of the masses; their revolutionary exertions had drained their energy and created a more skeptical mood in the country.[51] The peasants were exhausted by the continuous struggle, the war, the economic shortages and material sacrifices; in 1925–26 they wanted to keep their newly acquired land and were not interested in Trotsky's ultimate socialist aims; the working class had also lost its revolutionary zeal for similar reasons. Trotsky soon began to argue that it was these social and economic conditions that permitted conservative and reactionary elements to emerge in the party, under the banner of order, stability and power. In other words, these bureaucratic "opportunists" exploited the post revolutionary disillusionment of the masses and in fact, for Trotsky, they signified a return to capitalism and a "bourgeois restoration."[52]

The problem of underdevelopment of the Soviet Union—comprehended in its socio-economic and cultural senses—and socialism was a frequent theme in Trotsky's writing, before and after the Revolution. Like Lenin and other Marxists, he assumed that socialism was dependent on the highest possible development of the economy's productive forces and he was confident that economic crises would be solved after the overthrow of the bureaucratic autocracy of tsarism. Before the upheavals in 1905 and 1917 Trotsky tended to exaggerate the extent to which economic forces making for socialist change had evolved in Russia.[53]

In 1924, in a short but concise book, *Problems of Life*, Trotsky returned to the problem of backwardness and tradition. He warned the party of the "vengeance" of bureaucratic inertia, of meaningless church ritual, and the traditional Russian passion for vodka. He believed that a "workers' state" that could not eradicate poverty, increase literacy and culture, and obtain new technological know-how, would eventually fail. It was in these unresolved problems that in the 1930s he began to see the roots of Stalinist bureaucracy. In *The Revolution Betrayed*, Trotsky defined the roots in the following comprehensive terms:

> The basis of bureaucratic rule is the poverty of society in the objects of consumption, with the resulting struggle of each against all. When there are enough goods in the store, the purchasers can come whenever they want. When there are few goods, the purchasers are compelled to stand in line. When the lines are very long, it is necessary to appoint a policeman to keep order. Such is the starting point of the power of the Soviet bureaucracy. It "knows" who is to get something and who has to wait.[54]

Like Lenin's *State and Revolution*, Trotsky's *The Revolution Betrayed* asserted that once economic scarcity was eradicated and affluence achieved, bureaucratic problems would disappear. In 1917, Lenin predicted that the principle of self-government would be carried so far that in the future any cook could manage and rule the state.[55] According to his theory, since everyone was to participate in administering the state, everyone would become a temporary "bureaucrat," and therefore no one would be a real bureaucrat.[56] Lenin thus predicted that bureaucracy would die out. In his "Theses on Bourgeois Democracy and Proletarian Dictatorship,"[57] he also wrote that the elimination of governmental power was the principal aim of all socialists, and especially of Marx. Had not Marx drawn similar conclusions from the experiences of the Paris Commune? Unless this goal was realized, real democracy, that is, freedom and equality, could not be achieved. But in Lenin's view, the only practical way of obtaining this aim was through soviet or proletarian democracy, because the latter immediately began the "withering away" of the state by involving working class organizations in continuous and total participation in governmental administration.[58]

Trotsky took over utopian aspects of Lenin's and Marx's views, but he later explained that neither Marx—who never observed the problem of bureaucracy in the context of an underdeveloped society—nor Lenin had ever envisioned the serious, and ultimately destructive lack of culture which existed in the aftermath of the Russian Revolution. In *The Revolution Betrayed*, he elaborated in detail the comparison between Marx and Lenin; he also pointed out their visionary shortcomings:

> Before *The Communist Manifesto*, young Marx wrote: "A development of the productive forces is the absolutely necessary practical premise (of Communism), because without it want is generalized, and with want the struggle for necessities begin again, and that means that all that old crap must revive." This thought Marx never directly developed, and for no accidental reason: he never foresaw a pro-

letarian revolution in a backward country. Lenin also never dwelt upon it, and this too was not accidental. He did not foresee so prolonged an isolation of the Soviet state. Nevertheless, the citation, merely an abstract construction with Marx, an inference from the opposite, provides an indispensable theoretical key to the wholly concrete difficulties and sickness of the Soviet regime. On the historic basis of destructions of the imperialist and civil wars, the "struggle for individual existence" not only did not disappear the day after the overthrow of the bourgeoisie, and not only did not abate in the succeeding years, but, on the contrary, assumed at times an unheard of ferocity. Need we recall that certain regions of the country had twice gone to the point of cannibalism?[59]

Marx's shortsightedness was understandable. But Lenin too failed to draw the necessary conclusions as to the nature of the postrevolutionary Soviet state. According to Trotsky, Lenin's *State and Revolution* incorrectly assumed that "political measures" would be sufficient to eliminate "bureaucratic distortions."[60] Paraphrasing Lenin, Trotsky wrote that "it was assumed that along this road the bureaucrat, from being a boss, would turn into a simple and moreover temporary technical agent, and the state would gradually and imperceptibly disappear from the scene."[61] Here Trotsky was not in complete agreement with Lenin's prognosis. The roots of bureaucracy were not really administrative or political but rather social and historical. The vexing problem was that socio-economic underdevelopment was simply incompatible with a socialist state. What was necessary, according to Trotsky's line of argument, was to confront the underdeveloped state with a bold theory and a logical plan. If his ideas were not followed, it was obvious who would win:

It is perfectly obvious that the poorer the society which issues from a revolution, the sterner and more naked would be the expression of this "law," the more crude would be the forms assumed by bureaucratism, and the more dangerous would it become for socialist development. The Soviet state is prevented not only from dying away, but even from freeing itself of the bureaucratic parasite, not by the "relics" of the former ruling classes, as declares the naked public doctrine of Stalin, for these relics are powerless in themselves. It is prevented by immeasurably mightier factors, such as material want, cultural backwardness and the resulting dominance of "bourgeois law" in what most immediately and sharply touches every human being, the business of insuring his personal existence.[62]

Trotsky eventually came to view Stalin's bureaucratic victory as a result of this backward economic and cultural milieu. Of course, Trotsky recognized that the political struggle that followed Lenin's death, the political actors and their strategies, were all significant and played their part in Stalin's triumph. According to Trotsky, however, they do not tell the whole story. "A political struggle is in its essence a struggle of interests and forces, not of arguments. The quality of leadership is, of course, far from a matter of indifference for the outcome of the conflict, but it is not the only factor, and in the last analysis is not decisive. Each of the struggling camps moreover demands leaders in its own image."[63] What was crucial for Trotsky, then, was the social and historical context: the social and economic problems inherited by the Bolshevik regime after its victory over the autocracy.

All revolutions, Trotsky later admitted in exile in Mexico, psychologically and physically drain the strength, vitality and emotions of their people.[64] In a personal note to Christian Rakovsky, one of his closest followers and admirers, Trotsky remarked that a "revolution is a mighty devourer of human energy, both individual and collective. The nerves give way. Consciousness is shaken and characters are worn out. Events unfold too swiftly for the flow of fresh forces to replace the loss. Hunger, unemployment, the death of revolutionary cadres, the removal of the masses from administration, all this led to a physical and moral impoverishment."[65] In the same correspondence with Rakovsky, Trotsky further admitted that it was impossible to make rapid material improvements in the lives of the people in the immediate aftermath of the Revolution. Why? Because Bolshevik Russia of 1917–1925 was still a backward country; the civil war, the severe economic crises of "price scissors"[66] of 1923, the inefficient state industry and political isolationism, combined, according to Trotsky, to create ideal conditions for Stalinist bureaucracy.

In the light of Soviet Union's severe economic conditions after the Revolution, was Stalin's triumph and the bureacratization of the state therefore inevitable? Was Stalinism a necessary consequence of the Russian Revolution? Like some of his admirers and apologists, this is exactly what he is suggesting. Russia's socio-economic and cultural backwardness remained a key source of bureaucratism.[67] Yet he took every opportunity to emphasize that another political and social road was available to Bolshevism.

Writing in 1918 about the Russian socialist movement and about Lenin's concepts, Rosa Luxemburg recognized that socialist and cultural conditions necessary for a successful socialist state were lacking in Russia.[68] In 1920, Otto Ruehle, an influential member and cofounder of the German Communist Party characterized the conditions of Russia in much the same terms as Luxemburg. He also made the following interesting observations in 1921 about the Bolshevik adjustment to the country's unfavorable socioeconomic conditions. He concluded that the Bolsheviks

changed over to socialism with a magnificently daring leap. At least they persuaded themselves that it was sufficient for socialists to obtain political power in order to develop a socialist era. They thought they could achieve by overt action what had to evolve slowly, as a product of organic development. They saw the revolution and socialism first and foremost as political matters. How could such excellent Marxists ever forget that these are primarily economic matters? The indispensable prerequisites for a socialist economy, and for socialism as a whole, are highly developed capitalist production, developed technology, a trained labor force and the highest possible productive output. Where did such conditions exist in Russia? The rapid progress of revolution in the world would supply what is missing. The Bolsheviks did all they could to bring this revolution about. But it did not take place. Thus a vacuum was created. What they had was political socialism without an economic basis; a theoretical design; a bureaucratic arrangement; a collection of paper decrees; a few inflammatory phrases; and, above all, a dreadful disappointment.[69]

Lenin and Trotsky were obviously not in agreement with Ruehle's 1921 summary. Considering the poverty and malaise of the new Soviet state, they recognized that the restoration of the old bureaucracy was a possibility. But their supreme confidence in the role of the party as the embodiment of popular political will allow them to believe that such a return to autocratic rule would be prevented as long as power remained in reliable Bolshevik hands.

Lenin's and Trotsky's ideological theories of the revolution were maintained during this period and the party functioned as a unified organization. This was possible because Lenin's concept of leadership justified the utilization of bureaucratic regulations and policies, and because the party itself was transformed into a bureaucratic instrument. As mentioned earlier, it was also the source of recruits for the bureaucracy. Political power was concentrated in the hands of the party's secretary. The Eleventh Party Congress, held in April 1922, included a resolution pointing out that the party's organizations were in the process of being overwhelmed by the large administrative machine serving them. This machine, according to this resolution, had expanded gradually and had begun to absorb an excessive number of party members.[70]

When Lenin spoke of bureaucratic degeneration of the workers' state and the dangers of bureaucratic restoration, he was not referring to administrative deficiencies, to the snail's pace at which state business was accomplished, or to procedural delays. What he had in mind was the growth of an administrative machine which would try to govern rather than administer and which would have a claim on material as well as political privileges.[71] Conscious of this bureaucratic development, Lenin in 1923 attempted to alter its direction. He criticized the "invisible hands"[72] that had begun to control the wheel. By speaking out, he also hoped to halt the bureaucratization of unions and other worker organizations.

In *How Russia is Ruled*, Merle Fainsod pointed out that one out of twenty-five Bolshevik party members held fulltime administrative positions in the party in 1927 at the Fifteenth Congress.[73] Once the local party secretaries were subordinated to the central apparatus, from which they not only received their orders but on which they also depended for their promotion, the hierarchy became a special group in society. This development, according to Fainsod, was paralleled by a growing reverence for the state which replaced socialist concepts and goals.[74]

In *The Revolution Betrayed*, Trotsky was concerned with how the political power of the proletariat had "degenerated" and why Stalin's clique was able to gain political control. How could his and Lenin's "correct policies" have resulted in such a "parasitic" administration? How was it possible for Stalin to take the power away from the old cadres? As he proceeded to explain this development, it soon became clear that his arguments were inconsistent and contradictory.

The initial point of his investigation was the "official" claim that nationalization of property brought about by the Revolution had already transformed the Soviet Union into a socialist society. He rejected this theory at once. And in *The Revolution Betrayed* there is a direct challenge to Stalin's "official" doctrine:

To become social, private property must as inevitably pass the stage as the caterpillar in order to become a butterfly must pass through the pupal stage. But the pupa is not a butterfly. Myriads of pupae perish without ever becoming butterflies. State property becomes the property of the "whole people" only to the degree that social privilege and differentiation disappear, and therewith the necessity of the state. In other words: state property is converted into socialist property in proportion as it ceases to be state property. And the contrary is true; the higher the Soviet state rises above the people, and the more fiercely it opposes itself as the guardian of property to the people as its squanderer, the more obviously does it testify against the socialist character of this state property.[75]

What is significant here is that he points directly to the relationship of the "dialectic," which is always crucial to modes of production and distribution.[76] To alter ownership while keeping the same old principles of distribution is, as far as he is concerned, to make a mere "juridical change in proprietorship."[77] Social inequality, favoritism, and economic distinctions would not be alleviated but would in fact continue only under a different name. "In reality," Trotsky emphasized, it made little sense to the "day laborer" whether he was employed privately or by the state if at both locations the "conditions" of labor were identical.[78] An in Stalin's Russia, state ownership did not alter conditions of work.

What made Trotsky especially bitter was Stalin's introduction of large scale wage differentials and his brutal push for greater productivity. He vented his frustrations on the rise of "Stakhanovite" workers:

In the course of the few months an entire stratum of workers has arisen whom they call "thousand men," since their earnings exceed the thousand rubles a month . . . It would seem as though this divergence of wages alone establishes a sufficient distinction between "rich" and "unrich" workers. But that is not enough for the bureaucracy. They literally shower privileges upon the Stakhanovists . . . the number of suits, shoes, gramophones, bicycles, or jars of conserves this or that decorated worker has brought himself.[79]

As a result of the hierarchical relations, the flagrant differences of wages and benefits in the work force, Trotsky concluded that Stalin had introduced "sharp antagonisms" among the workers.[80] Most important, however, the bureaucrats were not in control, and the "free worker" no longer existed under state ownership, any more than he did under capitalism. Specifically what Trotsky meant was that workers were no longer running their industries and they could find no place in the "super-bureaucratic" system of management.[81] In his expressive words, the workers became subject to the decrees of the new "corps of slave drivers."[82] Only when the workers rise up and defeat the bureaucrats could the principle of "collective ownership" be introduced again and applied in the daily operations of workers industries and factories.

The end result of the above process, for Trotsky, was inequality in "social relations" and the eventual emergence of a new social stratum of bureaucrats, who appropriated to themselves all types of material benefits and privileges, while the majority of workers continued to struggle for economic survival. He therefore maintained that state ownership was moving farther away from collective ownership. In the meantime, the following "social inequalities" continued under Stalin:

From the point of view of property in the means of production, the differences between a marshall and servant girl, the head of a trust and a day laborer, the son of a people's commissar and a homeless child, seem not to exist at all. Nevertheless, the former occupy lordly apartments, enjoy several summer homes in various parts of the country, have the best automobiles at their disposal, and have long forgotten how to shine their shoes. The latter live in wooden barracks often without partitions, lead a half-hungry existence, and do not shine their own shoes only because they go barefoot. To the bureaucrat this difference does not seem worthy of attention.[83]

Although the above inequalities, economic hardships, and social differences continued to multiply in the 1930s, Trotsky nevertheless resisted the temptation to define the Stalinist system as capitalist. He believed that such a conclusion would have ignored significant historical differences which characterized Western European nations when compared and contrasted with the Soviet regime. He openly admitted, however, that a privileged "new caste," exploiting and living off the labor of others, had come to dominate the political and economic life of the country. Unlike Djilas, he contended that the "new caste" did not own the means of production, and that it could not amass or pile up wealth in the same manner as capitalists.[84] For Trotsky, the Revolution had done away with private property even though it still remained to be made "collective." In this respect, then, he argued, it did not make sense to apply capitalism to an economic system in which private "accumulation" or capital no longer existed and in which productivity was based on state regulation rather than free competition. Thus for Trotsky, as for Lenin, capitalism described a specific form of economic organization; to utilize it presently to give an account of the Soviet political and economic system meant abstracting the term from its historical and social context. The social inequalities of the Soviet regime and those of capitalism were analogous, and, on occasion even identical; yet, as far as he was concerned, the evil at work in capitalist and socialist societies was not and could never be the same.[85]

Trotsky's rejection of "state capitalism" as a theory emerges out of his personal conviction that the all-powerful Soviet bureaucracy could not form a class. As he had argued in *Biulleten Oppozitsii* in 1933 and in many debates with social democrats, state capitalism for him characterized fascist regimes in which the state intervened in the economy of the country in order to limit competition and obtain interests of monopolistic capital.

The suggestion that the Soviet Union had allowed a "new class" to come to power became in the late 1930s a subject of major theoretical controversy. As we shall see in the next chapter, Trotsky threw himself passionately into this debate.[86] But in the early 1930s he bitterly opposed such conclusions. As he wrote in *"Klassovaia Priroda Sovetskogo Gosudarstva"* in 1932-33:

A class is defined not by participation in the distribution of the national income alone, but by its independent roots in the economic foundation of society. Each class works out its own special forms of property. The bureaucracy lacks all these social traits. It has no independent position in the process of production and distribution. It has no property roots. Its functions relate basically to political technique of class rule. The existence of a bureaucracy in all its variety of forms and differences in specific weight, characterize every class regime. Its power is of a reflective character. The bureaucracy is . . . bound up with a ruling economic class, feeding itself upon the social roots of the latter, maintaining itself and falling together with it.[87]

Following Marx's analysis of the French bureaucracy in *The Eighteenth Brumaire of Louis Napoleon*, Trotsky came to the same conclusion about the Soviet bureaucracy: it could not constitute a class unto itself. He conceded that the Soviet bureaucracy had attained "in the full sense of the word the sole privileged and commanding stratum in the Soviet society."[88] Although many similarities and differences are mentioned between various bureaucratic states, including the recent Nazi example, he argues that the Soviet bureaucracy "has no tradition of dominion and command."[89] Like Hitler's and Mussolini's fascist bureaucracies which it most resembled, he further insisted that its power arose out of the tasks and functions that it performed. Unlike bourgeois society, its power is not derived from its economic and social institutions. He further explained:

The attempt to represent the Soviet bureaucracy as a class of "stage capitalists" will obviously not withstand criticism. The bureaucracy has neither stocks nor bonds. It is recruited, supplemented and renewed in the manner of an administrative hierarchy, independently of any special property relations of its own. The individual bureaucrat cannot transmit to his heirs his rights in the exploitation of the state apparatus. The bureaucracy enjoys its privileges under the form of an abuse of power. It conceals its income; it pretends that as a special social group it does not exist. Its appropriation . . . has the character of social parasitism.[90]

Like all previous bureaucracies, the Stalinist bureaucracy, in his view, served, and lived off, a class. Yet unlike previous bureaucratic systems, the Stalinist one arose and developed when its class, the proletariat, was only beginning "to achieve a degree of independence."[91] Therefore, the bureaucracy at one and the same time served and controlled the interests of the proletariat, its control a function of the weakness of the class. The end result of this relationship, in Trotsky's opinion, was neither the creation of an independent bureaucratic class, nor any type of class exploitation.

He attempted to explain this rather confusing conclusion in 1933 in "*Klassovaia priroda sovetskogo gosudarstva*":

The privileges of the bureaucracy by themselves do not change the basis of Soviet society, because the bureaucracy derives its privileges not from any special property relations peculiar to it as a "class," but from those property relations which have been created by the October Revolution and which are fundamentally adequate for the dictatorship of the proletariat . . . Insofar as the bureaucracy robs the people, who do not deal with class exploitation, in the scientific sense of the word, but with social parasitism, albeit on a very large scale.[92]

What then did the Soviet Union constitute? If it was neither socialist nor capitalist, did it represent some unique phenomenon, or was it merely a mixture of different forms? *The Revolution Betrayed* and Trotsky's articles in the 1930s illustrate that he was usually of two minds concerning these crucial questions. In theory and in principle he openly admitted that "the present Soviet regime in all its contradictoriness," was "not a socialist regime, but a *preparatory* regime *transitional* from capitalism to socialism."[93] This was a temporary designation. As long as classes and social inequalities continued to exist, he believed that the state bureaucracy would remain an unavoidable evil. He often repeated that "bureaucracy and social harmony were inversely proportional to each other."[94] In other words, it was possible for Trotsky to view the Soviet Union in traditional Marxist-Leninist manner, as possessing a "dual" character: "socialist insofar as the distribution of life's goods is carried out with a capitalist measure of value and all the consequences ensuing therefrom."[95]

But Trotsky never admits that he or Lenin had in any way contributed to the rise of and development of Stalinist bureaucracy. His policies and Lenin's were always "right" and the bureaucracy under Stalin had nothing to do with the "dictatorship of the proletariat" during the first five or six years after the October Revolution. The fact that the Bolsheviks exercised absolute control during this period, when he himself held a top-ranking foreign affairs and military position in the party, had nothing to do with Stalin, since the party under his leadership and Lenin's was the "advance guard of the proletariat."[96] Nor did Stalin's subsequent political clique ever obtain proletarian representation. If this was the case, why then did the "proletariat" remain silent during Lenin's rule? Trotsky never adequately answers this question except to state that the "proletariat" was a feeble political force, exhausted and disillusioned by the civil war, hunger and unemployment. As a result, it could not prevent Stalin from taking over.

Trotsky further assumed that a "workers' state" would evolve away from "capitalist" forms toward socialist ones. The state must be a bridge between a capitalist and socialist society, but a bridge open in one direction only. This was exactly where, in his view, the problem in defining the nature of the Soviet Union rested. In the early 1930s he could not make up his mind whether the regime was heading towards a capitalist or socialist administration. The growth rather than the reduction in the strength of bureaucratic organizations, the proliferation and intensification of Stalin's powers, as well as the perpetuation of bourgeois norms of material and political rewards suggested to Trotsky that the final character of the Soviet regime still remained in doubt.

In one section of *The Revolution Betrayed*, he dogmatically asserted that "character of the Soviet Union" had "not yet been decided by history."[97] In his expression, it "was a contradictory society halfway between capitalism and socialism."[98] *The Revolution Betrayed* does not posit any other alternative to future Soviet political and social development. Since he did not wish to believe that Stalin and his "opportunistic" clique could hold on to power forever, he refused to admit that any other alternative was open to Soviet society. That the Soviet Union, as an "intermediate" society might be ruled by and composed of bureaucrats for a long time was stubbornly rejected. According to Trotsky, even if Stalin were to consolidate the strength of his bureaucratic clique and rebuff the threat from the "left" and the "right", the end result would be a return to capitalism. As he remarked in 1937:

Let us assume—to take a third variant—that neither a revolutionary nor a counter-revolutionary party seizes power ... We cannot count upon the bureaucracy's peacefully and voluntarily renouncing itself in the behalf of socialist equality ... One may argue that the big bureaucrat cares little what are the prevailing forms of property, provided only they guarantee him the necessary income. This argument ignores not only the instability of the bureaucrat's own rights, but also the question of his descendants. The new cult of the family has not fallen out of the clouds. Privileges have only half their worth, if they cannot be transmitted to one's children. But the right of testament is inseparable from the right of property. It is not enough to be the director of a trust; it is necessary to be a stockholder. The victory of the bureaucracy in this decisive sphere would mean its conversion into a new possessing class.[99]

The idea of a "new possessing class" that Trotsky has in mind here has little in common with Djilas' "new class" or with other concepts which were espoused by various political thinkers after Trotsky's death in 1940. For Trotsky, the "new class" was essentially an older concept, a "bourgeois" creation—resembling capitalist "class" forms. If the bureaucrats held on to power, he argued that the society would sooner or later revert to capitalism. As we proceed with further analysis of his works in the 1930s, and especially with his newly formulated theories of Stalinism and the Great Purges, it soon becomes clear why he had to rework his views of Soviet bureaucracy.

NOTES

1. For an interesting examination of the clique network see, T. H. Rigby, "Early Provincial Cliques and the Rise of Stalin," *Soviet Studies*, Vol. 2, XXXIII, (January 1981).

2. Leonard Schapiro, *The Communist Party of the Soviet Union*, (New York, 1971), pp. 69-70.

3. For an examination of the precursors to this process see, Richard B. Day, *Leon Trotsky and the Politics of Economic Isolation*, (Cambridge, England, 1973), pp. 140-142.

4. Isaac Deutscher, *The Prophet Armed: Trotsky: 1879–1921*, (New York, 1965), p. 486.

5. Leon Trotsky, "Problems of the Organization of Labor," in *The Defence of Terrorism*, (London, 1935), pp. 118-145.

6. See Note 5 above.

7. Max Shachtman's *The Struggle for the New Course*, (Ann Arbor, 1965), pp. 121-148 evaluates and criticizes Trotsky's overall positions.

8. Trotsky, *The New Course*, (Ann Arbor, 1965), pp. 14-16.

9. Ibid., pp. 7-14.

10. Ibid., pp. 90-92.

11. Ibid., p. 92.

12. Ibid., pp. 16-25.

13. For a broader view and definition of the role of the secretary, see Shachtman's review, *The Struggle for The New Course*, pp. 121-148.

14. Trotsky, *The New Course*, pp. 39-47.

15. Marx, *Selected Works*, I, p. 33. Especially interesting and relative to our study are Marx's *Civil War in France* and *The Eighteenth Brumaire of Louis Bonaparte*.

16. Trotsky, *The New Course*, pp. 37-38.

17. For a detailed analysis of this problem in Ukraine, see Armstrong, *The Soviet Bureaucratic Elite*, pp. 35-45.

18. Trotsky, *The New Course*, pp. 15-21.

19. Ibid., pp. 27-39.

20. Ibid., pp. 30.

21. Statistical Table I in A. Bubnov, "VKP (b)," *Bol'Shaya Sovetskaya Entsiklopedia* (Great Soviet Encyclopedia; Moscow, 1930), XI, pp. 531-532.

22. Lenin, "Better Fewer, But Better," *Pravda*, March 4, 1923.

23. For a detailed account of the Comintern meeting, see E. H. Carr, *The Bolshevik Revolution*, Vol. 3, (London, 1971), pp. 381-421.

24. Lev Kritzmann, *Die Heroische Periode der Grossen Russishen Revolution*, (Berlin, 1929).

25. Ibid., p. 34.

26. For Trotsky's early thought on the soviets, see his *1905*.

27. Kritsmann, *Die Heroische Periode der Grossen Russichen Revolution*, p. 37.

28. John L. H. Keep, *The Russian Revolution*, (New York, 1976).

29. See André Stawar, *Libres Essais Marxistes*, translated from Polish, Jerzy Warszawski, (Paris, 1963), p. 187.

30. The magazine which Bukharin and Radek edited and others claimed that once the policy concerning workers was only concerned with reconstituting discipline, governmental structure would tend toward bureaucratic centralization and the establishment of all sorts of commissars. This would end by destroying the independence of local soviets. *Kommunist*, April–May, 1918.

31. Nikolai Bukharin, *Economika Perekhodnogo Perioda*, (*The Economics of the Transitional Period*), (Moscow, 1920). For recent commentary on this process, see Stephen F. Cohen, *Bukharin and the Bolshevik Revolution*, (New York 1973), pp. 87-89.

32. Rosa Luxemburg, *The Russian Revolution*, (Ann Arbor, 1971), p. 71. Also see the excellent introduction to Luxemburg's work by Bertram D. Wolfe.

33. Trotsky, *The New Course*, p. 18.

34. Ibid., p. 46.

35. Ibid., p. 49.

36. Ibid., p. 51.

37. See note 36 above.

38. Ibid., pp. 54-56.

39. Ibid., pp. 57-58.

40. Ibid., pp. 94-95.

41. See note 40 above.

42. Trotsky debated this issue with Christian Rakovsky. For Rakovsky's views see his "The Professional Dangers of Power," *Marxist Studies*, Vol. I, No. 3 (1969), pp. 18-29.

43. Trotsky, *The New Course*, p. 94.

44. Especially instructive in this respect is his article in *The New Course* collection entitled "Functionarism in the Army and Elsewhere," pp. 99-107.

45. Ibid., p. 36.

46. Ibid., pp. 92-94.

47. E. H. Carr in his multivolume study of the Russian Revolution has concluded for example that Leon Trotsky, although a superb orator, lacked political gifts in the narrower sense. He lacked the sense of timing, an absolute necessity to the working politician.

48. Trotsky, *13 S'EZD RKP* (b): *Stenograficheskii Otechet*, (Moscow, 1924), pp. 164-166.

49. Quoted in Max Shachtman, *The Struggle for the New Course*, (Ann Arbor, 1965), p. 154.

50. Trotsky et al., *Platform of the Joint Opposition*, (London, 1973), p. 47. The statement (written for the most part by Trotsky and Zinoviev) was never published because Stalin seized the opposition's presses. Trotsky published it later in exile under the title *The Real Situation in Russia*, (New York, 1928).

51. For various passages on this theme, see, Victor Serge and Natalia Sedova Trotsky, *The Life and Death of Leon Trotsky*, (New York, 1975).

52. Trotsky, *The Revolution Betrayed*, p. 251.

53. Trotsky, *The History of the Russian Revolution*, Three volumes, (Ann Arbor, 1960). For a brief analysis of this problem see, Irving Howe, *Trotsky*, (New York, 1978), pp. 27-33. For a thorough examination of the vexing problem of industrialization consult, Alexander Erlich, *The Soviet Industrialization Debate, 1924-1928*, (Cambridge, Massachusetts, 1960).

54. Trotsky, *The Revolution Betrayed*, p. 112.

55. V. I. Lenin, *State and Revolution*, (New York, 1971), pp. 43-44.

56. Ibid., p. 44.

57. Lenin, *On Petty-Bourgeois Revolutionarism*, (New York, 1974).

58. Ibid., p. 103.

59. Trotsky, *The Revolution Betrayed*, p. 65.

60. See note 59 above.

61. Ibid., p. 58.

62. Ibid., pp. 55-56.

63. Trotsky, *The Revolution Betrayed*, pp. 87-87.

64. For Trotsky's opinions in exile see, Jean van Heijenoort, *With Trotsky in Exile: From Prinkipo to Coyoacan*, (Cambridge, Massachusetts, 1978).

65. See excerpts of Rakovsky's acknowledgement of Trotsky's letter in Irving Howe's *The Essential Works of Socialism*, (New York, 1970), p. 370. For a more detailed view of Rakovsky's personal position on Soviet bureaucracy see his excellent essay, "Power and the Russian Worker," In *The International*, (November, 1934), pp. 105-109.

66. Trotsky, "On the Smytchka Between Town and Country, in *The New Course*, pp. 107-114.

67. In addition to his work on the Russian Revolution on this theme also valuable is Trotsky's article, "Problems of Devleopment of U.S.S.R.: Draft Theses of the International Left Opposition on the Russian Question," in *Writings*, (New York, 1973), pp. 203-233.

68. Luxemburg, *The Russian Revolution*, introduction by Bertram D. Wolfe. Luxemburg argued that conditions necessary for a successful socialist state were not available in Lenin's Russia. She observed: "In our opinion it is wrong to believe that the party majority rule by the enlightened workers, which is not yet feasible, could be 'provisionally' replaced by the absolute power of a Central Committee, nor that the missing open control by the workers of the party's organizations be replaced by the Central Committee exercising reverse regulation over the revolutionary proletariat. He (Lenin) reveals a much too mechanistic concept of the social democratic organization . . . when he praises the pedagogical importance of the factory, which accustoms the proletariat to 'discipline and organization' from the time they leave

home. The discipline to which Lenin refers is by no means impressed on the proletariat by the factory alone. It is also acquired in the army barracks, and from modern bureaucracy generally; in short, from the entire mechanism of the centralized bourgeois state."

69. Quoted in André Stawar, *Libres Essais Marxistes*, pp. 160.

70. Lenin, "The Conditions for Admitting New Members to the Party," 20 March 1922, *Collected Works, XXXIII*, pp. 256-258.

71. Ibid., p. 257.

72. For Lenin's critique of Stalin and Trotsky as future leaders see his "Testament." Lenin asserted: "Comrade Stalin, having become Secretary General, has unlimited authority concentrated in his own hands, and I am not sure whether he will always be capable of using that authority with sufficient caution. Comrade Trotsky, on the other hand, as his struggle against the CC on the question of the People's Commissariat for Communications has already proved, is distinguished not only by outstanding ability. He is personally perhaps the most capable man in the present CC, but he has displayed excessive self-assurance and shown excessive preoccupation with the purely administrative side of the work." Lenin, SOCH, Vol. XLV, p. 345.

73. Merle Fainsod, *How Russia is Ruled*, (Cambridge, Massachusetts, 1962), p. 156.

74. See note 73 above.

75. Trotsky, *The Revolution Betrayed*, p. 237.

76. Ibid., p. 239.

77. See note 76 above.

78. Trotsky, *The Real Situation in Russia*, pp. 15-54.

79. Trotsky, *The Revolution Betrayed*, p. 125.

80. Ibid., p. 126.

81. See note 80 above.

82. Ibid., p. 241.

83. Ibid., pp. 238-239.

84. Trotsky, "Not a Workers' State or a Bourgeois State," in *Writings 1937-1938*, pp. 90-94.

85. Trotsky, "Klassovaia priroda sovetskogo gosudarstva," in *Biulleten Oppozitsii*, (October 1933), pp. 1-10. Also see his references in *The Revolution Betrayed*, pp. 258-259.

86. In this debate, Trotsky's orthodox position was severely criticized by some of his most ardent followers in the 1920s. James Burnham, Max Shachtman, and James P. Cannon soon published articles and books which questioned Trotsky's orthodoxy.

87. Trotsky, "Klassovaia priroda sovetskogo gosudarstva," in *Biulleten Oppozitsii*, (October, 1933), pp. 6-9.

88. Trotsky, *The Revolution Betrayed*, p. 249.

89. Ibid., p. 248.

90. Ibid., pp. 249-250.

91. Ibid., p. 248.

92. Trotsky, "Klassovaia priroda sovetskogo gosudarstva," in *Biulleten Oppozitsii*, (October, 1933), p. 7.

93. Trotsky, *The Revolution Betrayed*, p. 47.

94. Ibid., p. 52.

95. Ibid., p. 54. Similar discussion of this problem can be found in his *The Transitional Program: The Death Agony of Capitalism and The Tasks of the Fourth International*, edited by Joseph Hansen and George Novack, (New York, 1973).

96. Ibid., p. 53.

97. Ibid., p. 252. Also see his article, "Not a Workers' State and Not a Bourgeois State," in *Writings 1937-1938*, (New York, 1970).

98. Ibid., p. 255.

99. Ibid., pp. 253-254.

The bureaucracy has in its possession the affairs of the state, the spiritual being of society; it belongs to it as its private property. The general spirit of bureaucracy is the official secret . . . Conducting the affairs of state in public, even political consciousness, thus appear to the bureaucracy as high treason against its mystery. Authority is thus the principle of its knowledge, and the deification of authoritarianism is its credo. But within itself this spiritualism turns into a coarse materialism, the materialism of dumb obedience . . . As far as the individual bureaucrat is concerned, the goals of state become his private goals: hunting for higher jobs and the making of a career . . . Bureaucracy has therefore to make life as materialist as possible . . . Hence the bureaucrat must always behave towards the real state in Jesuitical fashion, be it consciously or unconsciously . . . The bureaucrat sees the work as a mere object to be managed by him.

Karl Marx, *The Critique of the Gotha Program*

3

The Consequences of Stalin's Bureaucracy

In the previous chapter an attempt was made to explain why Trotsky initially believed that the victory of Stalinist bureaucracy was the consequence of Russian backwardness, war weariness and foreign isolation. How plausible was it for Trotsky to refer to the Soviet bureaucracy as Stalinist? We have seen that in the 1930s his explanation was simplistic and superficial, clearly omitting the political function of Lenin's and his own view of the socialist revolution and the bureaucratic-authoritarian character of the Bolshevik Party. Trotsky's theory of "objective conditions," especially low forces of production, lack of education and culture after the Russian Revolution failed fully to explain either the breeding ground of bureaucratism or its growth and eventual monopolization of political power under Stalin.

Merle Fainsod has described clearly the growth of bureaucracy under Stalin, on the regional level in *Smolensk under Soviet Rule*.[1] He recounts how Rumyantsev, the first secretary of Smolensk, ruled, modeling himself after Stalin: his portraits and photographs could be observed everywhere in the region, and even stores and factories were named for him and for his second secretary. He administered Smolensk with an iron hand and brooked no contradiction.

The relations existing between regional (Smolensk) party membership and Stalin's central administration were marked by both rewards and punishments. The central directives constituted pressure, they were "suspicious and capricious."[2] According to Fainsod, the central branches of government multiplied on paper and continued to function inefficiently. The Smolensk administration knew how to "build barricades against intervention by the central authorities."[3] Its key weapon was the "family circle"; that is, the occupation of important positions in the district by officials dependent on one another, who managed to suppress or control that criticism without which the central administration was unable to function effectively. Even when it came to electing delegates to regional (oblast) congresses, the Party secretariat handed down detailed instructions for procedure.

As Fainsod richly documents, this sort of regional administration suffered of necessity from corruption and other adverse governmental symptoms. However, there were also "periodic campaigns to root them out."[4] Rumyantsev himself finally fell victim to one such campaign. In spite of the losses incurred by embezzlement and corruption, the regional administration achieved its key goal. It projected central power into the districts and, while it often functioned inefficiently, on the whole it enforced the directives of Stalin. This limited but real success was accomplished at the price of constant tension, pressure and even physical threats, and the awareness on the part of the Smolensk administration that it would be considered expendable once it could no longer produce results.[5] Fainsod demonstrates clearly that the subordinated bureaucracy enacted central directives as the arbitrary representative of governmental power.

Fainsod also showed how each department of the Soviet bureaucracy attempts to manipulate its environment to be able to meet the demands made on it, and at the same time to receive as much political support as possible from higher authorities.[6] Therefore many efforts are made primarily for the sake of the department before they concern themselves with the subject issue. Khrushchev on 15 February at the Twentieth Party Congress referred to this situation when he spoke of officials who could be described as "busy loafers."[7]

Bureaucratic manipulation of the environment does not, however, eliminate the issues which contribute to social conflict. They often reappear as bureaucratic conflicts, perhaps as conflicts between territorial party secretaries and ministerial department sections. But Fainsod was able to illustrate, using the Smolensk archives, that governmental methods are purposely based on overlapping and duplicated functions. While there is a distinct demarcation between the upper and lower levels within each Soviet hierarchy, it is precisely by means of an extensive undelineated area of competence—especially among party officials and the general administration—that political decisions are implemented. One section of the administration always keeps an eye on another.[8]

Since Stalin's bureaucratic apparatus not only administered but also governed, power remained the motivating force in its relationship with the world surrounding it, regardless of the real purpose of its specific function.

It is the nature of all bureaucratic authorities to utilize a policy of manipulation and repression, which may vary in its intensity and the way in which it is applied. In the same way faith in the state continues to serve as the principle which molds the world according to bureaucratic concepts. This bears out Marx's statement that "bureaucracy asserts itself to be the final end of the state."[9]

Like Marx and Engels and many other socialist revolutionaries of nineteenth and twentieth centuries, Trotsky searched for historical events of the past in order to explain the bureaucratic developments in the Soviet Union under Stalin. Exiled to Alma Ata in 1929 and excluded from political decision making, he intensified his quest for historical comparisons and parallels. The central event was the French Revolution, which offered analogies, models and examples. From the point of view of its declared goals and the frame of reference within which it took place, the French Revolution was an extraordinary event in European history. Although different in social and ideological terms from the Russian Revolution, it nevertheless belonged to the same genus of events in modern history.

Trotsky came to be obsessed by the final fate of the French Revolution, especially its evolution from Jacobinism to Thermidor to Napoleon's dictatorship, and he became convinced that this evolution was to be repeated in the Soviet Union under Stalin. Ironically, when in the late 1920s the character of the Russian Revolution began to be debated by analogy with the French experience, it had been Trotsky who had strictly defended the Bolshevik-Jacobin tradition. Here I will analyze how he used this comparison and discuss in detail the significance of his utilization of Thermidor and Bonapartism.

It should be kept in mind that Trotsky's view of Thermidor were constantly revised in the 1930s. After all, he could not admit, as Djilas did in Yugoslavia in the 1950s, that the bureaucracy was to a large extent his own creation. The danger which he observed and against which he was determined to struggle to the end was what he called an "anti-revolutionary dictatorship."[10] Thermidor to him represented the ultimate danger; it had once destroyed the revolutionary zeal and spirit of French Jacobinism and now threatened what he, Lenin and the rest of the Russian revolutionaries had fought for.

Before his deportation from Alma Ata in Kazakhstan to Turkey in February 1929, Trotsky explained the meaning of Thermidor as he then understood it:

The first victorious stage of the counter-revolution, that is, the direct transfer of power from the hands of one class into the hands of another, whereby this transfer, although necessarily accompanied by civil war, is nevertheless masked politically by the fact that the struggle occurs between the factions of the party that was yesterday united. Thermidor in France was preceded by a period of reaction which unfolded while the power remained in the hands of the plebeians, the city's lower classes. Thermidor crowned the preparatory period of reaction by an out-and-out political catastrophe, as a result of which the plebeians lost power. Thermidor does not signify a period of reaction in general, i.e., a period of ebb, of downsliding, of weakening revolutionary positions. Thermidor has a much more precise meaning. It indicates the direct transfer of power into the hands of a different class, after which the revolutionary class cannot regain power except through an armed uprising. The latter requires, in turn, a new revolutionary situation, the inception of which depends upon a whole complex of domestic and international causes.[11]

As far as the Soviet Union was concerned, he argued later in 1930 in another article that:

When the Opposition [and Trotsky as its leader] spoke of the danger of Thermidor, it had in mind primarily a very significant and widespread process within the party; the growth of a stratum of Bolsheviks who had separated themselves from the masses, felt secure, connected themselves with nonproletarian circles, and were satisfied with the social status, analogous to the strata of bloated Jacobins who became, in part, the support and prime executive apparatus of the Thermidorian overturn in 1794, and thus paving the road for Bonapartism.[12]

Yet one year later in 1931 in his *"Problems of the Development of the USSR,"* he defined the concept of Thermidor rather more concisely as a "shift of power from the proletariat to the bourgeoisie, but accomplished formally within the framework of the Soviet system under the banner of one faction of the official party against another."[13]

The social basis of Thermidor in the Soviet Union, Trotsky initially argued, was the peasantry, whose influence resulted from the rural origin of much of the industrial work force and from the climate created by the New Economic Policy of the early 1920s.[14] He even appears for a brief period to have viewed the Kronstadt revolt of 1921 as constituting a possible prototype of the Soviet Thermidor.[15] Yet he himself was greatly influenced by the grave situation of 1921, when the Bolshevik army appeared to be the only effective organized force and contrasted sharply with the bureaucratic ineptitude of civilian planning and distribution. As Commissar of War during the Kronstadt debacle he favored the use and promotion of "bourgeois specialists" and the necessity of absolute discipline and order in suppressing Kronstadt sailors and any other tendency toward anarchy from below. He could even envision advantages in the utilization of Kronstadt battalions for reconstruction after the suppression of the revolt. In fact he became accustomed to issuing orders, to imposing discipline by terror.[16] He clearly had little time for tolerating different ideas on factory and soldiers' committees. As a result of Kronstadt and war communism generally he became identified with stern discipline. Indeed, he could not understand why the obedience demanded of the soldiers should not be extended to other workers, especially in the critically disorganized sphere of transport, or why trade unions should not be an integral part of the Soviet state.

In the minds of many party leaders and even many more ordinary citizens, Trotsky in the early 1920s was associated with militarization of labor, centralization and authoritarianism. Now in 1928, he had the audacity to argue that Stalin, like the Thermidorians of 1794 in France, had opened the gates to the regime of Bonapartism. He believed the process in the Soviet Union to be "a more open, riper form of the bourgeois-counter-revolution, carried out against the Soviet system and the Bolshevik Party as a whole."[17] For a brief moment in 1928, he naively suggested that a military coup could lead the country to a "bourgeois state," a ridiculous presumption, but suggestive of the degree to which he could not decide what to make of the Thermidorian comparison in relation to the Soviet Union. Up to 1929–30, he defined Thermidor as nothing less than a counterrevolution, in which power passed from one class to another, and which could succeed only through civil war; in his opinion, this is exactly what occurred in France, and why the sans-culottes had lost power, but had not yet happened in the Soviet Union. Although Stalin and his bureaucratic clique represented the "degeneration" of the revolutionary methods, the means of production, he stubbornly claimed, still remained in the hands of the state and had not been taken over by the bourgeoisie. This meant everything to Trotsky. There had been no counterrevolutionary civil war, and it was inconceivable to him that Thermidor could be carried out peacefully through quiet bureaucratic change. In an article in *Biulletin Oppozitsii* of October 1929, he rejected the view that the bureaucracy could form a new exploiting class while having no property of its own and fulfilling only managerial functions. In this period, he clearly insisted on viewing Thermidor as a right-wing bourgeois phenomenon to which Stalin's regime did not conform to its social structure and which remained a merely potential danger in the Soviet Union.

In 1934–35, Trotsky began to reformulate his conception of Thermidor. This was the crucial period of the assassination of Sergei Kirov, of the swing from the previous "left-wing" course in the Comintern to "popular front tactics," and of the new purge trials and terror.[18] In an article published a few weeks after Kirov's assassination Trotsky conceded that the Soviet administration had become "Bonapartist." But, as he understood only too well, Bonapartism in France had followed Thermidor and, as he would argue, it was in fact a higher, more politically entrenched form of Thermidor. If, therefore, Stalin was the "Soviet Bonaparte," if this analogy was to be maintained, it was essential and necessary to reexamine the character of the "Soviet Thermidor." In his 1935 article "The Workers' State and the Question of Thermidor and Bonapartism," Trotsky admitted that he had misunderstood the nature of the French Thermidor and as a result he had failed to appreciate fully its reincarnation under Stalin.[19]

What exactly had Trotsky been mistaken about? He now confessed that he had made the error of seeing the original Thermidor as a counterrevolution. To have been such, he argued, it would have had to restore feudal property relations which existed prior to the French Revolution. But nothing of the sort had occurred. On the contrary, Thermidor had anchored itself to the social foundations of the bourgeois revolution. What the Thermidor essentially amounted to, according to Trotsky, was a "reaction" within the revolution, the transfer of power from the left Jacobins to the moderate and conservative ones, from the great masses of the bourgeoisie to the well-to-do minority. Viewed from this perspective, it now appeared to Trotsky that the same Thermidorian process had been repeated in the Soviet Union under Stalin. As he concluded in another pamphlet:

It is impossible to ignore the fact that in the Soviet revolution as well, a shift entirely analogous to Thermidor, although much slower in tempo and more masked in form ... Socially the proletariat is more homogenous than the bourgeoisie; but it contains within itself an entire series of strata which become manifest with exceptional clarity following the conquest of power, during the period when the bureaucracy and a workers' aristocracy connected with it, began to take form. The smashing of the Left Opposition implied in the most direct and immediate sense the transfer of power from the hands of the revolutionary vanguard into the hands of the more conservative elements among the bureaucracy and the upper crust of the working class. The year 1924—that was the beginning of the Soviet Thermidor.[20]

In essence, Trotsky concluded that the Thermidor had been a "reaction in operation on the social foundations of the revolution."[21] So on this revised ideology, the Soviet Thermidor was no more synonymous with the counterrevolution than its French predecessor. A shift to the right, comparable with that which had occurred with the transfer of power from the radical to the more conservative Jacobins in 1794, had taken place with the eclipse of the Left Opposition in 1924 and Stalin's assumption of party leadership, initially with Zinoviev and Kamenev.

Trotsky argued, it was now, 1924, that marked the arrival of the Soviet Thermidor. He also began to assert that the doctrine of "socialism in one country" was in essence the doctrine of Thermidor.[22] The contraditions of a workers' revolution in an underdeveloped society, he insisted, could have been resolved only by his precise program of international revolution.[23] In brief, this meant a return to Trotsky's theory of "permanent revolution."[24] His highly original analysis examined the political economy of unevenness and backwardness in general and in Russia, in particular, and explained why the socialist revolution occurred in a time and place where the working class was a minority. In his own words, the "theory of permanent revolution" was based on "law of unevenness ... in the form of social and political peculiarities."[25]

Since this conception was rejected by Stalin and his followers, the contradictions were found to persist, and threatened to wipe out all that had
been achieved by the Bolshevik Party. Therefore, Stalin's doctrine of
"socialism in one country"[26] could have but one issue—the bureaucratic
domination of state and society. It undermined mass organizations, mass
participation and substituted a bureaucratic apparatus manned by managerial functionaries to support themselves and the "upper crust of the working class."[27] In this manner, "the dictatorship of the proletariat" was
replaced by the "dictatorship of the bureaucracy"; the latter, however,
was a dictatorship in the worst sense of the word, not that of a class but of a
ruling caste, and it was wielded for the purpose not of resolving social contradictions but of manipulating them politically.[28]

In the Soviet Union in 1924, as in France one hundred and thirty years
earlier, the Thermidorians achieved victory. As in eighteenth-century
France, Trotsky argued, Thermidor solidified itself on the basis of political
and social changes created by the French Revolution, so the Stalinist Thermidor based itself on the changes brought about by the great Russian upheaval in 1917. In *The Class Nature of the Soviet State* he argued that the
French Thermidor had resulted in a shift of power from certain factions in
the Convention to others.[29][2] What had occurred was not in fact, he insisted,
a counter-revolution. The French Revolution had itself been bourgeois, so
that:

The counter-revolution, corresponding to the revolution, would have had to attain
the re-establishment of feudal property. But Thermidor did not even make an attempt in this direction. Robespierre sought his support among the artisans—the
Directory among the middle bourgeoisie. Bonaparte allied himself with the banks.
All these shifts—which had, of course, not only a political but a social significance—
occurred, however, on the basis of the new bourgeois society and state.[30]

Trotsky concluded the article stating that the Thermidor had been "a reaction in the operation on the social foundation of the revolution."[31] According to this revised analogy, the Soviet Thermidor was no more synonymous
with the counter-revolution than its French predecessor. A shift to the right,
comparable with that which occurred with the transfer of power from the
radical to the more conservative Jacobins in 1794, had taken place with the
eclipse of the Left Opposition in 1924 and Stalin's assumption of party
leadership. According to Trotsky, it was now 1924 which marked the onset
of the Soviet Thermidor.

This reformulation, however, appeared to add comparatively little in
coherence to a concept which, on his own estimation, had hitherto "served
to becloud rather than to clarify"[32] the question of the essential nature of the
developments which had taken place in the Soviet Union since the death of
Lenin. The argument that the Soviet Union had experienced its Thermidor

in 1924 was hardly tenable. As Isaac Deutscher has emphasized in *The Prophet Outcast*, the defeat of the Left Opposition in that year could by no means be equated with the collapse and dissolution of the Jacobin movement but corresponded rather to the demise of the radical Jacobins which had happened some time before 9 Thermidor 1794.[33] Moreover, while the French Thermidor had marked the end of the revolutionary transformation of the social relations of production, this process did not come to a halt in the Soviet Union with the rise of Stalin, but actually witnessed its most radical and violent extension under his rule in the form of the forced collectivization of the peasantry.[34]

Trotsky's formulations as presented above amount to saying that he no longer viewed Thermidor as a "right-wing" bourgeois counterrevolution but as the bureaucratization of the Russian Revolution and of those social and political changes that the revolution had ushered in. He did not imply, however, that under Thermidor even those changes were permanently safeguarded. In his opinion, the bureaucratic dictatorship under Stalin did not constitute a permanent solution to the socioeconomic contradictions in Soviet society but merely an interim palliative whose dubious advantage was that it had created the illusion of internal order, stability and consolidation. Trotsky certainly believed that another social upheaval and a reversal to pre-Soviet society could not be ruled out. As the economic and contraditions become more and more irreconcilable, Stalin's political clique would discover how difficult it was to exercise total control by bureaucratic machinery alone. The French Thermidorians, faced by similar political contradictions, finally gave way to Napoleon Bonaparte; in the Soviet Union, Trotsky claimed, a similar development had taken place. So the Soviet Thermidor had not been succeeded by Soviet Bonapartism, a form of dictatorship which, though it kept its bureaucratic political structure, also added a component of personal rule.

From Thermidor, Trotsky turned to the related theme of Bonapartism. If Thermidor was the political consequence of the bureaucratic rule, then Bonapartism was its social culmination. Before the publication of *The Revolution Betrayed* in 1936, he had become convinced that the original French scenario would be repeated and played out in full within the Soviet context. He saw two possible takeover scenarios: either by a military coup d'état or by the achievement of total power by Stalin himself. If the military coup were to succeed, Trotsky believed it would be because the political regime had alienated its workers and peasants—its backbone and mass base—therefore establishing a power vacuum which the army could exploit.

The main goal of the coup would be the establishment and maintenance of order and stability. The secondary result would be to bring about a capitalist restoration. Although the army coup remained the most likely prospect, there was the possibility that Stalin, fearing the loss of his power, would strike first. If this occurred, one could surmise fairly accurately that the party would be transformed into a personal dictatorship. Collective and party rule would disappear and suppression of all opponents, real or imaginary, would be introduced. The consequence, Trotsky theorized, would be the undermining of all political institutions, not least the party and the bureaucracy, both of which would become subjugated to the personal whims of the dictator. Yet, such a personal dictatorship, he claimed, with Stalin as Bonaparte, would not in the long run be as counterrevolutionary as military rule; because of its political instability and constant crises, it too would eventually lead to the fall of socialism.[35] Of the two evils, it is interesting that Trotsky clearly favored the rule of Stalin. Under Bonaparte, in the Marxist analysis, certain of the achievements of the French Revolution were preserved. There are indications in his letters that to prevent a military coup d'état, he was prepared to unite with Stalin, and on several occasions he urged the Left Opposition not to rule out such a cooperation.[36]

Trotsky's theory of Bonapartism before Thermidor reappeared whenever the strategy was useful to his arguments and purposes in the 1930s. In 1931–32, for instance, he stated that Stalin's regime could not yet be identified with Bonapartism because the "degeneration" of the bureaucracy which had developed was only "one of the pre-conditions" for Bonapartism.[37] In contrasting and comparing the latter with Thermidor, he described it as a "more open, riper, form of bourgeois counter-revolution."[38] And he insisted that "the plebiscitary degeneration of the party apparatus undoubtedly increased the chances of the Bonapartist form."[39]

In 1932–33, it became clear to Trotsky that Stalin and not a military ruler would become the Soviet counterpart of Bonarparte. He now blamed Stalin for instituting the "principle of super-monarchical authority,"[40] and as a result of this principle hurling into doubt the character of the Soviet system. Yet even at this stage, he was prepared to affix a Bonapartist title to Stalinism only if it were perceived as a regime which continued to be grounded in the "Soviet experience."[41] In spite of his many previous statements that Bonapartism was a form of "bourgeois counter-revolution," he nevertheless insisted that Stalin had continued similarly to Bonaparte in the French Revolution, to preserve the nationalized character of the Soviet economy.[42] As a result, Trotsky seemed completely undecided as to whether Bonapartism was simply a political or a social phenomenon.

Karl Marx too had characterized Bonapartism as a political system in which the state apparatus acquired a considerable degree of autonomy from all classes in society. In *The Eighteenth Brumaire of Louis Napoleon*, Marx argued that Bonapartism became the most significant guarantor of the dominant relations of production. He maintained that the bourgeois state in the period of initial growth of industrial capitalism was a "weak state," in that this expansion was accompanied by the destruction of the feudal state apparatus which had hindered the expanded reproduction of capitalism.[43] And Marx added that "it was a feeling of weakness that caused them (the bourgeoisie) to recoil from the pure conditions of their own class and to yearn for the former more incomplete, more undeveloped and precisely on that account less dangerous forms of this rule."[44]

In *The Civil War in France*, Marx again analyzed the Bonapartist state in terms of the weaknesses of the bourgeoisie, but with a significant shift of emphasis, he argued that "it was the only form of government possible at a time when the bourgeoisie had already lost, and the working class had not yet acquired the faculty of ruling the nation."[45] The Bonapartist state was therefore superimposed on, and was actually the result of, a stalemate in the political balance of class forces, although it functioned to ensure the continued reproduction of capitalist social relations of production.[46]

In his 1935 article *The Workers' State and the Question of Thermidor and Bonapartism*, Trotsky attempted to extend Marx's concept of Bonapartism to encompass a "balancing" between internal and external class forces. As he explained:

The Soviet bureaucracy—"Bolshevist" in its traditions but in reality having long since renounced its traditions, petty bourgeois in its composition and spirit—was summoned to regulate the antagonism between the proletariat and the peasantry, between the workers' state and world imperialism: such is the social base of *bureaucratic centrism*, of its zigzags, its power, its weakness, and its influence on the world proletarian movement which has been so fatal. As the bureaucracy becomes more independent, as more and more power is concentrated in the hands of a single person, the more does *bureaucratic centrism* turn into Bonapartism.[47]

Here Trotsky conceptualized what he believed to be the dual role of Soviet bureaucracy: on the one hand, its defense of the economic base of the workers' state against world imperialism and internal reaction, and on the other, its conservative outlook (characteristic of all bureaucracies) and desire to maintain the "balance of power" in the international arena, in which the advance of world revolution and independent activity of the international proletariat would in any event threaten its own position. As a consequence, while the bureaucracy was obliged to arrive at a "working compromise" with imperialism if its rule was to remain secure, it simultaneously undermined the stability of the economic base upon which that rule was premised."[48]

In 1936, Trotsky once more redefined his position, coming to see a much clearer relationship between the Soviet Thermidor and Bonapartism. In his opinion now, the two systems had developed and arisen together, so that the conservative content of the Thermidorian regime was working hand in hand with the Bonapartist dictator. Initially bureaucratism had been enshrined, involving a shift to the right. It quickly conflicted with the needs of the masses and with the concept of the workers' state. As a result, the bureaucracy was deprived of mass support and it was therefore forced to acquire an independent power base in order to retain political control. As far as Trotsky was concerned, this was accomplished by a twofold measure: by "strangling" the party, the soviets, and the working class, and by establishing institutions of repression concentrated in the hands of the dictator. And the more this process moved along a course, argued Trotsky, the more did Stalinism turn into Bonapartism.[49]

Trotsky went to great lengths to illustrate that Soviet Bonapartism was not to be confused with the emerging fascist regimes in Western Europe in the 1930s. Fascism, as far as he was concerned, had arisen in response to crises of capitalism, and its essential aim was to restore and defend private property. In addition, fascism appeared at a time when bourgeois society was in disarray, declining and decaying. It represented to him the final, despairing gasp of a dying class. Soviet Bonapartism, on the other hand, was distinguished not only by its protection of noncapitalist, nationalized property, but by the fact that it emerged as this form of property was being created and as a "young" class, the workers, was coming to power. And he added another comparison:

We always strictly differentiated between the Bonapartism of decay and the young advancing Bonapartism which was not only the grave-digger of the political principles of the bourgeois revolution but also the defender of its social conquests . . . The present-day Kremlin Bonapartism we juxtapose of course, with the Bonapartism of bourgeois rise and not decay: with the Consulate and the First Empire, and not with Napoleon III and, all the more so, not with Schleicher or Doumergue.[50]

Stalin, then, was the Napoleon I of the Russian Revolution. He was thus the key to Trotsky's interpretation of Soviet bureaucratic developments in the 1930s. Although not entirely correct in his assessments and analogies, he continued to use various examples and parallels to illustrate how and why Stalin consolidated his rule.

Although Trotsky always distinguished between Soviet Bonapartism and Fascism, he admitted that both movements were in significant respects alike. Both, for example, represented a serious break between politics and society. He depicted Fascist Bonapartism as the final "stratagem" of a collapsing capitalist class; he also perceived that the capitalist class, by resorting to fascism to save its "skin," was relinquishing direct rule in favor of governmental leadership whose background was not capitalist but petty bourgeois.[51] When Fascist Bonapartist leadership obtained power it pretended to speak not in the name of a class but of an abstraction, the nation.[52] Fascist Bonapartism never intended to serve the nation but only the capitalist class; yet, it also encouraged the impression that it was politically independent, a regime drawing it legitimacy not from this or that class, but from a popular plebiscite supposedly rising above all individual or group distinctions. However illusory this was, in his opinion, there was a feeling that politics were above and separate from society: the capitalist class' clear willingness to sacrifice parliamentary institutions was followed by the fascists' formation of autonomous organs—bureaucracy, secret police, leader—over which there was no constitutional control. In this fashion, politics was given an independent base and came to dominate the entire society. The identical process, he believed, could be observed in the unfolding and coming to power of Soviet Bonapartism. The regime had been raised to power by the workers, but had renounced its class character by glorifying state power and by destroying the only legitimate popular institution, the party. The Soviet Bonaparte, then, replaced the party with the secret police, the bureaucracy, and the all-powerful dictator.[53]

Additional similarities were to be discovered between Soviet and Fascist Bonapartism. Both were "crisis regimes," societies enduring periods of pronounced socio-economic difficulties. Both suppressed opposition groups by force rather than by compromising on real economic issues. Both regimes owed their "birth to one and the same cause"—"the belatedness of the world revolution."[54] In the capitalist countries the same cause gave rise to "fascism . . . the dilatoriness of the world proletariat in solving the problems set for it by history."[55] Trotsky was therefore able to conclude that: "Stalinism and Fascism, in spite of a deep difference in social foundations, are symmetrical phenomena. In many of their features they show a deadly similarity."[56] And he added: "in turning its back to the international revolution, the Stalinist bureaucracy was, from its own point of view, right. It was merely obeying the voice of its own social preservation.[57]"

By this point in time, Trotsky had abandoned his earlier designation of Stalinist political practice as "bureaucratic centrism," having come to regard the bureaucracy as being, in its international relations, overtly counterrevolutionary. This, indeed, was the pretext for the formation, in September 1938, of the Fourth International, as well as being the basis for Trotsky's acceptance of the designation of the Soviet Union as a "counter-revolutionary workers' state."[58]

The implicit distinction between the partially progressive role of the bureaucracy (as the guardian of social relations of production established by the Russian Revolution) and its wholly counter-revolutionary international role was an awkward one. If the social formation remained a workers' state (albeit degenerated), it was difficult to see how this could fail to influence to some extent the bureaucracy's external relations, that is, how it could work consistently as an agency of counter-revolution. In fact, the elements of the solution to this dilemma were contained in certain of Trotsky's writings of 1939 and 1940, in which he attempted to elucidate the developments in the Soviet occupied areas of Poland, ceded to the Red Army as a result of the Nazi-Soviet Pact.[59]

In the meantime, it can be conceded that Trotsky's Soviet and Fascist Bonapartist analogy is a useful one for understanding the character and general role of the bureaucracy. The "deadly similarity" of the role of the ruler in the two societies made good sense. Like fascism, Soviet Bonapartism arose at the moment that institutionalized forms of rule no longer sufficed to protect a political system lacking popular support. The personality of the "Supreme Leader," whether he was charismatic or pretended to be, as in the case of Stalin, played a number of significant roles—he popularized an impersonal bureaucracy; he formed a national "symbol," above and beyond class differences, to provide a center for socialist identification; he concealed the regime's internal weaknesses by stressing stability, order and political unity. And it seemed to Trotsky that the more the bureaucracy ran up against social antagonisms of its own making, the more it resorted to the simple charismatic functions of Stalin to fend them off. As he wrote in *The Revolution Betrayed*:

Insistent deification of Stalin is, with all its elements of caricature, a necessary element of the regime. The bureaucracy has need of an inviolable super-arbiter, a first consul if not an emperor . . . That strength of character of the leader which so enraptures the literary dilettantes of the West, is in reality the sum total of the collective pressure of a caste which will stop at nothing in defense of its position. Each one of them at his post is thinking *l'etat, c'est moi*. In Stalin each one easily finds himself. But Stalin also finds in each one a small part of his own spirit. Stalin is the personification of the bureaucracy.[60]

The personification of Stalin's rule was only secondarily motivated by concern over its external image. Stalin's key ambition was of course his pursuit of a monopoly of political power and control regardless of the ruthless and brutal methods necessary to achieve these ends. It is in Stalin's thirst for power as well as his methods of coercion, according to Trotsky, that the full importance of the purges—the terror, the show trials and the physical regimentation of millions of people can be observed.[61] As he viewed it, Stalin and his psychopathological[62] bureaucracy were alienated from each other and from society, and as a result Stalin was driven to paranoia and distrust of even his closest followers.[63] A necessary but uneasy relationship continued to exist between the bureaucracy and Stalin during the purges because neither could survive without the other. Their alliance was in fact a partnership in crime.[64] On another level, the purges can be seen as logical, "functional," political instruments of the system and not simply irrational and psychological excesses of Stalin. Having since 1924 established the doctrine of "socialism in one country," having isolated the Russian workers and peasants from the outside world, and having thereby brought about severe economic hardships, the regime soon discovered that it had to use cruel, coercive methods in order to survive and rule.

Thus, Trotsky regarded terror as characteristic of a system which had gone back on its commitment to socialism. He admitted in *Their Morals and*

Ours that terror had been widely used against all "enemies" of Bolshevism in the early years of the Revolution, because it was necessary to subdue the civil war and to struggle against the autocracy. Then it was only a temporary measure, not characteristic of the system. But, now under Stalin, it had become a consequence of reactionary bureaucracy which had turned against those very elements that had once supported the revolution in 1917. Stalinism, therefore, perpetuated the terror which was meant only for a specific historical period and transformed it into a system of permanent dictatorship. According to Trotsky, this was not surprising since Stalinism engendered what was in effect a condition of civil war. Only by the constant utilization of terror could Stalinism survive.[65]

The new wave of purges, especially the "Yezhovshchina" involved a reign of terror without parallel in Soviet history.[66] The elimination of all important old Bolsheviks from 1936 to 1938 was a further illustration to Trotsky of the extremes which the Stalinist bureaucracy was forced to go in order to rule. In a speech on 10 February 1938 in Mexico City, he argued that:

A new aristocracy had been formed in the Soviet Union. The October Revolution proceeded under the banner of equality. The bureaucracy is the embodiment of monstrous inequality. The Revolution destroyed the nobility. The bureaucracy creates a new gentry. The Revolution destroyed titles and decorations. The new aristocracy produces marshals and generals.[67]

Trotsky believed that repression by Stalin's bureaucracy increased the resentments of the working class, especially as their social and economic hardships become worse. As social conflicts deepened, he was certain that the political system would become more and more unstable. To protect its hold on power, the regime had to resort to terror. It could not admit, however, that its methods of coercion were governed by its determination to defend its social status, nor that there existed any real estrangement between it and the people. Instead, Stalin and his "yes-men," were forced to deceive the "working class." One instance, he pointed out, was Stalin's pretense at "constitutionalism" and "legality," via the "Stalin Constitution" in 1936. In it every citizen was assured the most comprehensive array of individual and democratic rights. Universal suffrage and the secret ballot were the most significant proposals. Trotsky at once ridiculed the "constitution" and declared that these rights were entirely fictitious since the possibility of electing candidates other than the existing leadership did not exist.[68] He criticized the purely formal legal procedures. The more he learned about the trials, the more he argued against the illegal methods used to force confessions and assure convictions. The facade of the trials of the "frame-up-system," as he liked to refer to them, was crucial to Stalin because it created an illusion of legitimacy.[69] How else can one explain Stalin's motives?

According to Trotsky, trials and purges were central to Stalin's consolida-

tion of personal power and authority. He was unwilling to admit that his social and economic policies were dismal failures and so he embarked on a
witch hunt in search of "enemies of the people," Jews to divert attention
from his shortcomings. The blunders of the regime, therefore, could be at-
tributed, not to the bureaucracy and its "Supreme Leader" but to the
"traitors" who infiltrated the administration and the society, sabotaging the
"progress" of the Bolshevik Party. As a result, there was the obsession with
"Trotskyism"—therefore, the unending trials for everyone to observe;
therefore, the spectacular revelations of the Old Bolsheviks—Kamenev,
Zinoviev, and Bukharin—accused of being agents of foreign governments;
therefore, the "permanent purge" and violence.[70] Yet, according to
Trotsky, this did not signify that Stalin's regime did not feel threatened. On
the contrary, he stated at the "preliminary Commission of Inquiry" in 1937,
"fear imbues the Stalinist bureaucracy throughout so that the slightest provocation becomes a pretext for striking out."[71] The hysteria of the bureaucracy, then, partially explains "the mad character of its persecutions."[72]

Deception and victimization, Trotsky argued, were only part of a larger
drama. Along with numerous arrests and trials, there took place an enormous extermination of peasants, workers, soldiers and even lesser political
bureaucrats. Coercion was being joined to madness and insanity in order to
obliterate the unity of social groups and to uproot all areas of independent
human activity and thought.[73] At one stage, Trotsky believed that persecu-
tion was intended to prevent the formation and development of factions
competing for political power; at another, its goal was nothing less than the
entire elimination of all differences between the political and social centers
of authority. Of course, the same could be applied to the public and private
sectors. The final objective in each case was an undifferentiated and faceless
society but not a classless one. Since the Soviet Union, however, constituted
a heterogeneous society, that is, divided into classes or groups refusing to
adapt spontaneously, terror and coercion had to be used all the more frequently and cruelly. Indeed, economic differences, privileges and material
rewards became the cornerstone of Stalin's central and provincial administration;[74] however, economic power was not permitted to develop outside
the firm grasp of the bureaucracy. Social inequalities could continue
without giving rise to antagonism and dissension; classes could exist but in
a castrated form. At the same time, however, a fictitious idea was circulated
that the dividing line between classes was being destroyed; and if this was
the case, was there any need for politics? All that was required in terms of
popular participation was the unanimous "plebiscite," the expression of
conclusive consensus.[75] And this appearance of unity was to be both concretely and symbolically enshrined in the figure of Stalin, the "Supreme
Leader" who now represented complete ideological purity and political
legitimacy.[76]

In all of the evidence presented so far, Trotsky firmly believed, Stalinist Bonapartism was playing out the logic of its inherent character and nature. It had developed as a political stratagem against the disintegration of the social Thermidor. The more the Thermidor became untenable, the more did Stalin impose his tricks. However artificial the political homogeneity Stalin sought, he was relentlessly driving to obtain it. As a consequence, not only workers but social classes had to be undermined just in case they exploited their potential sources of political power; therefore, political organizations, including the top organs of the Bolshevik party, had to be eliminated in case they flexed their political muscles. The bureaucracy was thus turned into the dominating stratum and the secret police became the chief instrument of complete control. In other words, politics came to rule over society. As Trotsky summarized it: "the purpose of Stalin's faction was to destroy . . . subjecting the party to its own officialdom and merging the latter in the officialdom of the state. Thus was created the present totalitarian state. It was his doing the bureaucracy that not unimportant service that guaranteed Stalin's victory."[77]

As has been argued so far in this chapter, Trotsky's defenses of the Soviet Union, in spite of its social and political degeneration, was based on the economic structure, as maintained even by Stalin. Therefore, if for no other reason than the means of production had been nationalized and "forms" of capitalism checked, the Soviet Union, in his opinion, had remained potentially a "progressive" society. Though corroding socialism, the bureaucracy in spite of itself was unable to abandon the socialist foundations of society; however rudimentary these foundations they were enough to differentiate them from capitalism. The menace of Stalinism, of course, would threaten to devastate the structure. If that were to occur, Trotsky proposed that only one alternative remained—a return to capitalist relations and forms of property. He emphasized that the twentieth century offered a choice between two sides only—socialism or capitalism.

It is exactly this type of Marxist reasoning that at the end of the 1930s began to be questioned by Marxist intellectuals themselves. Such Marxists as Victor Serge, Max Eastman, James Burnham, Max Shachtman, and Bruno Rizzi in Europe and America, although partially influenced by Trotsky's own critique of the Soviet Union, could no longer accept on faith the standard Marxist analysis.[78] New sets of questions were being asked. How and why was the Soviet Union different? Was it really a paradigm of a new bureaucratized society? How was this phenomena developing and why was it throwing into doubt the old Marxist theory of capitalist-socialist division of the world? Was the bureaucracy still, as the Marxists would argue, in the service of one class or another? Or had the bureaucracy become a new ruling class?

Written in Italy and published in France in 1939, Rizzi's *La Bureaucratisa-*

tion du Monde initiated and directly challenged Trotsky's critique. Partly impressed but even more threatened by Rizzi's formulations, Trotsky immediately wrote a major article to dispute the issues raised by him.[79]

The central theory of *La Bureaucratisation du Monde* may be easily summarized, especially since James Burnham's *The Managerial Revolution* did a great deal to popularize the concept. Rizzi argued that the Marxist prediction that capitalism would be superseded by socialism had been proven to be false by developments in both the Soviet Union and in Western Europe. It was not socialism but a new type of bureaucratic rule that was evolving in such different political forms as Fascism, Stalinism and even New Dealism. What they all possessed in common, in Rizzi's opinion, was a bureaucratic elite determined to rationalize the organization of society and make economic production and distribution more efficient. In actuality, he believed the elite had already succeeded in both objectives, and this was the reason why it was able to shove the less efficient capitalist entrepreneurs aside and establish for itself such a huge monopoly of political and economic power. Opposed to the position that the bureaucracy could not form a class since it did not own the means of production, Rizzi insisted that in fact it was still a possessing class since it had total power over the state economy. Though the class was not the legal owner of state property, it nevertheless reaped enormous material benefits and privileges by controlling, supervising and distributing profits from state production. The distinction between the "new class" and the capitalist classes of the past was that the former flourished not as competing individuals but as a collective unit. Rizzi, therefore, proclaimed that the new epoch in world social development was that of "bureaucratic collectivism."[80] This was neither temporary nor accidental; it would preserve for a long period, and it was not historically rooted as capitalism had been in its own time. True, Rizzi concluded, bureaucratic collectivism would eventually give way to socialism, but for now it had little in common with it.[81] On the contrary, bureaucratic collectivism was a system in which workers toiled like slaves for the bureaucracy in order to achieve economic efficiency. The Soviet Union was not a "degenerated workers' state" but a society in which workers were under the guardianship of the ruling elite. The regimes of Hitler, Mussolini and Roosevelt too belonged to it as well. The bureaucratization of the Soviet Union had simply initiated the first step in the whole "bureaucratization of the world."[82]

In the Soviet Union, Rizzi claimed that the mode of extraction of surplus labor did not, as in the capitalist mode of production, consist in the appropriation of surplus value. He explained in detail:

Exploitation occurs exactly as in a society based on slavery: the subject of the State works for the one master who has bought him, he becomes a part of his master's capital, he represents the livestock which must be cared for and housed and whose reproduction is a matter of great importance for the master. The payment of a so-called wage, consisting partly of State services and goods, should not induce us into error and lead us to suppose the existence of a Socialist form of renumeration: for indeed, it only means the upkeep of a slave! . . . The Russian working class are no longer proletarians; they are merely slaves.[83]

Rizzi emphasized, nevertheless, that the "new society would lead directly to socialism, because of the enormous volume of production."[84] In explaining the disappearance of the state during the transition period between capitalism and socialism, he insisted that this would instead become a transition between bureaucratic collectivism and socialism. And he added that "the totalitarian state will more and more lose its political characteristics and retain only its administrative characteristics. At the end of this process, we will have a classless society and socialism."[85]

While retaining the designation of "bureaucratic collectivism", Max Shachtman rejected Rizzi's interpretation. He insisted that bureaucratic collectivism formed a "nationally limited phenomenon, appearing in history in the course of a single conjuncture."[86]

Trotsky had argued in 1936 that the Soviet proletariat had been politically expropriated by the bureaucracy, while nevertheless remaining the dominant class. This was an error, Shachtman maintained, because political and economic power in a workers' state was necessarily synonymous. As he explained in *The Bureaucratic Revolution*:

Thus by its very position in the new society, the proletariat still has no property, that is, it does not own property in the sense that the feudal lord or the capitalist did. It was and remains a property-less class! It seizes state power. The state is simply the proletariat organized as the ruling class. The state expropriates the private owners of land and capital, and ownership of land, and the means of production and exchange, becomes vested in the state. By its action, the state has established new property forms—nationalized or state-ified or collectivized property.[87]

And he added:

The economic supremacy of the bourgeoisie under capitalism is based upon its ownership of the decisive instruments of production and exchange, Hence, its social power, hence, the bourgeois state. The social rule of the proletariat cannot express itself in private ownership of capital, but only in its "ownership" of the state in whose hands is concentrated all the decisive economic power. Hence, its social power lies in its political power.[88]

It therefore followed, in Shachtman's opinion, that with liquidation of the soviets, the complete subordination of the trade unions to the state, and the total bureaucratic subjugation of the party, the Soviet proletariat was no longer "organized as the ruling class" and the state was no longer a workers' state. Therefore, he concluded that "the conquest of power by the bureaucracy spelled the destruction of the property relations established by the Bolshevik revolution."[89] Like Rizzi, Shachtman maintained that Trotsky should have rejected the view of the Soviet Union as a workers' state. And in addition, he emphasized that the transition from a workers' to bureaucratic collectivism was not such a gradual or nonviolent process:

The comparative *one-sidedness* of the civil war attending the Stalinist counter-revolution was determined by the often noted passivity of the masses, their weariness, their failure to receive international support. In spite of this, Stalin's road to power lay through rivers of blood and over mountains of skulls. Nevertheless, neither the Stalinist nor the Bolshevik revolution was effected by Fabian gradualist reforms.[90]

For Shachtman, therefore, the purges unleashed from 1934 to 1938 constituted the counter-revolution which served to consolidate the bureaucracy as a ruling class.[91]

Trotsky did not take long to respond to Shachtman's formulations. In one of his less bitter attacks, he refuted Shachtman's synopsis:

The U.S.S.R. question cannot be isolated as unique from the whole historic process of our times. Either the Stalin state is a transitory formulation, it is a deformation of a workers' state in a backward and isolated country, or "bureaucratic collectivism" . . . is a new social formation which is replacing capitalism . . . Who chooses the second alternative admits, openly or silently, that all revolutionary potentialities of the world proletariat are exhausted, that the socialist movement is bankrupt, and that the old capitalism is transforming itself into "bureaucratic collectivism" with a new exploiting class.[92]

Trotsky was more receptive to Rizzi's formulations. What appeared to impress him about Rizzi's theory of bureaucratic collectivism was the attempt by the latter to formulate a "major historical generalization."[93] It was also a challenge that Trotsky could not simply leave alone. His article "The USSR in War," published in 1940, took up the challenge. By agreeing with Rizzi on several issues, he also illustrated an unusual open-mindedness. Although he said that there was no reason to alter his personal views, he in one instance came close to abandoning the old "capitalist or socialist alternative" when in "The USSR in War" he described the future Soviet utopia. He proclaimed:

The historical alternative, carried to the end, is as follows: either the Stalin regime is an abhorrent relapse in the process of transforming bourgeois society into a socialist society, or the Stalin regime is the first stage of a new exploiting society. If the second prognosis proves to be correct, then of course, the bureaucracy will become a new exploiting class. However onerous the second perspective may be, if the world proletariat should actually prove incapable of fulfilling the mission placed upon it by the course of development, nothing else would remain except openly to recognize that the socialist program, based on the internal contradictions of capitalist society, ended as a Utopia. It is self-evident that a new "minimum" program would be required—for the defense of the interests of the slaves of the totalitarian bureaucracy.[94]

In a letter to an American "Trotskyist" James Cannon, on 12 September 1939, he expressed as he had never before an unusual pessimistic outlook:

Have we entered the epoch of social revolution and socialist society, or, on the contrary, the epoch of declining society of totalitarian bureaucracy? . . . It is absolutely self-evident that if the international proletariat, as a result of the experience of our entire epoch and the current new war, proves incapable of becoming the master of society, this would signify the foundering of all hope for a socialist revolution, for it is impossible to expect any other more favorable conditions.[95]

Trotsky's correspondence with James Cannon, Christian Rakovsky and the Mexican artist Diego Rivera[96] clearly shows that Trotsky's confidence of the future was severely jolted in 1939–40. Stalin's total control of the Soviet Union, the decline of the "Left" and the rise of the "Right" in Western Europe, the Nazi-Soviet pact, and the outbreak of World War II—all of these events must have had their impact upon him as unmistakable signs that the future did not necessarily belong to the "world proletariat." And even more interesting was the following personal admission:

War will provoke not revolution but a decline of the proletariat, then there remains another alternative: the further decay of monopoly capitalism, its further fusion with the state and the replacement of democracy wherever it still remained by a totalitarian regime . . . an analogous result might occur in the event that the proletariat of advanced capitalist countries, having conquered power, should prove incapable of holding it and surrender it, as the U.S.S.R., to a privileged bureaucracy. Then we would be compelled to acknowledge that the reason for the bureaucratic relapse is rooted not in the backwardness of the country and not in the imperialist environment but in the incapacity of the proletariat to become a ruling class. Then it would be necessary in retrospect to establish that in its fundamental traits the present U.S.S.R. was the precursor of a new exploiting regime on an international scale.[97]

Trotsky must have realized, in composing the above, that it acknowledged in effect that Marxist theory—concerning the growth and development of modern society in general, and the role of the "proletariat" in the Soviet Union in particular—might be proven to have been completely in error. In addition, the passage could be interpreted as implying that the true character of the Soviet Union—a "degenerated workers' state" or a new, bureaucratic, social system—was still in the balance; the "real" nature of Stalinism now arose—and a society which was neither socialist nor capitalist was a distinct possibility. It appeared as if he was suspending final theoretical judgment on these issues until political events themselves decided one way or another.[98]

Trotsky's article, "The USSR in War" then, was a significant revision of his previous views. His most loyal followers, including the American contingent, were quick to notice this change. As mentioned earlier in this chapter, they had arrived at similar destinations independently, but now they wanted "the Old Man" to formulate the vital and necessary conclusions.[99] Burnham, the most radical among the disillusioned American Trotskyists, proclaimed in *The Machiavellians* that Marxism in the Soviet Union and Eastern Europe had completely failed; and in 1940 he abandoned the Trotskyists to form a small anti-Marxist organization.[100]

Max Shachtman, less volatile and ideologically more stable. that Burnham, could also no longer endure Trotsky's arrogance or "defense theory" of the Soviet Union. A devoted follower since the early twenties, Shachtman came to regard the Soviet Union as nothing but a bureaucratic monster with imperialist policies no different from those of the capitalist West.[101] Others were convinced to follow suit by the Red Army's invasions of Poland and Finland. The final result of all this was that the Fourth International and the American Trotskyist movements were left in massive chaos and disarray.

In spite of a variety of concessions in his speeches and articles in 1939 and 1940, Trotsky declined to accept Shachtman's observations and he totally dismissed those of Burnham. He also instituted severe political attacks on all those who were abandoning the Soviet experiment or were contemplating on doing it.[102] Even though he conceded that his article, "The USSR in War," for a period of time, had taken bureaucratic collectivism and its theory seriously, he still insisted that his opinion remained the same and that his observations and predictions had been distorted.[103] He was correct insofar as his article had scorned various aspects of bureaucratic collectivist theory, and that it had not abandoned the future. As he remarked:

Marxists do not have the slightest right . . . to draw conclusions that the proletariat has forfeited its revolutionary possibilities and must renounce all aspirations to hegemony in an era immediately ahead. Twenty-five years in the scales of history . . . weigh less than an hour in the life of a man . . . In the years of darkest Russian reaction (1905—1917) we took as our starting point those revolutionary possibilities which were revealed by the Russian proletariat in 1905. In the years of world reaction we must proceed from those possibilities which the Russian proletariat revealed in 1917. We must not change our road . . . We must steer our course toward the world revolution and by virtue of this very fact toward regeneration of the U.S.S.R. and a workers' state.[104]

Though Shachtman's theory was characterized as superficial and schematic, his own articles also expressed naive confidence and wishful thinking about the future of socialism. He remained obdurate and dogmatic even though his views appeared increasingly out of touch with reality. He refused to compromise with any of his followers with the result that many left his cause.[105] He fought against "factionalism" in order to protect his "traditional" Bolshevik line of thought and action; and he insisted in defending the Soviet Union at all costs—going so far as to justify the invasions of Eastern Europe by force.[106] But the faith in the inevitable "laws of history" which had characterized his battles throughout his revolutionary career had been intensely shaken in 1940. The future utopia was not certain; although one should continue to struggle for the best, one should also be prepared for the worst. And for Trotsky, the worst meant either a complete "relapse into barbarism" or a total "eclipse of the civilization."[107] His commitment to socialism in 1940 was then of a moral and personal nature. If in the prerevolutionary period he had no doubts about the tide of history, he now contemplated a future lying in ruins; but the probability that socialism would be destroyed, and that the 1917 Revolution would consequently emerge as an illusory cause, would not hold him back. Until his death in August, 1940, he would remain a socialist, out of moral conviction if not out of "scientific" certainty: though socialism could no longer be said to be inevitable, it was still an ideal worth fighting for.

NOTES

1. Merle Fainsod, *Smolensk under Soviet Rule*, (Cambridge, Massachusetts, 1958).

2. Ibid., pp. 107-109.

3. Ibid., pp. 108.

4. Ibid., p. 94.

5. Ibid., p. 93.

6. Fainsod, *How Russia is Ruled*, pp. 386-421.

7. Strobe Talbott, ed., *Khrushchev Remembers*, (Boston, 1970), pp. 602-609.

8. Fainsod, *Smolensk under Soviet Rule*, p. 86. He also deals with this problem in *How Russia is Ruled*, pp. 390-410.

9. Karl Marx, *Critique of Hegel's "Philosophy of Right,"* Joseph O'Malley, ed., (Cambridge, England,1970), p. 46.

10. Trotsky, *The New Course*, p. 27.

11. Trotsky, "Thermidor and Bonapartism," in *Writings 1930-1931*, (New York, 1973), pp. 262-303.

12. Trotsky, "The Defense of the Soviet Republic and the Opposition," in *Writings 1929*, (New York, 1975), pp. 73-78.

13. Trostky, "Problems of the Development of the USSR," in *Writings 1930-1931*, (New York, 1973), p. 221.

14. For an analysis of Trotsky's views on peasantry and the problems of rural migration to the cities, see Richard Day, *Leon Trotsky and the Politics of Economic Isolation*, (Cambridge, England, 1973), pp. 114-120.

15. Trotsky, "The Danger of Thermidor," in *Writings 1932-1933*, (New York,

1973), pp. 71-81. For two very different views on the Kronstadt rebellion and the Bolshevik response to it, see Paul Avrich, *Kronstadt 1921*, (New York, 1970), and Ida Mett, *The Kronstadt Commune*, London 1967, Solidarity Press. (New York, 1973).

16. Avrich, *Kronstadt 1921*, p. 137.

17. Quoted in Laszlo Szamuely, *First Models of Socialist Economic Systems*, (Budapest, 1974), p. 44.

18. Trotsky, "Staliniskaia biurokratiia i ubiistvo Kirova," *Biulletin Oppozitsii*, (April 1935), pp. 1-9.

19. Trostsky, "Rabochee gosudarstvo, termidor i bonapartizm," *Biulletin Oppozitsii*, (April 1935), pp. 1-9.

20. Ibid., p. 8.

21. Trostky, "Not a Workers' and Not a Bourgeois State," in *Writings 1937–1938*, (New York, 1973), pp. 90-93.

22. Ibid., p. 90.

23. Ibid., p. 91.

24. Trotsky, *The Permanent Revolution*, (New York, 1965).

25. Ibid., pp. 11-17.

26. Trotsky, *The Revolution Betrayed*, p. 291.

27. Ibid., p. 294.

28. Ibid., p. 297.

29. Trotsky, *The Class Nature of the Soviet State*, (London, 1973), p. 4-34.

30. Ibid., p. 31.

31. Ibid., p. 30.

32. Ibid., p. 33.

33. Isaac Deutscher, *The Prophet Outcast: Trotsky, 1929–1940*, (New York, 1963), p. 316.

34. Ibid., p. 317.

35. Trostky, "Problems of the Development of the USSR", in *Writings 1930–1931*, (New York, 1973), p. 205. Also see, *Biulletin Oppozitsii*, (April 1931), pp. 20-21.

36. Trotsky, "The Defense of the Soviet Republic and the Opposition," in *Writings 1929*, (New York, 1975), pp. 261-265.

37. Trotsky, "Problem razvitiia SSSR," *Biulletin Oppozitsii*, (April 1931), p. 20.

38. Ibid., p. 21.

39. Ibid, p. 10.

40. Trotsky, "Otkritoe pismo prezidiumu Tslk a Soiuza SSSR," *Biulletin Oppozitsii*, (March 1932), pp. 1-6.

41. Trotsky, "Klassovaia priroda sovestskogo gosudarstva," *Biulletin Oppozitsii*, pp. 4-6.

42. Trotsky, "Not a Workers' and Not a Bourgeois State," in *Writings 1937–1938*, (New York, 1975), pp. 91-93. For different views on this theme, see E.H. Carr, *Socilism in One Country*, Vols. I and II, (London, 1959). Also see Max Shachtman, *The Bureaucratic Revolution*, (New York, 1962).

43. Marx, *The Eighteenth Brumaire of Louis Bonaparte*, (New York, 1963), pp. 130-135.

44. Ibid., p. 132.

45. Marx, *The Civil War in France*, (New York, 1969), p. 668.

46. For a theoretical discussion of Marx on this problem, see both Robert Tucker, *Philosophy and Myth in Karl Marx*, (Cambridge, England, 1972) and Shlomo Avineri, *The Social and Political Thought of Karl Marx*, (Cambridge, England, 1968).

47. Trotsky, *The Workers' State and the Question of Thermidor and Bonapartism*, (London, 1973), pp. 43-44.

48. Ibid., p. 44.

49. Trotsky, "Rabochee gosudarstvo, termidor i bonapartizm," *Biulletin Oppozitsii*, (April 1935), pp. 11-13.

50. Ibid., p. 12.

51. Ibid., p. 10.

52. Ibid., p. 11.

53. Trotsky, *The Revolution Betrayed*, pp. 277-278.

54. Ibid., p. 278.

55. Ibid., p. 279.

56. Ibid., p. 278.

57. Ibid., p. 278.

58. Trotsky, "The Fourth International and the Soviet Union," in *Writings 1935-1936*, New York, 1970), pp. 37-40. Also, see Trotsky "State," Ibid., pp. 91-101.

59. For some solutions to this problem see Trotsky, *Writings 1935-1936*, (London, 1970), pp. 30-39. See his two other articles in the same collection, "War and the Fourth International" and "On the Eve of World War II."

60. Trotsky, *The Revolution Betrayed*, p. 277.

61. For a detailed account of the purges and trials see, Robert Conquest, *The Great Terror: Stalin's Purge of the Thirties*, (London 1968) and *The Harvest of Sorrow*, (New York 1986). On the structure of the Bolshevik Party for the same period see, T. H. Rigby, *Communist Party Membership in the USSR, 1917-1967*, (Princeton, 1968).

62. Trotsky, "Rabochee gosudarstvo, termidor i bonapartizm," *Biulletin Oppozitsii*, (April 1935), p. 12.

63. Ibid., p. 14. Trotsky uses "paranoia" and "crime" constantly in this article.

64. For further insights on this theme, consult Conquest, *The Great Terror* or *The Harvest of Sorrow*.

65. See especially Trotsky's *Their Morals and Ours*, (New York, 1942).

66. Conquest, *The Great Terror*, pp. 38-47.

67. Trotsky, *The Revolution Betrayed*, (London, 1937). See especially the appendix of this edition entitled "I Stake My Life", pp. 292-312.

68. For his position and opinions on the 1936 constitution consult, *The Revolution Betrayed*, Chapter 10. Also see his article, "Novaia konstitutsiia SSSR," in *Biulletin Oppozitsii*, May 1936), pp. 2-7. Here he argued that opposition parties, though not anti-Soviet, should be allowed to participate in the political process.

69. Trotsky wrote numerous articles and pamphlets on this particular subject. For his specific comments on the Moscow trials, see, *The Case of Leon Trotsky: Report of Hearings on the Charges made Against Him in the Moscow Trials (Before the Preliminary Commission of Inquiry, John Dewey, Chairman)*, (New York and London, 1937). Also see, John Dewey's remarks, *Truth is on the March*, (New York, 1937), pp. 10-15.

70. Ibid., pp. 460-584.

71. Trotsky, *The Revolution Betrayed*, p. 283.

72. See note 71 above.

73. For use of coercion and fear to uproot and destroy the intellectual class in the 1930s, see, especially, Nadezhda Mandelstam, *Hope Against Hope*, (New York, 1970) and *Hope Abandoned*, (new York, 1974).

74. Trotsky, *The Revolution Betrayed*, pp. 199-120.

75. Ibid., p. 126.

76. Ibid., p. 185.

77. Ibid., p. 279.

78. See the disputes among the former Trotskyites themselves in Max Shachtman, *The Bureaucratic Revolution*, (New York, 1962).

79. Bruno Rizzi, *La Bureaucratisation du Monde*, (Paris, 1938). See Max Shachtman's interesting observations on Rizzi in " 1939: Whither Russia?" *Survey*, (April 1962), pp. 96-107.

80. Rizzi, *La Bureaucratisation du Monde*, p. 20.

81. Ibid., pp. 30-33.

82. Ibid., p. 35.

83. Ibid., pp. 72-74.

84. Ibid., p. 283.

85. Ibid., p. 284.

86. Shachtman, *The Bureaucratic Revolution*, p. 81.

87. Ibid., p. 43.

88. Ibid., p. 44.

89. Ibid., p. 49.

90. Ibid., pp. 45-46.

91. Ibid., pp. 61-73.

92. Trotsky, *In Defense of Marxism*, (London, 1971), p. 1.

93. Trotsky, "The USSR in War", *In Defense of Marxism*, p. 8.

94. Ibid., p. 9.

95. For correspondence and commentary see, Trotsky, *In Defense of Marxism*, (London, 1971).

96. See note 95 above.

97. Trotsky, "The USSR in War," p. 11; also see his "Once Again: The USSR and Its Defense", *Fourth International*, (August 1951).

98. See note 97 above.

99. On this issue, see Shachtman, *The Bureaucratic Revolution*.

100. In addition *The Machiavellians* see Burnham's resignation article entitled "Science and Style: A Reply to Comrade Trotsky and 'Letter of Resignation'," in Trotsky's *In Defense of Marxism* and "The Politics of Desperation," in *The New International*, (March 1940).

101. Shachtman, "1939: Whither Russia", *Survey*, (April 1962), pp. 96-107.

102. Trotsky, *In Defense of Marxism*, pp. 29–33.

103. Ibid., p. 32.

104. Ibid., pp. 15-16.

105. He lost such friends as Souvarine in France, Diego Rivera in Mexico, and Hook, Eastman and Shachtman in the United States.

106. His justification of the Polish invasion was that it was necessary for the inevitable confrontation with Hitler's Germany. For additional notes, see his *In Defense of Marxism*, pp. 131–136.

107. Ibid., p. 10.

4

Djilas and the Path to Yugoslav Communism

Since his removal from political life in 1954, Milovan Djilas has been preoccupied to a great extend with the past—his own and his people's. In a way, this is quite understandable. When a man has gone precipitously from the center of power to the solitary prison cell, he clearly does not have a very bright political future to anticipate. Rather than fritter away his time with musings about a future Utopia, he might reflect instead upon the path already traveled.

What is more unusual, I think, is that Djilas took occasional backward glances even during the time he was a leading figure in the Yugoslav Communist regime. We do not, of course, find the sort of extended recollection which he later practiced during his imprisonment at Sremska Mitrovica but there were already indications that the past was something which mattered deeply, even when he was reacting to and fighting against it. Our first purpose, then, is to attempt to uncover this heritage and the clues there provided to Djilas' subsequent development.

Milovan Djilas was born " on an unsettled afternoon at the beginning of the spring in 1911."[1] He was born a Djilas and a Montenegrin, which means that he was born into a mountaineer clan. He recalls that his mother had to give birth in hiding, for it was shameful to give birth within the walls of an unfinished house. His father was supposed to have had a vision the night before Milovan's birth that revealed to him that his new son would become more significant to the family clan than the other children. Djilas himself later asserted that many Montenegrins had similar visions regularly.

One of the most vivid aspects of clan organization was the hostility and rivalries that appeared to be inevitable. Commented Djilas:

Vengeance—this is a breath of life one shares from the cradle with one's fellow clansmen, in both good fortune and bad, vengeance from eternity. Vengeance was the debt we paid for the love and sacrifice our forebears and fellow clansmen bore for us. It was the defense of our honor and good name, and the guarantee of our maidens. It was our pride before others; our blood was not water that anyone could spill . . . It was centuries of manly pride and heroism, survival, a mother's milk and a sister's vow, bereaved parents and children in black, joy and songs turned into silence and wailing. It was all, all.[2]

Typically Montenegrin was the existence of blood feuds between the various clans:

The men of several generations have died at the hands of the Montenegrins, men of the same faith and name. My father's grandfather, my own two grandfathers, my father, and my uncle were killed, as though a dread curse lay upon them. My father and his brother and my brothers were killed even though all of them yearned to die peacefully in their beds with their wives. Generation after generation, and the bloody chain was not broken. The inherited fear and the hatred of feuding clans mightier than fear and hatred of the enemy, the Turks. It seems to me that I was born with blood in my eyes. My first sight was blood. My first words were blood and bathed in blood.[3]

Plenty of evidence exists without simply relying on his account that eventually every male member of Djilas' family "died at the hands of Montenegrins, men of the same faith and name."[4] Such practices, moreover, did not cease with the passing of the nineteenth and early twentieth centuries— other members of Djilas' household were to suffer death at the hands of counter-revolutionaries during World War II, as revenge for his personal leadership in the Communist movement and specifically the uprising in Montenegro in 1941.[5] At that time, partly because of his revolutionary dedication, partly because he was accustomed to bloodshed, he accepted the slaughter of his own family as inevitable and even logical under circumstances of war and revolution. But if we accept Djilas' account at face value, this was nevertheless a central point in his thinking, although it was not immediately registered in a different mode of action. When he returned in the summer of 1944 and saw his burned out home-place, he was by that time a mature Communist and leading Partisan in Tito's leadership. Djilas reflected:

What had brought me here? And what had driven me to investigate how it had all happened, though I could have dodged it and entrusted it to someone else? Who could tell? Was I not yearning to find even a crumb of my childhood and youth, of those moments of peaceful, joyful every day life? Was I not delving into the vast, un-resigned to its extinction to the impossibility of recreating in everyday life, of bring-ing it into the future?[6]

In short, what special meaning did this have for Djilas—the obliteration of his kin, putting the family home to flame?

Djilas' father had built the family home high on the hill. It had a com-manding view, and his father's main concern was that its chimney be clearly visible from afar, regardless of the season. His mother, on the other hand, was not particularly impressed with the location and found the winds dis-agreeable. There was an occasional squabble between them over this ques-tion, and Djilas' own choice is highly significant: "It seems impossible in life to have something both useful and beautiful. So men are divided. Some are for the useful, some are for the beautiful. I place myself on the side of beauty."[7] Committing the house to flames would seem to him, therefore, a wanton destruction of beauty. Two years after the event, when the chief per-petrator was being executed, Djilas realized that "there would never again be any comfort for me and that my past was lost forever."[8] "In these long postwar years," (it is not clear when this story was written), Djilas was tor-mented by memories. "The mutilated and unhealed past makes it impossi-ble for me to adapt myself to the present or to console myself with the ex-pectation of better times. I shall never be able to free myself from the past,"[9] that is, from recollections of youth, from happy family ties, from a standard of beauty. What one has thus far, then, is a powerful childhood cir-cumstance which elicits the notion that beauty is a value to be upheld and asserted. And this dialectic of beauty is a value to be upheld and asserted. And this dialectic of beauty and utility is one manifestation of the dualism that pervades Djilas' thought.

Djilas has no developed esthetic theory, but he does possess an esthetic sense which asserts itself at rather unexpected moments into his evaluation of men and events. It is unpredictable; one cannot anticipate to what objects Djilas assigns (or of what he will require) a criterion of beauty. But there is another area which provides a source for his attitude and embodiment of the value—Djilas' reaction to nature as something fundamentally esthetic and sensuous. "Aimless wandering though the mountains remains to me a memory of unspoiled beauty. The mountain draws a man to itself, to the sky, to man."[10] One of his autobiographical stories is especially instructive on this point. In 1938, he was sent back to his native mountain region to get in touch with some outlawed revolutionary remnants who "were waiting for answers and decisions for me, and only me...."[11] The dualism was again present though: as he and his local comrade guide start through the night, familiar forests, streams and hills brought back a rush of childhood memories. His own sense of being was intensified, union with the rest of na-ture made almost tangible. "My sole intention was to do my duty toward the (revolutionary) outlaws, and my sole desire was to rejoice in the lake. At any moment I could have moved away up the mountainside toward my duty, but I did not want to leave the woods and waters before I must."[12] The upshot was that he and his friend spent all night trout fishing. Djilas never informs us whether the revolutionary mission was accomplished.

In Djilas' description, his relation to nature is most intimate and friendly. As he wrote in the short story "Woods and Water":

For everything was as if it were the first day of creation—mine and that of everything living. I, too, moved and had my being in the life of everything living, perhaps of everything which was to live, a life indestructable and outside time, in the perception and consciousness of my own human existence, inseparable from and undifferentiated from other, living things.[13]

This vision has some significant implications. While Djilas is speaking of his experience of nature as immediate and pleasant, he also introduces the question of politics and revolution. Nature's forms, colors and smells, "had entered and taken root in the limitless cellars of my memory and thus acquired their own incontestable material existence. This was reality, known and irrefutable, but yet at the same time it was consciousness—myself."[14] However, "as for Spain, Spain was different; it was in my consciousness and yet far away from me, though I knew that I would live and die for Spain, either that Spain of the Iberian Peninsula or some other, any other."[15]

If we take his reference to Spain typologically, then politics is "in consciousness," whereas receptivity to and experience of nature is consciousness, self. The latter is "reality," while the former remains "thought" about something. There is a tone here suggesting that politics is something requiring a good deal of unpleasant effort, the realm of duty ("I would do my duty: I would not forget Spain."[16]), but nature is the sphere of joy, pleasure, and a sense of "at home-ness." It is Djilas' predicament to be suspended in an unhappy present; his native Montenegrin village "recalled to me a life without hatred and without torments, a life encased in memory or dreamed for a distant future that would never be mine."[17] Elsewhere he juxtaposes "my lake, childhood and my ideal Spain."[18] At this point Djilas appears unable to decide whether Utopia lies in the past or in the future. Despite his disclaimer that you can not literally go home again ("nor could I go back to my childhood, into a world and self that no longer existed,"[19]) and this does not necessarily preclude the future attempt to create and establish new conditions that would permit a life free of hatred and torments.

Another issue bears mentioning. If we attempt to phrase Djilas' outlook in terms of alienation, then the hostile subject-object dualism would exhibit itself in man's political life,[20] not including the realm of nature which is by contrast immediately experienced. This is a most unusual formulation for a Marxist and even for modern industrial man generally. It is not a matter of politics being hard and nature easy; both can require great exertions from man, but the mode of experiencing the two is very different.

Life on the mountain is not easier or more comfortable, but it is loftier in everything. There are no barriers between man and sky. Only the birds and the clouds soar by ... One goes to the mountain also for a holiday, to rest the body, and to give free rein to the mind, and to play and thus to melt nature and the universe. The beauty of the mountain is not merely in the clean air and diamond-cold water, which cleanse the body within. Nor is it in the easy life ... Its beauty lies in that ceaseless and all-pervading effort and exertion, which are not really oppressive. Stern in appearance, the cleanliness of its waters and air overpowering and yet invigorating, the mountain nevertheless dances in luster and color, and forces all creatures, above all man, into dances of spirit and body that are guileless with all their boldness and abandon.[21]

Nature is a sphere of union, between man and nature as between man and man; politics is divisive and has divisive influences even on the man-to-man response itself. For Djilas, man's relationship to nature does not take the form only of labor and manipulation, and accordingly his definition of man is not couched in terms that makes him so emphatically a laboring animal, burdened with pain and toil. This view has the merit that, if man could ever be emancipated from the necessity of labor, then Djilas' man will be able to take advantage of such a condition. At the least, his man is capable of enjoying free time and purposeless play. Furthermore, Djilas does not make nature something that is experienced antagonistically, something which must be mastered and dominated. It is not experienced as a "project" or a "provocation," the fundamental view of nature is behind scientific and industrial rationality.[22] In the political realm, however, he wrote that "I had to fight for ideals, for a world different from the one that existed."[23]

One is led to wonder whether this distinction between the natural and the political stands up. Djilas never discusses the problem in traditional terms of the differences between the natural and the conventional or artificial. However, he never seems to try to envelop both realms in an overall whole, subject to a single set of laws of development. I believe that in his thought (and certainly in his experiences) the contrast between nature and convention is entirely real. It appears that Djilas endows nature with greater independent objectivity than scientific rationality (and perhaps Marxist materialism) would allow. His view is more that of everyday common sense.

Part of Djilas' response to nature, as something to nurture rather than exploit, might be due to his class background. His father "belonged to that first generation of Montenegrin officers who had any sort of education,"[24] but who nevertheless remained peasant to the core. Djilas' class origin, therefore, was "an environment of peasant civil servants, more peasant that anything else, like so many Montenegrin intellectuals of my generation."[25] Nature, in this melieu, is taken not as an object to be torn and violated, but as a plot to be tended so human life can grown and flourish.[26]

Djilas' father's generation had its heyday during the two Balkan Wars, 1912–1914. By the time of the First World War, these men were faced with an emergent political question that was to throw them, and their conventional modes of life, out of joint: the question of whether Montenegro was to be united with a Greater Serbia or remain an independent kingdom. Upon an answer to that question depended their status, their self-image, very frequently even their careers.

A moderate opponent of Serbo-Montenegrin unification, Djilas' father "nevertheless accepted service as gendarmery commandant,"[27] after it came to pass in 1918. However, he found no greater satisfaction in the new political order than he would have had he returned to a position of private citizen and peasant. One of his actions as commandant was to assist in putting down a rebellion among antiunification clans, with his gendarmes exercising more than the necessary cruelty.

This is a significant episode as Djilas interprets it, because what his father really had done was to violate his own integrity, the consequences of which were far worse than a reduction in civic status. According to Djilas, he

found himself in the tormenting position of having to act against his thoughts and desires. The course of history was changing, and one could not manage to warm himself at two fires at once. Choosing between conviction and a better life, most including Father, decided in favor of the latter. Having accepted the job and its duties, he had led on despite his will—the fate of all those who have renounced their convictions for the sake of the necessitites of life without becoming convinced that their convictions are wrong.[28]

That Djilas is acutely aware of this issue of truthfulness to oneself, is further indicated by the fact that the longest part of his *Montenegro* is given over to its exploration. One significant dimension of the problem is that long-run and short-run duties (or even self-interests) do not always coincide.

The story revolves around one Miloš Milosević, whose brother had killed an Austrian officer during the occupation following Montenegro's capitulation to Austria in January 1916, and Miloš did nothing to prevent his escaping to the hills. For this Miloš was imprisoned and sentenced to the gallows. The subjects of Djilas' examination are reflections of this man living in the shadow of certain death at a definite point in time, his relations with his fellow prisoners and particulary his dialogue with himself.

An Austrian Commissioner has offered Miloš his freedom if he will only publicly renounce his brother's action and condemn it as an act of rebellion. This circumstance sets in train Miloš's agonizing self-analysis, one of the most powerful and emotionally exhausting pieces Djilas ever wrote. Miloš struggles with the question of precisely where does the higher duty lie: to himself, or to his blood brother and clan loyalties? To life itself, the necessary condition for everything else one wants to do? Or is there a circumstance when death is the greater obligation? Would disagreeing with his brother appear to be agreeing with the detested foreign occupier? Throughout endless questionings and doubts, Miloš repeatedly comes back to an irreducible integrity of his self, whose opponents are more than individual wishes and desires:

To accept your proposal would mean for me the destruction of my personality, of my moral wholeness, of my core. If I did, I should cease to be a Serb, and a son of my clan and of my country.... Everything comes down to that destruction of the personality which you mentioned. I should cease to be what I am if I were to accept your proposal, since by doing so I should be agreeing to utter a lie deliberately and aloud. And that I cannot, I cannot do! But this is a question of something else. By the declaration you are asking of me I should not be deceiving you and Austria, but myself. I should have to say deliberately and publicly that I believe in something in which I do not believe, in something I am not—and I cannot do it. There are people who can do even a thing like that. But I am not one of them. I can't. If I did such a thing, I should become a different person, someone unfamiliar and repulsive to me—a crawler, soulless, consciousless, faceless, I should become a living corpse, a corpse walking the earth conscious of my corruption and my shame.[29]

One notes that Miloš thinks not just in ethical terms—what it is that one ought not to do—but that it is also a question of knowledge in the final resort; what it is that one can and cannot do. Such knowledge is not a priori; it is discoverable only under stress. "A man has to find himself under special circumstances to find out what is unchangeable in his personality and what it is that makes him an individual."[30] Nor is such knowledge neatly reduced to logical categories; the Austrian Commissioner accuses Miloš of lacking defensible standards, of acting in a contradictory way if he permits himself to die and thereby destroys the only standard, life, by which one can value personality and individuality. To which Miloš replies:

Indeed I have not, Mr. Commissioner. A standard is something rational. But here is a case of an inner resistance that is as much instinctive as conscious. Some might call it faith in victory, others national or some other sort of consciousness, others conscience.[31]

Not the victim, but the tormentor, is the rational one:

Standards! The man who measures does not give, does not sacrifice himself. It is those who drive people to death who calculate. The future is the only measure that will tell who has been a fool and who farsighted. My duty is not to betray myself. There is no measure for the immeasurable, for the things in which passion and chance play an inescapable part ... I do not know whether, or how much, my death will help my country's struggle, but I am sure that I shall remain clean in my own eyes and before the laws of my own personality—by my own categorical imperative, if you like.[32]

This view of ultimate moral dilemmas represents Djilas' most mature reflections on the problem. As we shall continue to see, his approach always contains a generous portion of personal and individual valuations—that is, both his attraction to a disillusionment with various facets of Communism. On one occasion when he attempts to account for a major personal decision in Marxist terms, it strikes one as quite vulgarized.[33]

This digression on the problem of integrity has taken us away from the starting point; Djilas' relation to his father and some of the lessons he draws from the latter's actions. To pick up the thread—his father was eventually pensioned and found himself with no meaningful outlet for an abundance of energy. He tried his hand at being a merchant, at digging irrigation ditches; he even grew a beard and flirted with a superficial religiosity. But his restlessness reached floodtide in the affair of one Boško Bosković. In background and position, this man was one of the younger Montenegrin officers, a war hero, and clan chieftain. He and Djilas' father were not always on the best of terms but they shared both the exhaustion of battle and confinement in the enemy's prison.

Some years later, in the mid-1920s, Boško was ambushed in circumstances that appeared to implicate the nearby Moslem population, and Djilas' father threw himself into the resulting massacre as one of a sizeable mob bent on destruction and reprisal. In a sense, the way for this bloodletting had been prepared by the otherwise positive fact that his father was the first of his forebears to transcend clan consciousness and give primary allegiance to nation and state. Consequent upon this, however, was a heightened loathing for the foreigner, particularly the Turk (all Moslems were "Turks").

What is the importance of all this for our study and for Djilas' father as well? An answer to this question forces us to consider how important myth and legend are for the people of Montenegro. A myth is not an untruth, but rather a kernel of truth that is embroidered and magnified beyond the original starting point. The relationship between the Ottoman Turks and the people of the Balkans is of course a matter of historical record. But, according to Djilas, "time washes and wrings from tales all that is unimportant, all the daily humdrum, and leaves only the essential, that which gives body, expression, and meaning to life over the generations."[34] And so, "people live just as much in the past and in illusions about themselves as they do in the realities of every day."[35] Djilas' fathers' participation in the massacre of the Moslems, then, was one more episode in the Montenegrin revenge upon the Turks for their five-hundred year domination over the Balkans.

Every one of the "great myths" which Djilas enumerates has some relationship to this central issue. As he points out vividly in *Njegoš*:

a doomed Serbia, the flight of its nobility into the Montenegrin mountains after the fall of the empire of Kosovo, the duty to avenge Kosovo ... the irreconcilable struggle between Cross and Crescent, the Turks as an absolute evil pervading the entire Serbian nation.[36]

These legends and historical episodes constituted the first examples of culture and education given the young Montenegrin when Djilas was growing up. The greatest of them, moreover, was transmitted in the form of folk or epic poetry, handed down and embellished from generation to generation. It is for this reason the Djilas can say the men of Montenegro "swear by God and their gusles," the latter being the stringed instrument on which they accompanied their recitations. If one guslar stopped, another would pick up the story, especially "The Mountain Wreath," of Prince Bishop Njegoš, practically without pausing.

What we see here is a peculiar mingling of two separate factors. If the past is typically preserved in poetry and poetry operates according to esthetic criteria, then we find the past and beauty becoming at least partially identified. Individual incidents of the past are not "pretty," but the ongoing poetic expression and recollection of them is beautiful; and the past is lofty and reverberates with the heroic struggle of a people.[37] Djilas as a youth believed that he might be able to write poetry, but he cannot decide whether this is a fitting action for a person, such as he, who thinks of himself as a young radical.

Who would dare? I would be discovered and ridiculed. Even my best friend, Mihailo, would make fun of me. He had inherited from his Communist uncle Milovan a tendency to ridicule poets and to look upon poetry as something worthless. Poet's life, he would say; their poems have nothing real in them. And on and on. Maybe Mihailo and his uncle were right. Still, poems are beautiful things, and one would hardly live without them.[38]

So the milieu in which Djilas grew up facilitated a spilling over from the realm of the factual into artistic representation, or a partial confounding of the true and beautiful. I think it unnecessary to enter here into the argument over who gives a more adequate description of the babbling brook, the poet or the physicist. Suffice it for our purpose to admit that they exemplify two modes of representing a matter and that Djilas tends to play one argument against the other. This may not be the ordinary way of looking at things, according to either common sense or Marxist ideology, but for the Montenegrin there is evidently nothing unusual about it.

In the Montenegrin creative genius there are two separate strands—beauty and truth—just as there are in every other creative genius. But in others they are fused. In Montenegro they are separate themes, two different faces. Njegoš wanted to unite them, and succeeded in doing so, though not always or everywhere. Still, he did succeed, and in a unique way. Njegoš, as no one else did, made wisdom into beauty.[39]

It is possible to ruminate endlessly over the meaning of this cryptic pronouncement. The primary difficulty, I think, stems from the fact that we are unaccustomed to thinking of social realities in esthetic terms, but Djilas obviously asserts some sort of connection between the two. In the statement above, he does not make clear whether Njegoš "united" truth and beauty in his individual life or in his social action and the polity over which he ruled. Njegoš was both prince and poet, thus manifestly dualist in the salient characteristics of his life, and there is a lasting dialectic between the man of letters and the man of action. The Njegoš archetype, its unity of poetry with power, seems to be the pattern for which Djilas yearns throughout his career. By contrast, all his own political experience tells him that politics is most properly characterized by its divisive qualities.[40]

Despite the pervasive vagueness of the statement above and indeed of the entire problem, I believe it possible to extract a kernel of meaning from Djilas' main references to beauty. What factors lead him, perhaps unconsciously, to attribute beauty to one area rather than another and what possible implication can this have for his vision of the political world? A careful reading seems to indicate that it is the presence of free activity or free response—voluntary, uncoerced, self-determined—that is associated with his judgements of beauty.

In *Land Without Justice* and in *Montenegro*, for example, one discovers such sentiments as these: it is "aimless wandering through the mountains" that remains a memory of "unspoiled beauty." "There are no barriers between man and the sky." Human life becomes "less ashamed of its passions, less withdrawn, like a herd of horses galloping freely across endless pastures in a time when they had not yet been subdued by man." All creatures, particularly man, are forced "into dances of spirit and body that are guileless with all their boldness and abandon." And finally, the beauty of it all "lies in that ceaseless and all-pervading effort and exertion, which are not really oppressive."[41]

The tone of "Woods and Water" is more responsive and receptive, less active. Djilas notes more than once his feeling of union with the natural environment, and contrasts his desire to remain by the lake and his duty to the revolutionary comrades; the latter tears him from the former and from the union to which it conduces. At various times he recalls the obligations of practical affairs, "the world that did not permit me to be absentminded ... the world of man's relation to man ... with duties and decisions."

Nature is a realm of free activity: "How rapidly and inevitably does nature renew itself?"[42] As to the family home, his father obviously did not have to build it high in the hills; to do so was to defy utility, as Djilas himself notes,[43] and choice of this site over some other was a free act. Poetry likewise embodies the free play of invention, going beyond the reality of life's necessities: "One could not live without poetry." This is a reality of life's necessities: "One could not live without poetry. This [Montenegrin] land may not be good for living, but it is fine for telling tales."[44] And the recitation of these heroic folk stories is never static and fixed; any *guslar* worthy of the name would not confine himself to the printed version which in many instances did not exist anyhow. Instead, an essential element of heart is the ceaseless improvisational development of the tale with each retelling.[45]

If Njegoš really expressed the essence and destiny of Montenegro (as Djilas claims he did), some background evidence can be taken from that source. Njegoš propounded a dualist cosmology in terms of several dichotomies; light against darkness, God against Satan, and good against evil. God's creativity was treated by Njegoš as an artistic, poetic act by which inchoate matter is infused with order and beauty. Therefore, assuming that Djilas shares in the Montenegrin outlook, his use of the term "beauty" might also perhaps be taken as a kind of cosomological image standing for a principle of creativity and generativity.[46]

If we are correct in this view that Djilas' reference to something as beautiful indicates that presence of a substantial ingredient of free activity, we must note further that not every one of his uses of this quasi-esthetic judgment—in the context in which it occurs—exemplifies the thesis here asserted. Some of his references are brief and casual, a statement made, but then never followed up, and contextually insignificant.[47] There is nothing about the references and their contexts, however, that contradicts the present view. Even on occasions when he is concerned wholly and explicitly with a political matter, a statement suddenly intrudes itself that something is beautiful or ugly.

Especially in *Land Without Justice, Njegoš, The Leper and other Stories, The Stone and the Violets,* and in the novel *Montenegro,* Djilas illustrates the influence of his ancestral legacy and the ties of his native soil in the intellectual development of his personality. His description of Montenegrin people, the depiction of the "blood ties" of the various clans and tribes, and the demonstration of the powerful emotional bonds between Montenegrins and Russians in time of war are developed in his most recent work, *Wartime.* Djilas' own agnosticism remains in a complex fashion a legacy of his native land: a country in which the bishops were warriors and the warriors bishops and where Christianity was one aspect of the struggle against the domination by the Ottoman Empire. Clearly the fiery and bloody history of the various clans of Montenegro shaped his spirit and temperament. He greatly admired the fierce independence of Montenegrins, who alone of the south and west Slavic peoples were able to retain their independence from foreign enemies; he venerated the idealism and toughness necessary to survive the hardships of a rugged and hostile land; he respected the profound sense of active kinship that linked men and enabled them to withstand their enemies, both natural and human.

As we have already seen, Djilas took great pride in a melange of Montenegrin fables, legends and folk ballads. He himself joined the family clan—the Kuči.[48] The rich folk-ballad tradition of the Kuči tribe and of other Serbian and Montenegrin groups served to further Djilas' growing convictions. The works of Njegoš and later Marko Miljanov,[49] two self-educated nineteenth-century Montenegrin statesmen, aroused his commitment to the search for freedom, truth and justice. He had in fact memorized all of Njegoš's famous ode to freedom, *The Mountain Wreath*, by heart, as well as hundreds of folk ballads.

At the time of Djilas' birth, his other hero, Marko Miljanov had been dead for a decade. But the legend of this hero of the same Kuči tribe was green, despite governmental disapproval. As Djilas was to be, Marko Miljanov was in the thick of the battles of his day. A fighter against the Turks from the tender age of fourteen, he was most responsible for the Montenegrin victory at Fundia in 1871.[50] Later he broke with his sovereign over matters of principle. Ostracized and enveloped by official silence, the craggy hands of this Nestor became sufficiently accomplished in wielding the pen to produce a magnificent classic in 1901, *Examples of Manliness and Heroism*. The epic heroes of this record of pure virtue live in Djilas's own literary works, especially in *Montenegro*, and perhaps in more complex and psychologically subtle ways. So do the obvious political parallels between these two men, often best drawn by Djilas himself.[51] Through these examples and others, Djilas rejected the utilitarian for the beautiful, in a way that was characteristic of many Balkan romantics and revolutionaries.

In fact, we may say that romantic nationalism or "clan" patriotism pervaded Djilas' soul, and as has already been pointed out, Djilas often referred to the beauty and influence of romanticism in his life. To understand Djilas we must comprehend his struggle with poetic beauty, art and politics. In the course of his development, poetry, art, and literature came to represent the personal, while revolution (politics) stood for the social. While serving his sentence in the Sremska Mitrovica Prison under Tito, he attempted to explain this duality.

Politics is, in fact, the creation of a new reality, as is art, but politics is in all reality, unlike art. But only in reality. Artists are not good politicians, and politicians are not good artists either. And I have been torn all my life between art and politics, as if I had two natures in me. I recall that conflict between desire and duty, and it seems to me that I am simply made that way.[52]

Although at an early age, Djilas decided in favor of duty to society it was in fact a number of years before he had to make a real choice. He remained torn, and as we shall see on other occasions, his responses appeared to be dictated by neither desire nor duty but by what was most beautiful. Like many young intellectuals of his time, he was beset by moral dilemmas: his personal desire to write and the sense of the beautiful was in conflict with what he felt to be moral obligations to work for a better society, a society of justice and social equality. As he explained much later in his "Prison Diary," "it was more important and even more beautiful to 'make a revolution' than to describe it."[53]

Milovan Djilas was acutely aware that one could not remain permanently in a state of childhood "innocence" and gratification. Whatever may be its specific forms, change does supervene, and no condition or style of life can be frozen or made immune to the flux of human living. Furthermore, if one cannot "stay at home" neither can he "go home again."[54] From a variety of sources and at several levels of experience Djilas was impelled into an active response to his personal and social world, and ultimately into Communism. As I have suggested, young Djilas took seriously the myths, stories and legends recorded in folk poetry. He identified with its heroes; distinctions between art and life, past and present, fantasy and reality, became blurred. The "Song of Vuk Lopuština," in particular, moved him as example and in-spiration. The beauty of the song and the heroic exploits of its central figure were incorporated into "forboding that the beauties and the events of the song could never happen again; but I could create fresh beauties and in fresh unforeseen events still be great in the inimitable manner of Lopuš-tina . . . I strained, as what human being does not, to create my own reality, to create new worlds."[55]

We may view Djilas' sensitivity to his poetic heritage as extraordinary, but there is nothing unusual in the youthful urge to remake the world and in the belief that it will submit. Simply put,

Young people—each in his own way—pose questions and seek answers. It would ap-pear that the solution lies in this constant search. But everyone wants to find nothing less than the final solution in his own time—especially those among young people who are dissatisfied with the state of affairs they find, and who are sufficiently strong and serious to look social reality straight in the eye.[56]

So much for the general energizing sentiments that lay behind Djilas' rest-less desire to become an active participant in the world around him. Nevertheless, this restlessness was far from a specific commitment to the Communist party of Yugoslavia. Djilas' inclination toward Communism was induced by a multitude of decisions and circumstances, individually of varying significance but cumulatively powerful. The reader may laugh—

Djilas recalls that everyone else did—to learn that he became a Communist at the ripe old age of seven.[57] His godfather, Mihailo Vicković, had impressed Milovan by the fact that "he was a Communist because he loved justice, like Christ,"[58] and Djilas' own gentle nature appeared to respond to this: such a posture had definite shock value and it was enjoyable to be interesting in front of others.

On the whole, Djilas' political evolution into a mature Communist was fostered by the influence of individuals, usually indirect, by the political environment of the period, and to a lesser extent by his reading. Apart from the case of his godfather, most of Djilas' relevant personal encounters had nothing directly to do with Communism. Rather, what was gleaned from these experiences was an appreciation for social justice and mercy; and adherence to a Communist point of view was a derivative of these prior values. An example of this process was Djilas' relation to one Archpriest Bojović who gave religious instruction in his secondary school. The Archpriest's arguments were designed to turn students away from the new radicalism and violence of Communism, but his nontheological and man-centered explanations "were completely in harmony with the youthful disposition for justice and mercy,"[59] and Djilas always felt later that he had an unpaid Communist debt to the Archpriest.

Similar indirect influence stemmed from his reading. An ostensibly radical piece, Chernyshevsky's famous *What is to be Done?* struck Djilas only as unconvincing and somewhat shallow. *Uncle Tom's Cabin* and *Les Miserables* each had a powerful impression while one was reading, but it disappeared as soon as the book was put aside. And therefore, for Djilas:

It was classical and humanistic literature that drew me to Communism. True, it did not lead directly to Communism, but taught more humane and just relations among men. Existing society, and particularly the political movements within it, were incapable even of promising this . . . The only thing that could exert any influences, and indeed it did, was great literature, particularly the Russian classics. Its influence was indirect, but more lasting. Awakening noble thoughts, it confronted the reader with the cruelties and injustices of the existing order.[60]

It is important to see what vision of Communism these influences led Djilas to espouse. For him at age seven, "Communism is something just and for poor people."[61] By the time his was in secondary school he reflects that "were not the first impulses toward Communism those arising out of a desire to put an end to the world of force and injustice and to realize a different world, one of justice, brotherhood and love among men?"[62] This is, of course, an extremely idealistic and rather simplistic attitude. While his views later became much more ideologized and politicized, a remnant of this early position will occasionally crop up. As he wrote in 1952, in one of his *Borba* articles:

in the end socialism in nothing other than, simply putting concern for people, their life, health, future, eduation—concern for the common working man.[63]

In the same article Djilas continues to discuss and evaluate such everyday issues such as the rate of industrial accidents, and wages.

It is evident then that Djilas' adherence to a Communist standpoint did not result from any process of conversion. No one accident turned him, nor did his reading or his acquaintances lead him to formulate a rational body of doctrine. What we see instead is a highly personalized response to, and appropriation of, certain elements in his environment. From all the evidence available, Djilas' case was a highly personal one.[64] For that matter, as Djilas himself implies, there was no body of doctrine to adhere to in 1920, no local organization and leadership to which he could profess. His childhood villages, Berane and Kolašin, were isolated intellectually, and "Communism" tended to be whatever one happened to call it, usually no more than vague yearnings for justice and a better economic life. Another Montenegrin source has mentioned this specific lack of ideological refinement.

There always had been Communists, Anarchists, Tolstoians and Socialists among Pastrovići (an area, as well as a group of clans), but they had kicked the precepts of Marx and other teachers around to suit themselves.[65]

What appears to have saved Djilas from ineffectual localism was the fact that he traveled to Belgrade and attended the University, where there was an organized body of discontent and a defined political situation to react to.

While still a secondary school student in Berane, Djilas had already closely followed political developments in Belgrade and Zagreb, and through his older brother Aleksa had participated vicariously in some of them. Djilas always has spoken of his brother in terms of profoundest love and devotion. Of course they had their disputes but they were similar in personality and agreed on political questions. One incident was taken especially personally by Djilas. In the fall of 1928, Aleksa was involved in a riot against the ratification of the Nettuno Convention with Italy.[66] In a political situation increasingly polarized along ethnic lines, many of the activists in the riot, in addition to being hostile to Italy, were opposed to Serb-dominated central government in Belgrade, thereby making all participants suspect to the government. A hospital attendant rescued Aleksa just in time to prevent a policeman from carrying out his declared intention to "knock the fellow over the head with a rifle butt to teach the others a lesson."[67] This was an important event for Djilas because "it was the first great political experience we shared. I participated in it through my love for him. I was moved against the regime particularly because the gendarme wanted to bash in my brother's head for no good reason, and during a patriotic demonstration at that."[68] As we can see, Djilas' political discontent is beginning to focus on a specific government and its actions as the obstacle to that social justice and better life he hopes to help make.

Following this incident, the next major political crisis was the assassination of Stjepan Radić.[69] Leader of the Croatian Peasant Party from 1921 to 1928, and taken by many as the conscience of the country, Radić was seriously wounded on the floor of the Parliament in June 1928 and died two months later. Djilas was the only member of his school class that read newspapers and he avidly followed *Politika's* report of events leading to the assassination. He and his brother saw in the event not just an attack on a single political leader but an attack on Parliament itself. King Alexander[70] would and could do nothing constructive, because he was himself implicated in the plot.

Eventually came the proclamation of a royal dictatorship in 1929. Yugoslav democracy had been largely ineffectual since the formation of the Yugoslav state in 1921, and on the surface the dictatorship did not appear to make any great difference in daily life, except for the fact that the dictatorship made "an end to free speech, which most people apparently value as much as bread."[71] Otherwise, the real government—the police—were no more ruthless than before. For Djilas personally, King Alexander's action did not crystallize his thinking in a way that led to any definite line of action. However, he did begin to draw some preliminary conclusions:

At first and also later, the dictatorship only intensified my somber state of mind and discontent. It was the cause of my spiritual wanderings and of my dissatisfaction with social conditions. It seems to me that it was precisely these repressed dark moods, this psychological base tht provided for a political and social discontent which was all the more profound because it was moot and unconscious.[72]

From the evidence presently available to an historian, I do not think it possible to determine with any certainty what Djilas' view of parliamentary institutions and government is now, or what it was during the late 1920s. But there is a discussion on *Montenegro* that is quite sympathetic. The difficulty is that Djilas did not speak in his own person and the semifictional form of this work makes it impossible to ascertain his preferences. At any rate, one of his characters argues that parliamentary democracy "sprang from the natural desire of human communities for diversity and competition and made possible their unimpeded, inevitable progress."[73] In some ways this is not unlike Djilas' account of himself:

He had in his head a mixture of what he had acquired—Western liberal doctrines and Serbian parliamentarianism—and what he had inherited—the patriarchal harmony and equality of the family group and the tribe. This mixture did not strike him as either unnatual or artificial. He was deeply convinced that the Serbs were democrats by nature, so to speak, and that outside influences alone, combined with the selfishness of certain individuals, particularly rulers, were to blame if there had not always been freedom in the Serbian state. As soon as the Serbian nation grew strong and united, people would yield to their natural inclination for freedom and all denials of freedom would cease to exist.[74]

Although we cannot be absolutely certain that Djilas is referring to himself in the above statement, the latter part of remarks would aptly apply to King Alexander and his dictatorship. We shall see that the same will later apply to Tito and the Party or the new class. Dictatorship or not, "existing society, and particularly the political movements within it, were inescapable . . . more humane and just relations among men. It was that state of society itself that provided the prime and most powerful impulse."[75]

By logically following Djilas' arguments, the only alternative left was the Communist Party. After all there was a living example of its success in action in the Soviet Union. Djilas soon familiarized himself with these revolutionary forms, especially at the university[76] and later in the underground movement of the 1930s. As he explained:

If anyone wished to change it—and there are always men with such irresistible desires—he could do so only in a movement that promised something of the kind and was said to have succeeded once through a great revolution. The guardians of the *status quo* only made something like this attractive to a young man by their stories about the Communist specter and by their panicky preservation of old forms and relations. Communism was a new idea. It offered youth enthusiasm, a desire for endeavour and sacrifice to achieve the happiness of the human race.[77]

In other words, the movement promised a better and happier life. Was this not the life without hatred and without torment which Djilas had previously thought of as "encased in memory or dreamed of in a distant future that would never be mine?"[78] To Djilas, it apparently now appeared that a future can be won for a new reality, transcending but embodying old values, if he would take to heart the Communist movement as a vehicle for transformation. Harking back to his prewar attitudes Djilas stated "that the revolutionary tasks of our Party are tasks within which we should and must seek happiness, meaning that the joy and beauty of this life alone."[79] There is a direct connection here between the Communist Party and Djilas' childhood values.

But before he entered the University at Belgrade, Djilas had already considered himself an "active Communist."[80] His first active political involvement came in January of 1932, when he was a leader in a student demonstration against elections which had provided voters only a single list of candidates the previous November.[81] In the aftermath of this rebellion, Djilas earned his full revolutionary credentials—a three-year prison term in Sremska Mitrovica. His descriptions of the prison and the state officials are found in the second part of his autobiography, *A Memoir of a Revolutionary*. His experiences in prison only confirmed his desire to change the state and society.

To disclose a theme to be treated in greater detail later, there is a tone here to much of what Djilas claims about himself which I believe implies that he is the victim of circumstances—that choices are only in the most tenuous sense consciously and freely made, which would tend to confirm that nature, not politics, is the realm where man acts, responds and experiences most freely. In the present context, the issue arises from Djilas' remarks about attempting to decide between a political and literary career. And he commented on this personal dilemma:

Every man, especially a youth, yearns after various paths in life, and frequently he is forced to take the very one he never quite felt to be his own . . . I was the only one of my schoolmates who quite definitely regarded himself as a Communist. But I wished to be a writer. Finding myself even then, and especially later, with the dilemma of choosing between my personal desire and those moral obligations that I felt I owed society, I always decided in favor of the latter. Of course, such a decision is a pleasant self-deception: every man wishes to portray his role in society in the best possible light and as the result of great personal sacrifice and inner dramas. Yet it is true, even where this is so, that man who rejects self through a struggle nevertheless does only what he has to do, conditioned by the circumstances in which he finds himself and by his own personal traits.[82]

It is extremely difficult to specify the exact date when Djilas became a Communist but from the above statement suggests around 1925; and in any case it was "especially later" that he felt the dilemma. We know that his father had participated in putting down a rebellion among antiunification clans two or three years before 1925. It must be recalled that Djilas' father at the time was a "gendarmery commandant." In the light of that incident, Djilas passed the rather harsh judgment that his father had transgressed his own integrity and convictions.[83]

It appears that Djilas has worked himself into an inconsistency here. If his decision was made because of what he had to do, "conditioned by the circumstances in which he found himself and by his own personal traits," then presumably the same generous view should apply to his father. On the other hand, if his father chose freely to do what he did, and if he deserved to be reprimanded for allowing himself to be led on, "conditioned by the circumstances in which he found himself and by his own personal traits," then Djilas was himself free to choose otherwise and he should know better than to argue in this manner. For him, there is a conflict between personal desire and obligation to society; for his father the conflict is between conviction and a better life. The internal relation has been reversed: Djilas is struggling with a personal desire (literature) and a social duty (moral obligations) to society; his father contends with a personal duty (his relative position to unification) and a socially oriented wish (a government position). For Djilas, duty calls him outward, to participate; for his father, the duty is to withdraw from political activity. But all this is quibbling in the face of marked difference in emphasis: when Djilas is judging himself the accent is on necessity;[84] when he judges his father, it is on free choice.

It is possible to relieve some of the tension if we take another look at Djilas' formulation of the matter. He claims that he "decided" in favor of social obligation, but that this was a "self-deception." Man does only what he has to do. But what determines what he has to do? The circumstances in which he finds himself and his own personal traits, which presumably would entail his values, his energy, the strength of his commitments. In short, man never acts fully; his action is often determined by his personal traits.[85] Djilas' personality illustrates this in the following comment: "For our times, it was and is more important and more beautiful to 'make than to describe' revolution."[86] To Djilas, Communism offered a special dynamic for a purposeful social and political change.

NOTES

1. Milovan Djilas, *Land Without Justice*, (New York, 1958), p. 6.

2. Ibid., p. 107.

3. Ibid., p. 8.

4. See for example, Duško Doder, *The Yugoslavs*, (New York, 1979), pp. 177-195.

5. Djilas, "Fire and Knife," *The Leper and Other Stories*, (New York, 1964), p. 134.

6. Ibid., p. 137.

7. Djilas, *Land Without Justice*, p. 23.

8. Djilas, "Fire and Knife," *The Leper and Other Stories*, p. 150.

9. Ibid., p. 123.

10. Djilas, *Land Without Justice*, p. 110.

11. Djilas, "Woods and Water," *The Leper and Other Stories*, p. 33.

12. Ibid., p. 33.

13. Ibid., p. 42.

14. See note 13 above.

15. Ibid., p. 39.

16. See note 15 above.

17. See note 15 above.

18. Ibid., p. 41.

19. Ibid., p. 36.

20. Djilas' concepts and views of political life will be explored in greater detail later.

21. Djilas, *Land Without Justice*, pp. 110, 111.

22. For the development and importance of some of these ideas, see Barrington

Moore, Jr., *Reflections on the Causes of Human Misery*, (Boston, 1970), and also H. Arendt, *The Human Condition*, (Garden City, 1959).

23. Djilas, "Woods and Waters," *The Leper and Other Stories*, p. 35.

24. Ibid., p. 34.

25. Ibid., p. 36.

26. Herbert Marcuse, *Eros and Civilization*, (Boston, 1955), pp. 197-198.

27. Djilas, *Land Without Justice*, p. 89.

28. Ibid., pp. 89-90, p. 97.

29. Djilas, *Montenegro*, (New York, 1963), pp. 257-258.

30. Ibid., pp. 258-259.

31. Ibid., p. 263.

32. Ibid., p. 264.

33. At the critical point of his conflict with the Party in 1953, Djilas claimed that he was forced to become overtly critical because he was the victim of objective social processes. See, "Reply," *Anatomy of a Moral*, (New York, 1959), pp. 101-103.

34. Djilas, *Land Without Justice*, p. 4.

35. Djilas, *Montenegro*, p. 348. Djilas points out that Njegoš was " a poet who experienced myths as realities—for this is what they really were in their hidden meaning, compressed realities and myths." *Njegoš*, p. 316. "The kolos (circle dances) sing of the past as though it were still alive—and indeed it is in the Montenegrin outlook and struggle. Ibid., p. 361.

36. Djilas, *Njegoš*, (New York, 1966), p. 11.

37. Djilas' remarks on the very difficult life of a mountain people and probably the clans.

38. Djilas, *Land Without Justice*, p. 132.

39. Djilas, *Montenegro*, pp. 190-191.

40. On this see, "The Leper," *The Leper and Other Stories*, where the village headman puts it bluntly to the village poet: "Song is yours; authority mine." The poet, importantly, is the leper—beyond the pale of the real world of human community.

41. Djilas, *Land Without Justice*, pp. 110-111.

42. Djilas, "Woods and Waters," *The Leper and Other Stories*, pp. 34, 36, 56.

43. Djilas, *Land Without Justice*, p. 23.

44. Ibid., p. 137.

45. Djilas, "The Song of Vuk Lopuština," *The Leper and Other Stories*, p. 161.

46. See Djilas' interpretation of Njegoš's "The Ray of the Microcosm," in *Njegoš*, pp. 266-309.

47. For some examples: Yugoslavs are a "heroic and beautiful people" deserving the highest patriotism ("Govor ministra savezne Milovana Djilasa," *Borba*, 25 April 1948, p. 1). Jews are a "small, unfortunate, but beautiful people." ("Antisemitizam," *Borba*, 14 December 1952, p. 5). Communism is a beautiful idea, whereas capitalism, bureaucratism, and Cominformism are ugly ("Ljudski komunistički odnosi," *Borba*, 1 January 1952, p. 2; and "Ideološki ratovi," *Borba*, 17 May 1953, p. 1). Man is the "most beautiful and most graceful creation of nature whose serious injury or death means the incapacity to enjoy all the beauties of life or to create new beauties" ("Briga o ljudima," *Borba*, 4 August 1952), p. 1.

48. Djilas, *Land Without Justice*, p. 167.

49. Djilas, "About Marko Miljanov," *The Stone and Violets*, (New York, 1971), pp. 212-238.

50. Ibid., p. 216.
51. Ibid., p. 219.
52. Djilas, "Prison Diary," in Milovan Djilas *Parts of a Lifetime* edited by Michael and Deborah Milenkovitch HBJ, 1975 p. 111.
53. Djilas, "The Brothers and the Girl," *The Stone and Violets*, p. 53.
54. Djilas, "Woods and Waters," *The Leper and Other Stories*, p. 36.
55. Djilas, "The Song of Vuk Lopuština," *The Leper and Other Stories*, p. 182.
56. Djilas, *Land Without Justice*, p. 310.
57. Ibid., p. 126.
58. See note 57 above.
59. Ibid., p. 304.
60. Ibid., pp. 353, 353.
61. Ibid., p. 126.
62. Ibid., p. 305.
63. Djilas, "Briga o ljudima," *Borba*, 4 August 1952, p. 1.
64. There is nothing unusual about all this; see for example the discussion by Arthur Koestler and Ignazio Silone in: Richard Crossman, ed., *The God that Failed*, (New York, 1959).
65. Milla Z. Logan, *Cousins and Commissars*, (New York, 1949), p. 69.
66. Djilas, *Land Without Justice*, p. 316.
67. Ibid., p. 316.
68. See note 67 above.
69. For a comprehensive analysis of this very important event and its implications, see Bogdan Krizman, *Stjepan Radić and the Croatian Peasant Movement*, (Zagreb, 1975).
70. See note 69 above.
71. Djilas, *Land Without Justice*, p. 351.
72. Ibid., p. 352.
73. Djilas, *Montenegro*, p. 36.
74. Ibid., p. 35.
75. Djilas, *Land Without Justice*, p. 354.
76. For an interesting but somewhat one-sided analysis of the university life in the 1930's see, Pero Morača, *Studentski dani prvo drugog svjetskog rata*, (Belgrade, 1978).
77. Djilas, *Land Without Justice*, p. 353.
78. Djilas, "Woods and Waters," *The Leper and Other Stories*, p. 33.
79. Djilas, *Legenda o Njegošu*, p. 4.
80. Djilas, *Land Without Justice*, p. 321.
81. Djilas, *Memoir of a Revolutionary*, (New York, 1973), p. 106.
82. Djilas, *Land Without Justice*, p. 349.
83. See note 82 above.
84. Djilas, *Memoir of a Revolutionary*, pp. 303-312.
85. Similar solution is interestingly given by the liberal philosopher John Stuart Mill
86. Djilas, *Legenda o Njegošu, p. 5.*

The social origin of the new class lies in the proletariat just as the aristocracy arose in a peasant society, and the bourgeoisie in a commercial and artisans' society. There

are exceptions, depending on national conditions, but the proleteriat in economically underdeveloped countries, being backward, constitutes the raw material
from which the new class arises.

                                                    Milovan Djilas, *The New Class*

We Yugoslav Communists, headed by Comrade Tito, have therefore acted not
merely in the interest of the Yugoslav peoples, but in the progress of socialism in
general, in opposing both the Soviet aggressive and hegemonist pressure and the
anti-socialist ideology produced by the Soviet ruling bureaucracy to the level of
State-capitalist bureaucratic despotism. The forces of international socialism must
have both daring and ability to take the lying mask of that system so that they themselves can go forward.

                                                    Edvard Kardelj, *Socialist Democracy*

5

Marxism and the Rise of the New Class in Yugoslavia

In order to comprehend the political and social system established in 1945 by the Yugoslav Communist Party, we must first briefly examine Yugoslav Marxism before its seizure of power. What was the path which led the Yugoslav Communists to power? What were the key stages and obstacles to the movement? Secondly, when and why did Djilas come to realize that Party rule had resulted in bureaucratization, the rise of the new class of technocrats, scientific elite, rigidity, routinization and arbitrary exercise of power? What were his initial objections? Finally, what is the nature and style of the new class?

The Yugoslav Communist Party was formed in the aftermath of World War I. Established by the Party Congress of 1919, the Yugoslav Party, like all other European Communist Parties, began its life as a carbon copy of the Marxist-Leninist Communist Party of the Soviet Union. Total subservience to the Soviet Union through the Comintern and nontolerance of dissent within the Party were the order of the day. Those who disobeyed were either reprimanded or expelled. Freedom was a means and not an end for the Party and its members in the period when it was out of power and fighting to seize power. Freedom remained an instrument most of the time after it had seized power, and until it faced Stalin's wrath in 1948–49. Then, for a brief period of time the Party behaved as if it believed that while freedom in external policy must be a goal, so that the country can remain independent, in internal policy it should remain more an instrument than a goal—for Party and non-Party members alike.

Yugoslav Marxism passed through three significant and turbulent periods from 1919 to Hitler's invasion in April 1941. The first period from 1919 to 1921 began with the founding of the Party—known then as the Socialist Worker' Party of Yugoslavia—which was officially affiliated with the Comintern. This legal party blindly followed the zig-zags of the Third International. It supported confrontation with the bourgeois political system in Yugoslavia through strikes and other militant actions. It advocated the free redistribution of land to peasants and the unification of the workers' movement to combat the bourgeoisie. As a legal and political party in the new state it participated in the parliamentary elections of November 1920—receiving 201,539 votes and 58 seats in the parliament.[1] It was the third largest party in Yugoslavia, with strong support in the underdeveloped regions of Montenegro, southern Serbia and Macedonia. The Party in 1920–21 had over 70,000 members and controlled the trade-union movement with 200,000 members.[2] Filip Filipovic was its first general secretary.[3]

Lenin's twenty-one conditions for the admission to the International were adhered to by the Party. The Leninist "democratic centralism" (the resolution on Party Unity) passed at the Tenth Party Congress of the Communist Party of the Soviet Union (CPSU), in March 1921, cemented the subservience of lower Party bodies to the Central Committee. These two documents were fundamental pillars of support for the elitist, monolithic and disciplined Leninist communist parties, including the new Communist Party of Yugoslavia (CPY).

Lenin's purge of the Bolshevik Party at the Tenth Congress of the CPSU was also sweeping through the Yugoslav organization. At the Vukovar Congress of the CPY (June 1920) the statute was adopted which foresaw "the total centralization of the Party, the abolition of regional committees, and the creation of distinct councils with secretaries appointed by the Central leadership . . . Stricter criteria for the admission of new Party members were prescribed."[4] At the same time, the "centrists" were also purged from the Party leadership. Laws to ban legal activities by the Party were passed by the Yugoslav parliamentary government in December 1920 and August 1921.[5] The Party was forced underground, emerging only after Hitler's blitzkrieg in 1941.

The second period of the Yugoslav Communist Party, from 1921 to 1935, is marked by an intense internal struggle and the emergence of Lenin's Third International. This gives rise to the leadership of Šime Marković and the right-wing faction of the Party.[6] When the Committee of the Third International tried to coerce the Party to accept the thesis that Yugoslavia was an artificial creation of the Treaty of Versailles, the pawn of Western imperialism, and hence it should be dismembered. The Party was encouraged to forge an alliance with the powerful Croatian Peasant Party and to concentrate on nurturing dissatisfaction among Montenegrins, Albanians, Macedonians, Hungarians, Croats, Serbs and Moslems.

In fact, the Serbian bourgeois centralization of Yugoslavia was attacked through two communist parties—the illegal one and the Independent Worker's Party of Yugoslavia, a legal labor party created in 1923.[7] Two central committees ran the Party—one at home and the other abroad, in Paris or in Vienna. Throughout the 1920s, Party leaders were arrested, and morale and discipline continued to decline. By 1928 many local Party organizations, like the Zagreb one where Tito was an important functionary, condemned the Party leadership for allowing factionalism. Slovenian and Croat communists, following the Third International policy of breaking up Yugoslavia, explicitly demanded that separate Slovenian and Croat communist parties should be formed. They were only attempting to carry into practice the International's "Resolution on Central Europe and the Balkans: The Yugoslav Problem" passed at the Fifth Comintern World Congress in 1924. That resolution condemned "Serbian imperialism" and advocated "separating Croatia, Slovenia and Macedonia from Yugoslavia and creating independent republics of them."[8] In March 1925, Šime Marković had a spirited exchange with Stalin about the same question—one of the last challenges that Stalin received from a foreign communist leader.[9]

The Communist Party of Yugoslavia was most severely shaken during the royal dictatorship of King Alexander I from 1929 to 1932. But it stabilized itself after 1935, and popular-front and anti-fascist alliances with other progressive forces soon took form. The withdrawal of the Party leadership abroad, by order of the Third International, made efficient work in the country impossible. By 1932, the subservience to Moscow was complete. Milan Gorkić, the new Party secretary, complained to the Yugoslav representative in the Soviet Union with the International, a certain Vladimir Čopić, how difficult it was to follow the "correct line" when "one does not know in which direction the wind blows from above." He pleaded: "You must inform us about each new matter, new question, new tactical position, new article that contains directives, each new speech that offers guidance . . . send us at least constant even if unofficial information."[10]

The third stage in the prewar Party's existence was when Tito reigned supreme, from 1936 to 1941. Tito's absence from Yugoslavia never diminished his prestige. It was a period of great factional infighting, encouragement of separatist tendencies among Croat and Slovenian communists, imprisonment of many leading Party members, successful infiltration of progressive organizations opposed to cooperation with fascist countries, especially Germany, and testing of revolutionary tactics by the large number of Yugoslav communists who fought in the Spanish Civil War. Tito was in fact not only running the Communist Party of Yugoslavia from Paris, but also coordinating the Comintern Spanish recruitment activity there. Often in and out of Yugoslavia, he was mostly associated with the Croat section of the Party. He also spent time in the Soviet Union, where he attended the special training school of the Comintern and worked in the Yugoslav section alongside a number of his future administrators and officials.[11]

Tito in some ways played Lenin's role in forging Yugoslav communism into a Marxist-Leninist model. He preserved the Party's Leninist structure, adding and subtracting theoretical and organizational forms whenever he felt it necessary. He was also a graduate of the toughest political school—Stalinism. He learned well and survived purges, whereas his opponents did not.

In essence, that part of the prewar period during which Tito ran the Party was a time of the successful rebuilding of the Party along Stalinist lines. Tito, as a superb balancer of the Serbian centralist and the Croat separatist tendencies, provided the Yugoslav Communist Party during the Second World War with the claim that the communist represented the only genuine force that could rebuild Yugoslavia as a federated community. The earlier communist tacit toleration of the *Ustaša* in the early 1930s was forgotten, as was the more benign view of fascism after the Nazi-Soviet Pact of 1939.[12]

Tito rebuilt the elitist Party which in 1936 had 3,000 members. More than 2,000 of them were in and out of jail.[13] But things began moving. By the order of the Comintern, a consultation of the Communist Party leadership took place in Moscow in the summer of 1936. In June 1937, Tito was named organizational secretary of the Party, while Gorkić was renamed general secretary. The Central Committee was to be transferred to Belgrade. The Comintern agreed with Tito's suggestion that parties for Slovenia and Croatia ought to be created as a move to reassure those dissatisfied nationalities that more genuine rights would be given to them in a communist Yugoslav state.

The principal task of that antifascist period was to weaken the influence in Croatia of the Croat Peasant Party and of the Croat fascist *Ustaša,* through a renewal of previous communist tactics of cooperating with Croat nationalists. Djilas described this strange relationship between the communists and "Croat national revolutionaries" while he was imprisoned with the *Ustaša* leader Josip Rukavina in 1933–34:

They [Ustaša] preferred to call themselves Croatian nationalists. The gap between us Communists and the *Ustaša* was not nearly as great as it was to become in the late 1930s and during the war. The Central Committee and the Comintern emphasized the importance of cooperation with "national revolutionaries" in certain areas. At one point negotiations were concluded with them, but no agreement was reached. The prison atmosphere explains in part our relatively good relations with the *Ustaša.* We had a common enemy: the government and the regime. And we lived under much the same conditions. But there were other more important reasons as well. First of all, both groups believed that Yugoslavia should be broken up into its component parts. The *Ustaša* wanted a series of independent states, whereas we Communists had a somewhat vaguer concept. We believed that each one of those independent state units would join the Soviet Union, which is to say, the Balkan Federation. We Communists did not blame the *Ustaša* for their reliance on Italy and Hungary, although we didn't approve it either. We instinctively felt that the *Ustaša* action could help further our own cause: the destruction of Yugoslavia. When he ran into Communists in the street during the war, his former prisonmates, he did not report them to the authorities. However, he exterminated Serbs all over Lika [region near the Adriatic], and with gusto, believing that to be his mission in life. He hated Serbs far more than Communists. When Zagreb was liberated, our authorities caught him and executed him. He asked for nothing, and he expected nothing.[14]

By 1939 Tito was in sole charge of the Communist Party of Yugoslavia. After persuading the Comintern that their desire to abolish the Yugoslav Party he turned his attention to the Croat separatists including the Croat Peasant Party and the fascist *Ustaša*. As he dealt with them, he began to strengthen the organization and centralization of the Party in Serbia, Bosnia, Macedonia, Montenegro and Vojvodina.

By Hitler's invasion in 1941, "the Party had 7,000 members and the numbers and the number of young communists was around 25,000. The Party dominated the United Trade Union with its membership of 150,000 . . . and despite having 3,000 communists in concentration camps" in 1940, "the government failed to arrest all those they wanted. They did not know many uncompromised communists, and the leading Party cadres returned to underground work and continued their political tasks."[15]

One may conclude that in the immediate prewar period the Yugoslav Communist Party under Tito's guidance was indeed getting stronger; it had more professional revolutionaries and was forced to rely upon its own ideas, never forgetting that the Comintern was the highest body and that Stalin was watching what was going on within the Party and within Yugoslavia. Examples of imitiation of Marxist-Leninist characteristics within the Communist Party of Yugoslavia are frequent in the official correspondence between Tito's advisers and the Comintern. In addition to Djilas' memoirs, Svetozar Vukmanović-Tempo and Edvard Kardelj provide similar emulations in their memoirs and political statements.[16] Tito's remark that "I have never been anyone's man but only the Party's and so I shall be",[17] addressed to G. Dimitrov, the head of the Comintern, in the spring of 1938, is an example of complete allegiance and dedication to the service of the Communist Party of Yugoslavia. During the coup d'état of March 27, 1941, when ties with the Axis were broken, Vukmanovič-Tempo's temperamental response that the new government of General Simović should invite the Communist Party to share political power with the Popular-Front forces angered Tito. He deliverd a severe lecture on Marxist-Leninist tactics: "The masses mostly lag in their comprehension of developments behind the vanguard, thus the revolutionary must be patient and actively help the situation to ripen; never must he run too much ahead in front of the masses because he will isolate himself from them and be beaten for sure."[18]

Especially in *Conversations with Stalin,* Djilas elaborated on the spirit of international and financial cooperation between the European Communist Parties and the Comintern. Financial aid from the Comintern was handled through a "phony" agency called "Red Aid," whose name was later changed to "People's Assistance," both to make it sound more legal and to keep it in the spirit of the popular vocabulary.[19] Djilas commented subsequently on the gradual rise in economic independence from Moscow: "By 1940 our financial independence was such that we were able to give assistance to our Italian comrades, who had stopped in Yugoslavia on their way from Moscow."[20] Djilas best describes Marxist-Leninism-Stalinism when he proudly remarks at a conference in Bosna 1940, that Yugoslav Communist Party leaders

were fully aware that the Fifth Conference would finally solidify the Comintern's confidence in our party. To be able to hold an illegal conference, attended by such a large number of people, with so many reports and discussions, was in itself proof of consolidation of power that no other illegal Communist party had achieved. We knew it and we felt it.

A Soviet intelligence man had accompanied Tito on his trip from Moscow. He had brought a radio with him; thus we were in regular contact with Moscow. Tito had also brought some money with him. The Comintern had been giving the party regular monthly financial assistance. But after Tito came back, this stopped. For one thing, it was technically impossible to get it. But it was not only that. In truth, for a year or two we had not received from Moscow any financial aid.[21]

During the preparation for the seizure of power, from 1941 to 1945, the Yugoslav Communist Party operated firmly within the framework of Marxism-Leninism and Stalinism. The major consolidation of the new revolutionary system occurred, however, when the total reliance upon its own power base and the total lack of physical contact with, or aid from, the Soviet Union during most of the war, solidified Yugoslav independence from Moscow. A relatively short period of cooperation with the Red Army (less than a month of actual Soviet military presence on Yugoslav territory before and after the liberation of Belgrade) as well as significant and prolonged Western aid could not influence a political and military order which possessed its own tradition, ideology and Party apparatus, all of which created a genuine basis for the emergence of Yugoslav national communism.

Although the Yugoslav Communist Party was tightly controlled from above, a more relaxed atmosphere existed within organs of authority, where communists were emphasizing the antifascist national liberation struggle rather than the communization process. The Popular Front strategy headed by Dušan Simović, where all patriotic forces and all nationalities should participate, was stressed. The short-lived military alliance with the remnants of the Yugoslav army in Serbia under colonel Draža Mihailović in the summer of 1941 ended in open civil war—lasting with greater or lesser intensity until the end of the war, when the noncommunist Serbian forces were finally defeated. Once more, the superior strategic capacities of Marxist-Leninist revolutionaries triumphed over the decentralized, less disciplined, regionally oriented and even separatist nationalist elements.[22]

After their victory in 1945, the Yugoslav Communist Party surged ahead, attempting to achieve socialism with such dizzying speed that even Stalin felt it was going too fast. Industrialization and agricultural collectivization began immediately in 1946–47. The active support of the Greek communists and the shooting down of an unarmed American military plane illustrated the intensity of Yugoslav bellicosity against the West.

All that came to a standstill, when "Uncle Joe" charged Tito and the Yugoslav Party with national deviations and with allowing bourgeois trends in Yugoslavia to emerge. The falsity of the charges united the majority of the Party leadership in their determination to resist Soviet imperialism.

This period of Stalinism continued until 1948 when Tito replaced it with his own style of rule. For the first time Yugoslav Party leaders were forced to think outside the prescribed Stalinist system. It dawned on them that the freedom of thought should be a natural right for every communist party. Not merely Djilas but Tito himself had come to that conclusion in 1952 at the Sixth Party Congress. Under Comintern "guidance" there were no alternatives, only the Stalinist dogma. As Pero Morača and Dušan Bilandžić indicate, the Communist Party of Yugoslavia "could not freely develop its own political thought before the conflict with Stalin. The higher interests of the world communist movement did not recognize the freedom to seek one's own road to socialism."[23]

In the process of seeking freedom of self-expression "the new ideological-political conception about the further development of socialist social relations began gradually to emerge. The conflict with Stalinism gave Party cadres the incentive to reflect about all problems of socialist theory and practice. And all Stalin's works were ultimately rejected as "etatist ideology."[24]

The Fifth Party Congress of 1948 rejected Soviet accusations and declared that a search for the authentic Yugoslav road to socialism was on. The Yugoslav Party leadership declared in 1949 that

The change of the general Party line in socialist construction . . . the state socialism is replaced with self-management socialism . . . The Party must stop the ongoing process of etatization of Yugoslav society, because it threatens to undermine the authority of the working class by strengthening bureaucratic power. Inspired by the ideas of Marx, Engels and Lenin concerning the withering away of the state, the

highest Party leaders following the conflict with the Cominform came to the conclusion that one must begin without delay that process of realization of that most important idea of Marxism-Leninism ... Those classical measures were named at the
time "decentralization" and de-bureaucratization.[25]

The Sixth Party Congress of November 1952 officially altered the name of
the Party to the League of Communists of Yugoslavia. Instead of an elitist
Party, the aim was now to form a more open, mass Party. From a Party that
grew to 200,000 members during the Second World War (of whom 60,000
died in the conflict), a Party of 150,000 members, most of them peasants,
came to power. At the time of the conflict with Stalin, the Party had 500,000
members but, by June 1952, the membership grew to almost 900,000 members. The change of the name of the Party to that of League was done in
order to formally change it from a classical political organization of the
Stalinist type and to identify it with the Marxian League of Communists.
The League of Communists of Yugoslavia was pledged to abandon "gradually the method of direct guidance and decision-making"[26] and to become
the ideological vanguard of the working class which, in turn, would become
the direct self-managing force of society. Decentralization of the Party and
governmental organs would guarantee the abolition of the "hierarchial
relationship of local organs toward the higher ones."[27]

The League of Communists of Yugoslavia must "fight for the strengthening of individual rights and civil rights."[28] Parliament passed the new constitution in 1953 which provided for social and economic ownership of the
means of production and the self-management of producers. The Council
of Producers was elected directly by those employed in production; the
Federal Council was elected by the republican and regional assemblies. The
Executive Council ran the nation. The goal of this new relationship, of
course, within the League and the state, was to "prevent tendencies that
might lead toward Stalinist despotism as well as toward liberal bourgeois-
democracy."[29]

In 1954–55, practice showed that workers' self-management existed in
theory but not in reality, where etatistic tendencies triumphed. The pressure
for a speedy reemergence of the free market led to tendencies for restoration
of old capitalistic socioeconomic relations. "Contradictions emerged between progressive, revolutionary, humane ideology of workers' self-management and the very cruel and callous social reality which suited more
autocratic, centralistic and bureaucratic tendencies."[30] All this created an adverse reaction among those communists who really believed that the
freedom of thought which had been cautiously planted within the League
of Communists in 1949, should receive even more nurturing. Here Djilas
sharply criticized the etatistic forces and his views, according to the League
of Communist leadership, "were evaluated as a call for a multi-party system
existing in Western nations."[31]

The sudden death of Stalin in March 1953 and Djilas' call in the autumn, which struck an enthusiastic response among the rank and file of the League and the public at large, aroused the leadership from the mistaken belief that freedom of thought could be controlled and the new Yugoslav model of Marxism-Leninism would remain unchallenged. The second largest postwar Party purge in the aftermath of the Soviet-Yugoslav dispute in 1948 brought about little freedom of thought. Tito and his leadership expelled over 55,000 party members.[32]

Now that we have examined briefly the rise to power of the Yugoslav Communist Party, several queries should be raised. What were Djilas' major objections to Party structure and rule? What were his visions and hopes for the new state? How did his initial criticism develop into a more thorough analyses? How did he explain the growth and rule of Party bureaucracy?

INITIAL CRITICISM

The first piece of Djilas' early criticism of the nature of the Yugoslav state bureaucracy, which served to expose him as an "enemy of the Revolution" appeared under the title of *Anatomy of a Moral*. In a series of eighteen articles written for the central Communist Party mouthpiece *Borba (Struggle)*, and then in the highly theoretical journal *Nova Misao (New Thought)* during the last days of December 1953, Djilas successfully managed to cause a turbulence in the political life of the country. The articles, written in Djilas' extremely philosophical and rambling style, initially attracted very little attention. His declaration that the revolution in Yugoslavia had to be defended by more democracy, his attacks on Stalinism, his warnings against the dangers of dogmatism and opportunism—all of these things had been said before by Tito and his subordinates. But slowly the articles took on a sharper turn. It was almost as though Djilas was convincing himself at each stem that he must go still further, almost as though, scenting conflict, he became more eager for it. Suddenly he began to train his fire on sacred concepts.

Djilas did not regard himself as attacking communism, he wanted rather to purify and purge it of all its non-Communist trappings. Communism as a goal should be abandoned, he wrote on December 2, 1953. In the struggle against bureaucracy, the goal of "complete Communism" was too distant to be meaningful and only "distracts our attention from bureaucratic reality." In any event, Communism as a conscious goal was superfluous "because in the end it will come anyhow" once socialism and democracy have taken hold. Instead of Communism, Djilas vigorously argued, the goal must be "concrete measures, realizable from stage to stage."[33] The goal now, he insisted, had to be "quick progress of socialism and democracy through concrete and feasible forms—not Communism."[34]

In an article entitled *New Concepts,* Djilas expounded on a need for the Communist Party of Yugoslavia to realize that the revolution was over and that Yugoslav society must find "new forms." In his view, the revolution was not transforming itself into any type of democracy or socialism and, worse, the fruits of revolution were being destroyed. Instead of leading Yugoslavia towards socialism and democracy the new group of professional revolutionaries had usurped power and was no longer interested in its professed goals. A despotic and privileged political bureaucracy was being created in the name of the revolution.[35]

Djilas charged that revolutionary forms vital to preserve the fruits of revolution were no longer necessary since the revolution was securely won. What remained was the process of social democratization. Especially intolerable and odious to Djilas was the obvious fact that individuals received appointments and favors in the party administration and economy not on the basis of their qualifications and abilities but from party officials acting as "protecting sponsors." "The people are the ones who must pay for all these illegal and unjustifiable goings-on, favoritisms, and frauds. Most of all, the working class pays."[36] Herein lay the inner conflict existing within Milovan Djilas. As a chief Marxist theoretician and critic he could not reconcile power and privilege at the cost of the common man with his position of power and privilege in the Communist Party of Yugoslavia. Party bureaucratism had wiped out democratic and socialist principles and individuals were no longer able to receive positions in the government and economy on the basis of merit alone. Instead, bureaucratism developed in a special way and favoritism and arbitrariness proliferated throughout the administration. Thousands upon thousands of officials obtained special appointments, illegal party pensions, and other allowances. In addition, the best friends of party officials were awarded with scholarships, housing transfers, and special medical treatment.[37] Djilas was deeply upset that even his best friends were behaving like greedy "capitalist" bureaucrats.

Asserting that the weapons for the protection of the social democratic processes existed, Djilas in 1953 called for "new forms" as opposed to old and prerevolutionary ones. "A free socialist economy calls for an appropriate form; socialist democracy."[38] The "new forms" elaborated in the *Borba* article had to be debated in an atmosphere of free discussion among Communists and non-Communists as well to become effective. According to Djilas, "We must, therefore, learn to respect the opinions of others, even if they seem stupid and conservative to us."[39]

The forms under discussion by Djilas were laws, social and moral norms, established habits in human relationships, and new ways for socialists and communists to reach political and economic decisions. Since these forms were already in existence, claimed Djilas, to harmonize them with the social base, property, was the essential task which confronted all good Communists: "To harmonize new forms means today to nurture and develop democracy, but also something greater, a more permanent, and more far-reaching form of democracy."[40] He further insisted that the Soviet political and economic development should not be imitated any longer simply because Stalin's socialist experiment had failed. Although the Soviet Union had nationalized its industry and trade it had not been very successful in nationalizing human social relations. In fact, Djilas vigorously stressed, in the Soviet Union the forms of social relations were imposed upon the people by Stalin's crude methods of manipulation, fraud and outright force.[41] Clearly, claimed Djilas, the Yugoslav Communist Party ought to avoid Stalin's path to democracy.

As far as Djilas was concerned, Tito's Yugoslav Communists had themselves a long way to go in eradicating social and human injustices. He provided the top party leadership with several concrete examples. For instance, he vividly recalled a story of a man who was arrested for having engaged in "hostile propaganda" against the state. He and his wife were ordered to vacate their apartment. The wife appealed her case, arguing that since her husband had not yet been found guilty they had the right to live in their large apartment. The Supreme Court of the Republic decided on the basis of the law that the apartment should indeed be retained by the original occupants. The Committee of the League of Communists reasoning that since they knew this gentleman better than the court, the apartment should be let to a deserving family rather than have the lady take up the whole apartment by herself. So the decision of the Supreme Court was never implemented.[42]

The point made by Djilas is that although it would seem the human thing to do on the part of the Communist League, it is neither formally nor actually correct: "No matter what the court decision, when it is not carried out, the will of the committee, of the Party organization, actually rules."[43]

Djilas simply contends that with two kinds of justice, one for the Communist bureaucrats and another for the noncommunist citizens, the struggle for socialism and the individuality of men will never be achieved—he emphatically declares that democracy is for all, even the bourgeoisie. Furthermore, the law must be applied equally to all. Nothing can or should be done to the bourgeoisie or any other class outside the legal framework: Additional laws are not required: "Hence, real equality before the law is the only thing which can prevent arbitrariness and, thereby, the destruction of the borderline between socialist and reactionary forces."[44]

Clearly recognizable is Djilas' overt criticism of what Tito and the Party officialdom called Cominformist (former Party members supporting Stalin) enemies of democracy and bourgeois reactionaries. Both labels were extremely useful in getting rid of one's enemies, even when it would be difficult to differentiate Cominformists and bourgeois reactionaries from some Party officials. These catagories, Djilas asserted were not worthy of the juris-

diction of the law. The law, therefore, applied only to those whom the Party
deemed fit. In this sense the Party became the supralegal organ of the administration. Upset and deeply hurt by this creation, Djilas lashed out at the
ruling caste: "They believe freedom must be confined to them, because they
consider themselves the leading and most progressive forces in the country,
and ardently wish to be considered as such by others as well."[45] Freedom for
the bourgeoisie while necessary, did not mean that the true Communist
should not fight against all bourgeois ideas or against the restoration of
capitalism.

In his short but succinct essay "Is There a Goal?" Djilas proclaimed that it
was necesary for the Communist Party of Yugoslavia to place goals in their
proper perspectives. Unlike Tito and Kardelj, for Djilas, goals such as power
were proximate as opposed to ultimate ends. Once, he continued, political
power was the chief ambition of the Communist Party. New goals arose
and were subsequently realized. The whole political and revolutionary
movement led toward the one ultimate goal—true Communism:

> Now when we already have socialist power and a new socialist economy, when we
> live under socialism and democracy—though young and underdeveloped, we live
> with and in them—what can be the final goal? In any event, communism.[46]

Djilas revealed his essentially Marxist character when he insisted upon
the historical progression, vis-à-vis the dialectic, to ideal Communism:
"Socialism-communism is the inevitable progressive movement of contemporary society toward liquidating its own contradictions, no matter what
form that process takes."[47]

At the same time Djilas continued to indict Party leaders for repeatedly
promising the "golden future" while forgetting the present economic and
social ills of Yugoslavia. In front of Tito and other high ranking officials, he
boldly stated that this also occurred in the Soviet Union under Stalin and
was similarily affecting the course of Yugoslavia. In addition he insisted that
the presence of "subjective forces" were no longer justified in modern
Yugoslavia. While "subjective forces" were desirable during the revolution
and in fact were of critical importance since they were representatives of the
"objective process," they tended to view themselves after the Revolution as
effective replacements for the "objective forces." And Djilas concluded
"concretely" that "No one group or party, nor even a single class, can be the
exclusive expression of the objective imperatives of contemporary society.[48]

What was, therefore, needed was to curb and weaken the political monopoly of the Communist Party of Yugoslavia over the life of society. The
forces of production, so well depicted by Marx, must be less and less subordinate to subjective ideas and interests shooting out in contrary directions,
the forces of production must serve to obtain and direct the aims of socialist
society. In order to achieve this harmony of interests, democracy, more

freedom of discussion, more free elections to social, state and economic organizations and more strict adherence to the law would be necessary. No single subjective force, selfish by nature, must be permitted to react against social progress.

In a decisive article in *Borba* on January 4, 1954, entitled "League or Party," Djilas virtually demanded a denial of the Party's role as the ruling force in Yugoslav politics. It was no longer necessary, according to the *Borba* editorial, for the Party Committee to keep all the power in its hands, administer the socialist consciousness of the masses, order how and what ought to be done, and hold exclusive responsibility for the ideological and political levels: "The League of Communists is no longer the old Communist Party because everything is no longer centralized in its hands."[49]

In other words, the role of the Party was not to be the abstract and exclusive mouthpiece of the self-appointed leadership, but rather the guiding instrument for elevating the socialist consciousness of the masses, and more importantly, educating the masses for legality, to the rights of citizens and democracy.

At the center of most of Djilas' arguments for the new role of the Party was his faith in the socialist consciousness of the majority of the people of Yugoslavia. The revolution and the civil war, he continued, had been successfully completed and the old ruling class had been so thoroughly destroyed that there was no longer any danger of counterrevolution. Socialist relations had on the whole been established, except among the private peasantry.[50] Large segments of the population, especially among the workers, supported the policies of the administration and had in fact attained a high level of socialist consciousness. Djilas, therefore, concluded that more effective methods for the achievement of the new role of the Party could not be realized in an atmosphere which lacked free discussion and debate. If that road was followed, Djilas warned, Yugoslav society could only move into one direction—Stalinist bureaucracy:

There [in the Soviet Union] they teach and are taught what Stalin said, what Marx and Lenin preached, but there still exist the shedding of innocent human blood, despotism, famine and backwardness . . . These methods are excellent for keeping people backward.[51]

To the disbelief of his comrades, Djilas again indicted the Soviet Union for having espoused Marxism while perverting its "real goals." "No one would be more astonished," argued Djilas, "than Vladimir Ilyich if he saw what remained of his works and ideas in his own country."[52]

The *Borba* editorials and the articles in *Nova Misao* provided Djilas' most biting account of the Yugoslav Communist society. *The Anatomy of a Moral* sparked a huge debate as soon as it appeared on the Belgrade and Zagreb newsstands and, apparently, it was promptly bought up by the public before

Kardelj, Tito and Ranković knew of its existence. This article remains one of the most devastating satires of the Communist society ever published by a person belonging to it. The two chief characters were Djilas' Montenegrin friend, Colonel Peko Dapčević, Chief of Staff of the Yugoslav Partisan Army, and Milena Vrsajko, the Colonel's twenty-one year old actress bride. Although no one was named in the article, these two were described with sufficient detail for the public to identify them, and Dapčević later said the identification was correct.[53]

The Anatomy of a Moral was primarily a condemnation of the "caste" snobbishness of the wives of high government and Party functionaries. These "selfish monsters" who had once been heroic women, wrote Djilas, greeted Dapčević's young bride with "insidious hatred, scorn and icy boycott" because she was an actress and because she was not prominent in the Communist Party. They also held it against her that she had not fought with the Partisans, in spite of the fact that she was only thirteen at the end of the war.

While Djilas devoted most of the scorn to the wives of key Communist functionaries, he did not leave the husbands unscathed. Concerning the attitudes of the male members of the "inner circle" toward the young actress Djilas wrote: "The men were, or pretended to be, indifferent to the newcomer in their hallowed and secluded class, which, when not loafing in its magnificent, parvenu offices, moved from place to place, lived in its own select and restricted summer resorts, gathered in its own secluded houses, sat in its own exclusive theatres and stadium boxes."[54]

Djilas' fellow members of the Central Committee must have burned at his references to the "closed world" which "had automobiles and Pulman cars, got its food and clothing from special stores, spent its holidays in special Adriatic villas and summer resorts." This "inner circle," he further claimed, maintained its solidarity "not so much from ideological and moral unity but rather from the same way of living and similar interests, from the nature of power and the manner in which it was attained."[55]

The *Nova Misao* article was in a way the culmination of Djilas' attack on the whole Communist political system in the Soviet Union and Yugoslavia. Disguised as fiction, *The Anatomy of a Moral*, clearly set up and opened his mind to the nature of communist state power and ultimately drove him to write *The New Class.* Greed, immorality, consciousness of rank and luxurious living were pictured by him as widespread among the Communist hierarchy. The heroes of the Yugoslav Revolution had become not only despotic bureaucrats; they were also "sham aristocrats." Both in their private lives as well as in their official capacities, they were "enemies" of the real democracy. Djilas' piece of "political pornography," as Moša Pijade called *The Anatomy of a Moral,* constituted a frontal attack on the very group of Communist functionaries who would eventually try his case. It was as if Djilas, in a final gesture, deliberately attempted to rob himself of any support he may previously have had among the members of the Central Committee.

The Anatomy of a Moral was the last straw. If Djilas had been concerned earlier that the Plenum of the Central Committee would be convoked to discuss his "heresies," he must have realized that this article made it inevitable. Tito's analysis of Djilas' actions at this point may very well be correct:

Comrade Djilas was acquainted with my negative opinion before he published his latest article in *Nova Misao.* He published it in a rush. And what was to be achieved by it . . . The intention was in fact to disqualify us, the "circle" which he attacked in *Nova Misao,* from the moral point of view.[56]

There was no point in attempting to cover up the dispute any longer. On January 10, 1954, *Borba* published an announcement and in a serious tone declared that Djilas' articles were "contrary to the opinion of all other members of the Executive Committee." The whole subject, it was said, "would be discussed at the forthcoming Plenum of the Central Committee."[57]

The Third Plenum held at Tito's resort island of Brione in 1954 put Djilas on trial. Unlike other meetings of the Central Committee, the proceedings were fully reported in the press and many of the speeches were broadcast to the public over the radio. For two days various members of the Central Committee attacked Djilas, and only one defended him—his close friend, Vladimir Dedijer, the official biographer of Tito, and former member of the Yugoslav delegation to the United Nations.[58]

The brunt of the attack, however, was launched by Tito and Kardelj, with the other speakers mostly repeating or elaborating the identical points. Tito made it clear at the beginning of the sessions that Djilas' primary sin was his call for the liquidation of the Communist League. But while criticizing Djilas on this point, Tito made the rather surprising admission that he himself had been the first to speak of the "withering away of the Party." He emphasized, however, that this would be a long process, not something which could take place in six months or a year or two. The Communist League, added Kardelj to Tito's remarks, could not be converted "into some sort of debate club without any internal discipline."[59] Nor was Yugoslavia ready for a multiparty system, which Djilas was accused of favoring.

According to Tito, a disciplined Communist League was essential as long as it was still necessary to wage class warfare. "Until the last class enemy is eliminated," Tito pointed out at the Third Plenum, "Socialist consciousness embraces the wildest masses of our citizens at large, there can be no question of the . . . liquidation of the Communist League, because the Communist League is responsible for the fruits of the revolution."[60] In the meantime, concluded Kardelj, the Communist League is the "exclusive expression of the interests of the whole society."[61]

While Djilas had earlier written with optimism about the acceptance of socialism by the majority of the people, his critics found themselves in the rather awkward position of having to argue that most of the population was not behind the government. Kardelj emphasized especially the prevalence of anticommunism among the peasants in the countryside, who represented "over seventy percent of the population," in addition to other "class enemies" in the cities. Tito and Kardelj both illustrated by their statements that they had not been fooled by the results of the national elections of November 1953, in which eighty-five percent of the voters had cast their ballots for the regime in supposedly free voting.[62] They also openly admitted that the administration of the government depended upon coercion to maintain its rule and carry out its social and political program. "We are forced," said Kardelj, "to retain even in economic relations, let alone in political life, certain elements of coercion in order to get away from old and backward ways as soon as possible."[63] To extend democracy to the bourgeoisie, declared Tito, would lead "to anarchy, to a terrible uncertainty . . . If we permitted this, in a year's time our Socialist reality would not exist: it would not exist, I tell you, without a bloody battle."[64] On this particular point of popular opposition to the regime there seems little doubt that Djilas was the visionary optimist, while his opponents were hard-headed realists.

While Djilas had emphasized throughout his articles and editorials the primary necessity of immediately extending democracy, his former comrades and friends insisted that socialism was a prerequisite for further development of democracy. Djilas, said Kardelj, had put forward the old slogan: "First of all democracy, and only after that socialism." "Such a slogan," said Kardelj, "is senseless, especially under our conditions where any kind of democracy is impossible without socialism, even bourgeois democracy."[65] "True democracy," according to Tito, "can not exist without socialism nor socialism without democracy. But to preach and write about democracy for the sake of democracy, and at that about democracy of the Western type—formal democracy—is going back to old forms rather than going forward."[66]

To place such emphasis on democracy, said Kardelj, was especially dangerous when, as in the case of Djilas, "democracy is reduced to the formula of free discussion." Such a proposal, he continued, "means supporting petty-bourgeois—anarchist tendencies which are just as serious a hindrance for the development of socialist democracy as bureaucratism itself."[67]

Tito and Kardelj also accused Djilas of "reformistic opportunism" in the tradition of the famous revisionist of German Marxism, Eduard Bernstein. They declared that Djilas had imitated Bernstein's ideas when he advocated the renunciation of communism as a final goal. Djilas' ideas were not new, they argued, but merely a restatement of the well-known phrase of Bernstein: "The final goal of Socialism is nothing, evolution is everything." Djilas desired to renounce the goal of Communism, Kardelj charged, because in fact he no longer wanted Communism. By calling for the abandonment of Communism as the final goal he was "taking the compass from the hands of the Communists" and permitting the smuggling in of "various tendencies consciously or unconsciously aimed at disrupting or weakening the ideological unity of the Communists."[68]

Kardelj denied Djilas' charge that bureaucratism as a system had established itself in Yugoslavia:

We have shattered gradually the bureaucratic system of the first years by a number of measures of decentralization, by developing social self-management, by organizing workers councils, by new methods of work in People's Committees with production of councils, by the democratic organization of workers which will enable every citizen to participate fully in the political system.[69]

Thus, concluded Kardelj, was the way to construct socialist democracy and not, as Djilas appeared to indicate, "through intellectual arguments and disputes in debate clubs."[70]

NOTES

1. Ivan Božić and Vladimir Dedijer, eds., *Istorija Jugoslavije*, (Belgrade, 1970), p. 430.

2. Ibid., p. 432.

3. Ibid., p. 430.

4. See note 3 above.

5. See note 3 above.

6. Mihailo Pisanjuk, *Pregled istorije komunista Jugoslavije*, (Belgrade, 1966), p. 61. Also see Ivan Avakumovic's account of Marković's career in *History of the Communist Party of Yugoslavia*, (Aberdeen, 1964), pp. 29-32.

7. Ferdo Čulinović, *Stvaranje nove Jugoslavenske države*, (Zagreb, 1959), pp. 29-75. Also see the account of the Independent Workers' Party in Phyllis Auty, *Tito, a Biography*, (Harmondsworth England, Pelican Books, 1974), pp. 84-88.

8. Čulinović, *Stvaranje nove Jugoslavenske države*, p. 32.

9. Auty, *Tito*, p. 86.

10. Pero Damjanović, *Tito na čelu partije*, (Belgrade, 1968), p. 47.

11. For Djilas' observations on Tito in the Soviet Union see, Djilas, *Tito: The Story from Inside*, (New York, 1980). Also see, Vladimir Dedijer, *Josip Broz Tito: Prilozi za biografiju*, (Belgrade, 1953), and Branko Lazitch, *Tito et la Revolution Yougoslave*, (Paris, 1957).

12. See Djilas, *Memoir of a Revolutionary*, (New York, 1973), pp. 131-147.

13. For an interesting analysis of the experience of Yugoslav Communists in Russia in the 1930s see especially, Anton Ciliga, *The Russian Enigma*, (London,

1940). For Tito's remarks see his *Govori*, (Belgrade, 1960), and Dedijer's, *The Beloved Land*, Routledge and Kegan and Paul (London, 1940).

14. Djilas, *Memoir of a Revolutionary*, pp. 136-37.
15. Djilas, *Wartime*, (New York, 1977), p. 61.
16. Svetozar Vukmanović-Tempo, *Revolucija koja teče, memoari*, (Belgrade, 1971), two volumes. Also see Kardelj, *Problemi nase socijalističke izgradnje*, (Belgrade, 1960).
17. Quoted in Auty, *Tito*, p. 154.
18. Svetozar Vukmanović-Tempo, *Revolucija koja teče*, p. 162.
19. Djilas, *Memoir of a Revolutionary*, p. 355.
20. See note 19 above.
21. See note 19 above.
22. For an excellent account of the Partisan-Chetnik debacle, see Walter Roberts, *Tito, Mihailović and the Allies*, (New Brunswick, 1973).
23. Pero Morača and Dušan Bilandžić, *Avangarda*, (Belgrade, 1968), pp. 120-36.
24. See, especially, Dr. Vladan Cvetković, *Moć i kriza étatizma*, (Belgrade, 1978), pp. 44-57.
25. Morača and Bilandžić, *Avangarda*, pp. 125-26.
26. M. Hadži-Vasilev, *Pregled istorije saveza komunista Jugoslavije*, (Belgrade, 1970), p. 488.
27. Morača and Bilandžić, *Avangarda*, p. 132.
28. See note 27 above.
29. Ibid., p. 133.
30. Ibid., pp. 140-43.
31. Ibid., pp. 152-54.
32. Ibid., p. 154.
33. Djilas, *Borba, (Struggle)*, (November 18, 1953), p. 5.
34. Ibid., p. 5.
35. Djilas, *Borba*, (October 11, 1953), p. 2.
36. Djilas, *Borba*, (November 22, 1953), p. 4.
37. See note 36 above.
38. Djilas, *Borba*, (November 1, 1953), p. 1.
39. See note 38 above.
40. Djilas, *Borba*, (November 8, 1953), pp. 3-5.
41. Djilas, *Borba*, (November 29, 1953), pp. 2-4.
42. Djilas, *Borba*, (November 30, 1953), p. 5.
43. See note 42 above.
44. See note 42 above.
45. Djilas, "Respect for the Law," *Borba*, (November 17, 1953), p. 2.
46. Djilas, *Vjesnik u srijedu*, (Zagreb, 1954), p. 6.
47. Ibid., p. 6.
48. Ibid., p. 8.
49. Ibid., p. 7.
50. Djilas, *On the New Roads of Socialism*, (Belgrade, 1950), p. 12.
51. Ibid., pp. 5-8.
52. Ibid., p. 6.
53. Speech by Colonel Dapčević at the Third Plenum on January 19, 1954.

54. Djilas, *Nova misao*, (January 1, 1954), p. 3.

55. See note 54 above.

56. For Tito's speech at the Third Plenum see, *Politika*, (January 19, 1954), p. 4.

57. The proceedings of the Third Plenum of the Central Committee of the Yugoslav Communist Party were reported in detail in the January-February 1954 issue of *Komunist*. *Borba* and *Politika* also published most of the key speeches.

58. Vladimir Dedijer, "The Party Needs His Strength and Talent," Speech at the Third Plenum. Not one member of the Yugoslav Communist Party supported Dedijer. Djilas himself immediately repudiated his speech.

59. Kardelj, Speech at the Third Plenum, (January 18, 1954).

60. Speech by Tito at the Third Plenum, (January 18, 1954).

61. Speech by Kardelj at the Third Plenum, (January 18, 1954).

62. See note 61 above.

63. See note 61 above.

64. Speech by Tito at the Conclusion of Djilas' Trial, (January 18, 1954).

65. Statement by Kardelj at the Third Plenum, (January 18, 1954).

66. Statement by Tito at the Third Plenum, (January 18, 1954).

67. See note 66 above.

68. See note 66 above.

69. See note 66 above.

70. See note 66 above.

In history, it is not important who implements a process, it is only important that the process be implemented. Such was the case in Russia and other countries in which Communist revolutions took place. The revolution created forces, leaders, organizations, and ideas which were necessary to it. The new class came into existence for objective reasons, and by the wish, wits and action of its leaders.

Milovan Djilas, *The New Class*

6

The New Class in Power

Although Milovan Djilas' analysis of Soviet bureaucracy under Lenin and Stalin is considerably different from Trotsky's, it appears unlikely that Djilas was completely unaware of *The Revolution Betrayed* and perhaps other works, although he certainly failed to take them very seriously in the 1940s, because of resilient ideological reflexes activated by the mere mention of Trotsky. Whatever may be the case, the result was to leave Djilas to evaluate the problem for himself.

Djilas' first references to bureaucratic distortions in 1950 are almost disguised or concealed in long-winded sentences of criticism of certain practical mistakes that surfaced in the work of Yugoslav Peoples' Committees.[1] Many of these involved vaguely defined "hostile elements," "reactionary groups and classes." These statements, considered alone, would ordinarily be understood as referring to the bourgeoisie or the elements of the old regime—and that was clearly part of Djilas' intention. In 1951, he becomes more specific and warns of separating the "authorities from the masses":

This occurs in the most various forms, such as for instance a callous and bureaucratic attitude towards people, a lack of concern for the vital interests of the masses, the adoption of a policy whereby clerks assume the role of the committeemen and thus separate both the committee and the committeemen from the masses, etc.[2]

Djilas complained bitterly that committeemen, who were the appointed officials and administrators of the Yugoslav Communist Party, had a way of taking all the issues into their own hands, and therefore managed to reduce party's plenary sessions to a formality. Their goals should have been to implement the widest possible democracy. The "callous attitude" that Djilas observed is perhaps best seen in the inappropriate combinations of "the method of persuasion and method of coercion."[3] People should not be treated like objects, argued Djilas; coercion should be avoided at virtually any cost, although it must be employed against "negative individuals" if democracy is not to turn soft-headed. Nevertheless, in 1952, he stated that "to abandon the method of persuasion results in the degeneration of authority into a bureaucratic instrument for ruling the people in a heartless way."[4] In another formulation in early 1953, Djilas was clearly viewing enemies that were very different from the customary "bourgeois" variety. "Local committees are said to contain" careerists, speculators and all sorts of corrupt officials. "That is why the intensification of the struggle in the committees—their purity, principled attitude, consistency in the fight against favoritism, corruption and bureaucratism—is one of the most significant tasks."[5]

From the early sources of Djilas' writing on the problem of bureaucracy in 1950-51, the above observations typify his understanding of the problem. His criticism was not conceptualized or placed within any sort of theoretical framework. Nevertheless, despite subsequent alterations in his position, he does introduce a point with which he will be preoccupied continuously and at times consumed—that bureaucratism is capable of existing and developing at lower levels of government. As he began questioning:

in the new Yugoslavia . . . the greatest number of irregularities originate precisely from the lower organs into which hostile elements have made their way . . . And, in truth, the laws that emanate from the higher levels are good and just; the measures are good and beneficial, but they are distorted when they come to be applied.[6]

In early 1953, by which period Djilas' own beliefs had crystallized considerably, he wrote: "Bureaucratism as an anti-democratic and anti-socialist force today is expressed particularly in localism, in losing sight of everything that is not within its district, its firm, its commune, and even its own republic."[7] Djilas' affirmation makes perfectly good sense here. The problem of any government is to gain administrative compliance, in the first place from its citizens, but also from those "bureaucrats," specialists, and other functionaries, who are charged with reducing general rules to specify application. After all, no government can dispense with public administration. In the modern state especially, specialists and bureaucrats have come to occupy crucial positions in the functioning of the government. And Djilas soon realized that an instruction manual can only be so thick, and then the administrator's individual discretion unavoidably takes over. How will the bureaucrat act on his own? Will he act within the framework of legal norms?

Djilas' developing interest in the rise and functioning of the bureaucratic phenomenon was clearly provoked by Stalin and the ensuing Yugoslav-Soviet dispute in 1948. For the most creative intellectual of the Yugoslav Communist I .rty, the need subsequently developed to explain the theoretical issues. What exactly were the effects of bureaucratic practices on human relations in the Soviet Union? Was Yugoslavia ready to follow the same pattern? Prior to the political events of 1948 and his personal meetings with Stalin, Djilas' references to bureaucratic developments or bureaucratic elitism were indeed rare and casual, although there were of course frequent complaints of political and economic mismanagement, and of administrators providing bureaucratic excuses for work delays and shortages.

Djilas' contribution to the argument with the Soviet Union and with Stalin, in particular, in 1948 centered upon his disenchantment with the late arrival of the Red Army to aid Yugoslavia during World War II. He was subsequently upset with the behavior of Soviet army officers in Belgrade but the conflict did not move beyond that point at that time.[8] He did not raise the problem of bureaucracy with Stalin since the latter had promised earlier to Tito to look into the situation.[9] He was confident that the conflict would be eventually resolved. Only in April 1949 did Djilas come to realize that Stalin wanted to impose on Yugoslavia the same terms of political control and economic exploitation that characterized his relationship with other Eastern European states. In fact, Djilas had great admiration for Stalin after his second round of conversations in March 1948:

—even an uncontrolled admiration. Probably the world enforced this admiration which I had earlier taken on from the Party because at the eve of the war the Yugoslav party was completely devoted to Stalin's line in policy, his foreign policy and his general policy—absolutely. I cannot today say that I was a Stalinist nor can I say that I was not. Stalinism was, for me, the same thing as communism, as Marxism. Therefore, he embodied all that progress: Marx, Engels, the Marxist revolution, communism, Stalinism were all personified in and identified with Stalin. Just say that I was a Stalinist. But for me Stalin represented nothing that was contrary to communism, to Marxism.[10]

But it was not long before Djilas began again to have doubts about the practice of Marxism. Stalin's attempts to bully Yugoslavia shocked him, and he soon began to criticize Soviet tactics and policies. In 1950, in an article entitled "On the New Roads of Socialism," he strongly advocated complete equality as the only acceptable basis for relations between socialist states. With his Montenegrin pride and stubborness, Djilas, the rebel poet, was willing not only to challenge but fight Stalin to death. In this article, he argued against Stalin and he maintained that forms of revolution and revolutionary transition to socialism must differ because of the historically conditioned particularities of each nation and of its rights to self-determination.[11] Such differences must be recognized by all socialist leaders. To Djilas and to the rest of the Yugoslav leadership, Soviet behavior was completely unacceptable because it attempted to impose "unequal relations" on the other countries by underestimating their achievements and their particular political and social problems.

Strangely enough, the bureaucratic issue was never really mentioned throughout Djilas' disagreement with Stalin from 1948 to 1949. The nearest he comes to it is to accuse the Communist Party of the Soviet Union of a "nationalist" intention to proclaim its own revolutionary forms universally and then to expect other nations to submit to these "unequal relations." In the heat of the debate, of a life and death struggle it was only natural for Djilas, to fall back initially to old Leninist doctrines. This was also the method Trotsky used in 1924 in his struggle against Stalin.

In the aftermath of the 1948 Soviet-Yugoslav dispute, Djilas further developed his critique of the Communist Party of the Soviet Union. He now depicted the leaders and the character of the Soviet regime in rather different terms. At an important Party meeting in 1950 in Titograd he stated:

The matter concerned, among other things, their attempt to kill the initiative of the masses in our country, to terminate the further development of socialist democracy, to establish instead of the real power of the masses the rule of a monopolistic bureaucracy which would be obedient to them—in a word, they are trying to suppress the initiative of the masses and are abandoning the principle of socialist democracy.[12]

Were they also betraying the people in Yugoslavia and establishing a bureaucratic power? Djilas commented in 1950:

What kind of internal enemies are we dealing with? . . . Who are they and what do they want? To rise to such positions and secure for themselves a privileged position in society. They manage socialism as the mastery of a privileged caste of bureaucrats; and since they cannot take root in the people and the Party, they seek it outside in the Soviet and satellite governments. In order to gain for themselves a privileged position, they are prepared to betray their country, their people and struggle for socialist construction to the Soviet government which is doing its utmost to take over our country and exploit it. They are people without a heart, without conscience or honor, who are interested only in mastery over their people.[13]

Djilas deliberately placed the internal social structure of the Soviet Union in this bureaucratic category. He vociferously argued that the Cominform Resolution illustrated that "bureaucratic elements in the Soviet Union who have frozen their privileged position, are attempting to find the solution to the internal crisis in the outside world, that is, to hush it up temporarily by foreign successes, by exploitation and subordination of other socialist countries."[14]

Although the specific shape and nature of bureaucratic development in the Soviet Union and Yugoslavia still needed investigation, the possibilities, according to Djilas' study of *The New Class* of Marx and Lenin, could lead to serious dangers for the working class in socialism. He showed concern with the overthrown bourgeoisie and its own bureaucracy.[15] In order to explain the bureaucratic phenomenon further, however, Djilas claimed that one had to trace and determine its sociohistorical status—whether a bureaucracy constitutes a class or a caste.

Djilas in 1951 claimed that two key elements determined whether a group constituted a class—its position in the process of production (whether its members worked or lived off others labor) and its ownership or nonownership of the means of production. The Soviet bureaucracy, of course, while it was supported by others' labor, did not own the means of production.[16] Of central importance was the fact that Soviet and Yugoslav ownership was collective, and therefore a bureaucratic caste could not entirely resemble previous classes, which had all been based on private, individual property. In addition, there was no individual inheritance of bureaucratic positions. While it was true that there was a sort of group self-perpetuation, illustrated by the fact that students in higher schools were frequently the sons of functionaries, it was still true that each functionary was not personally replaced by one of his immediate descendants.[17] Simply put, "ownership is not the essential question—this form or that—but the management of ownership, or differently put—to whom belongs the right to distribute the surplus labor."[18] Indeed there was and remains a condition of incipient conflict between the working class and the state monopolistic manager and distributor of the national surplus. And "this external form tells us that we are dealing with a caste rather than a class, because the struggle is not about ownership itself, but about the management of the same."[19]

Like Trotsky, Djilas in 1951 argued the existence of that state was momentarily inevitable as the epiphenomenon of "remnant of class society and class relations."[20] Relying entirely on Marxist terminology to explain the transition from capitalism to socialism, Djilas ardently argued that the state had to assume a host of new responsibilities as regulator, organizer and planner of the nation's economy. This interpretation of the newly extended state finally led Djilas to see the bureaucracy in terms of function. Since the context was no longer that of private property relations, however, he realized that the bureaucratic phenomenon had to be something completely new and the best name for it was "caste." "Of a caste, one can say that the essential characteristics are privileges of all kinds on the basis of functions performed, not on the basis of ownership."[21] He became even more specific:

"and privileges on the basis of management and distribution were and remain the basic, classical characteristic of a caste."[22]

At this stage of Djilas' analysis, the caste embodied the negative remnants of all old classes—the absolutism of the feudal class, the bourgeoisie's insatiability as portrayed by Marx, and the "ugliness" of them all. But since its functions would not last forever, neither would the caste. Nevertheless, the caste's privileged position would not be short lived: to speak of its function as temporary and traditional was to describe "not a certain length of time but its process."[23]

Although collective property was the foundation of Soviet and Yugoslav society, exploitation was not automatically abolished with its achievement. Djilas feared that the bureaucracy would like to establish a new, nonsocialist form of its own. So this was no longer a crisis of socialism, as some of his comrades in the Party argued, but a new phenomenon which arose on the ground and within the framework of socialism itself.[24] Through the analysis of his *Borba* articles from 1950–53, we shall examine how and why he came to these conclusions.

To what extent did his personal participation in politics make him aware of the crisis? Only several months after his first *Borba* article on this issue in 1950, Djilas pointed to the Soviet Union's continuing monopoly role in the "creation and distribution of surplus value" and the lack of any withering away of the state. Djilas asserted that the Soviet Union was state capitalist, having undergone a "restoration and a counterrevolution of a special type" special "because this counterrevolution did not restore the old capitalist individual ownership," but involved instead a "transformation into state, in fact capitalist, property."[25] This meant, according to Djilas, the "total negation" of socialism, because "socialism implies . . . certain social relations (the democracy of the producers and their exercise of power—without the state—over the forces of production, etc.)"[26] Two years later Djilas was still to maintain that state capitalism "is not socialism, but, as Lenin used to say, the anteroom of socialism. The Soviet Union has not moved from that anteroom."[27] Throughout the above discussion in the *Borba* articles and in other journals Djilas basically maintains the "caste" nomenclature.

There are three significant reasons why Djilas did not push his critique further at this time. The suggestion has already been made that he emphasized control and management, rather than ownership, as fundamental to his definition of caste. But from another angle, the opposite could be equally true; he made ownership primary in the sense that the revolution closed the question once and for all by "expropriating the expropriators."[28] With the arrival of collective ownership, even though he does not always consider it socialist, a new dispensation was introduced and any analysis made must take account of the fact that this basic category of property has undergone a fundamental change. Like Trotsky throughout his career,

Djilas claimed in 1950 that abolition of private property meant the disappearance of the owning class, and thereby the exploitation of man rooted in class structure. To follow his hypothesis one step further, since classes no longer existed, the new ruling stratum had to be something else. So it was through an examination of the funtional role of the new group that governed that Djilas derived the concept of the caste. In a special article on this issue entitled "Class or Caste," Djilas explained:

There is no formal private property in the Soviet Union, and that is why there are no longer any classes, but the State apparatus (which includes, beside the socially superfluous bureaucrats, a number of socially necessary officials) . . . can have only the nature of a caste. The essential characteristic of the caste is that privileges of all kinds are accorded on the basis of functions performed, and not on the basis of ownership.[29]

Djilas therefore concluded that a "classless" society is not necessarily egalitarian, and that abolition of private property and the capitalist economic and social structure of class privileges need not involve the abolition of all privileges. Unlike Machajski, he did not claim that social and economic inequality could be based on something other than the physical means of production.

In addition to the assumption of the distinctness of collective and capitalist property, Djilas' strong loyalty to Marxist analysis of property and class structure clearly held him back from the obvious conclusion that a class structure had been reborn. It is evident from Djilas' writing that he was torn by Marx's statements on this problem:

He proved in his *Capital* that it is impossible, after capitalism and capitalists, for a class to develop and come to power . . . But Marx at the same time saw . . . that two dangers threaten the victorious proletariat: restoration of the overthrown bourgeoisie, and its own bureaucracy.[30]

It is quite clear that Djilas at this point was most concerned with the correct application and realization of theory, rather than the utility of the theory itself. There was another significant reason for Djilas not holding that bureaucratic power and domination was equivalent to class domination—although extremely critical of the Soviet Union, he could not afford to write off the whole of the Soviet history, with which pre-1948 Yugoslav Communists were so intimately connected. The importance of the struggle and the achievements of the Russian Revolution had to be retained. Djilas wrote in "Class or Caste":

The nationalization of capitalist enterprises in the Soviet Union carried out by the dictatorship of the proletariat under Lenin's direction, was a progressive and revolutionary act, and really a qualitative leap from old capitalist relations to new socialist relations.[31]

According to Djilas, one had to understand and appreciate that the Soviet Union had suffered a degeneration subsequent to what in fact had been a fairly solid beginning under Lenin. While Yugoslavia had a close call with a similar set of circumstances and perhaps fate, he was optimistic enough to claim that his own country and its configuration of social and economic forces were on the correct path.[32]

Nevertheless, from the evidence of his own writing at this time, there exists a major difficulty with Djilas's optimism, which he failed at the time to appreciate completely. Marx explained that the rise and development of the new class was impossible, he "came to such a conclusion on the basis of an analysis of the level of productive forces developed by capitalism, which gives society the capacity gradually, after the expropriation of expropriators, to abolish classes and class exploitation."[33] But what if Marxism came to power in a less developed or even "backward" society where there had not existed a very active expansion of the forces of production? Djilas clearly did not appreciate either the theoretical problem of the substructure or the pragmatic issue of economic development. Some of his ideas in this respect can be observed in his book entitled *On the New Roads of Socialism* written in 1950:

people, not machines are the major thing. And truly, although the struggle for socialist construction presupposes the development of modern technics, and although the oppression of these technics is even, in a certain sense, a condition of that construction, we must be aware that technics, by themselves, are not basic in socialism but social relations are basic. If socialist democracy does not stop in its development and in its struggle against bourgeois reaction and bureaucracy, if the initiative (of the masses) is freed, then free people,—regardless of all difficulties— will be able to create technics and enable their further development.[34]

It is probably going too far to view in all of this a romantic attitude that places great faith—"regardless of all difficulties"—in backyard steel mills, but there are problems nevertheless. Social relations may be "basic" in the sense that their amelioration and humanization is the most significant goal that socialism sets to accomplish. But clearly they are not basic if the meaning is historical or ontological priority: rather, "they correspond to a definite stage of development of material powers of production," and Djilas himself had asserted that the construction of socialism "presupposed" a certain technical level.[35] To be certain, people can "create technics," but they can do so only on the basis of productive forces already in existence; if the latter in turn are inadequate to a satisfactory level of socialist democracy, then society will be confronted with the distortions characteristic of an unavoidable transition period, and then the nation is thrown back into the bureau-cratic whirlpool from which it began. If mass initiative must be freed by kicking down bureaucratism, but bureaucracy is itself merely symptomatic of the "transitional" fact that conditions are not now present for democratic initiative, then Djilas was simply reasoning in a circle. He also assumed that the creation of "democractic forms" must await material transformation.

At the same time, Djilas emphasized the importance of the economic base. In his discussion of this problem with the economic specialists of Yugoslavia in 1950 he said to Kidrić and Kardelj:

We all agree that the roots of bureaucratism should not be sought in the subjective weakness (lack of consciousness) of revolutionaries and the revolutionary move-ment, but above all in objective reality. But have we overcome that reality? Does sub-jective reality still hold dangers of bureaucratism, or not? We all agree, I think, that it does—and not only from without, from Soviet aggression, but also from within from the predominantly peasant character of our country and other forms of backward-ness, from as yet unformed socialist democratic relations.[36]

If the root of bureaucratic development lies in objective conditions, as Djilas has formulated them here, then to alleviate the former, the latter must be altered. Therefore, if we understand Djilas properly, it is impossible to "abolish" bureaucratism in any sense other than that its historic function must eventually be outlived. Djilas' discrepancy between the context of Marx's well-known analysis of developed productive forces and the context of its pragmatic application in a predominantly peasant society in Russia and Yugoslavia were not immediately clear to him. We shall observe that in *The New Class* he pays a lot more attention to the theory in industrialization and modernization.[37]

It should be clear from the above that Djilas' treatment of economic forces and substructure between 1948 and 1950 was not always consistent. In 1950, he also placed a lot of stress on consciousness:

because the tendencies towards domination by bureaucracy in the transition period are a phenomenon by law, they are actually at the same time an anarchical, spon-taneous process. That is why serious efforts of "genius" are not necessary for them to prevail.[38]

This is a confusing statement. How can a historical tendency manifest and embody an objective law and simultaneously be anarchic? An objective law in the Marxian sense is analagous to a scientific or natural, rather than an ethical, law. Its knowledge is independent of human knowledge, whereas such knowledge is indispensable to the operation of an ethical law. An ob-jective law of social development, in other words history, involves a teleol-ogy and at least some broad pattern of stages of development which are not fortuitous or "anarchic" but are the unfolding of an objective necessity. This evolution may "just happen" without men's comprehension of their role in it—or it may be "spontaneous"—but still progressive in terms of the process itself. According to Djilas, spontaneity becomes the law "in itself." But not always even that: since it is not necessarily based on a rational grasp of the objective law, spontaneity may involve error and develop in ways other than those which actualize the law. It is then at best a dubious ally of the objective process—their coincidence is unreliable, and an identification of them is not necessarily warranted. Nevertheless, the supposition is that the law is knowable, which knowledge introduces the factor of "consciousness" that in some degree apprehends the process and, by manipulating spontaneity—borrowing before it or putting brakes on it—can assist the objective process along.

In his philosophical statements, Djilas often attempted to equate objective law with anarchy and spontaneity. Like the examples above, they frequently entailed a remarkable confusion, if not contradiction. Beginning in 1952, Djilas shifted the emphasis from what he had asserted elsewhere—that the bureaucracy had its objective foundation in the economic backwardness of the Soviet Union and Yugoslavia. The economic condition had not simply been "there," unexplainable or accidental. Rather, it existed because of the prior domestic and imperialist evolution of capitalism, which had not been spontaneous but which had unfolded along the lines disclosed by scientific Marxism-Leninism. But by means of this confusion of objectivity with anarchy, Djilas was led to assert a powerful role for consciousness. In order for bureaucratic tendencies to triumph, Djilas wrote in *On The New Roads of Socialism:*

It is enough to stop the conscious struggle against them to have the state monopoly over management of material production, necessary in the struggle against capitalism and in the beginning of socialist construction, become a social monopoly, that is, to drag in its wake privileged distribution of the surplus of social products and attempts at monopolization of all phases of life and social activities. However, if bureaucratic anarchy is reined in by conscious activity—then the monopoly over management is stopped, and by that fact every other kind of monopoly.[39]

The above analysis suffers from the identical dilemma just discussed. How can conscious activity tighten the reins on bureaucracy when the underlying problem remains economic backwardness? Did it not originally give rise to bureaucracy?

Two or three possible solutions might get one out of this dilemma. One would be simply to obliterate objectivity by claiming that consciousness can accomplish everything. Djilas did not opt for this solution; he was still too much of a Marxist for that. Without venturing too far, Djilas and for that matter the entire Yugoslav Communist Party, like the Communist Party of the Soviet Union, did come to place increasing reliance on injecting consciousness into the proletariat from the outside. In line with this point of view, the Sixth Congress in 1952 changed the name of the Party to the League of Communists and called for a much more active educational role in society for League members with a corresponding de-emphasis of the "method of command."[40]

Along with the change of the Party name and a greater demand for inter-Party discussion, Djilas openly argued that the objective factors had also been altered; the locus of consciousness had in part shifted to the masses themselves. He does not fully assert that the masses have become either completely conscious or the vanguard suddenly mindless, but more modestly that Communists no longer hold a monopoly on socialist consciousness. This was clearly the line of argument that carried Djilas to a head-on collision with his Party colleagues, because the inescapable conclusion is that the Party has partially outlived its usefulness.

To a great extent, then, Djilas arrives at the problem of bureaucracy in a rather circuitous manner. It has already been pointed out that bureaucratism is rooted in the economic backwardness of the transition period. If the productive forces were to be strengthened, it had to be the result of socially necessary forces of labor. In this connection, Djilas on 3 May 1952 made an observation that was not extremely flattering to his fellow bureaucrats:

Productive forces . . . are created above all through the physical labor of the workers and working people in general, and also by the mental labor of engineers, educational workers, doctors, etc., in a word—technicians and scientists. Socialism is above all the work of the physical labor of the working class. The Party and organs of authority can not have any essential role except (a) protectors of the process of labor and of the working class from enemies of socialism; (b) as the conscious mobilizer of the masses and the propaganda of the ideas of socialism and socialist social relations. This is understandable because they do not create . . . material goods necessary for society to become socialist.[41]

In Marxist thought and terminology, it is quite true that a "non-productive worker" is not necessarily a social parasite, but rather an individual not engaged in an activity which results in a product. Strictly speaking, he is a "non-product worker," and all service functions fall under this category. But it is unusual to see the Party and government examined in this manner and with such candor—especially by a leader of that Party and government—hinting that, after all, the workers really make a greater contribution to socialism than do the cadres. Djilas presents here a preliminary theoretical crack in the bureaucratic wall.

According to Djilas, new analytic ideas always originated with a minority. In his case, these new ideas included a struggle with bureaucratism. Furthermore, he added in an article in *Borba* on 4 January 1954: "Every new idea . . . reflects some reality, some change either in the material world, or in scientific discovery or artistic creation."[42] What are these newly emerging realities and social forces that are finding their reflection in new ideas? If the social reality is constantly changing, how do human beings influence it in order to "live and progress" in the new conditions? Are the "new" political, scientific, or even artistic ideas arising from these realities formulated by individuals or groups? Even though Djilas was not certain how to respond to all these questions, he was very clear on one thing: "No one party or group . . . can be the exclusive expression of the objective imperatives of contemporary society."[43]

Djilas, of course, explained that during the period of war and revolution in both the Soviet Union from 1917 to 1921 and in Yugoslavia from 1940 to 1945 complete political monopoly and concentration of power and forces was absolutely necessary in the organized, disciplined and conscious element of the society—the Party. But at present, since the forces of production have reached a higher stage of development and social relations today are not resolved by force of arms, the methods of work and struggle likewise cannot remain the same. What is essential for socialism and for every little bit of real democracy is greater flexibility and relaxation of Party's authority.[44]

In addition, Djilas argued, people cannot expect any fresh ideas from the ranks of functionaries. Self-examination and voluntary adjustment to "new social reality" have never been their strong point. In fact, the horizon of the bureaucracy is severely limited by what Djilas considered its historic function. As he explained: "They have centralized and regulated everything from ethics to stamp collecting . . . many communists have still not succeeded in changing their own opinions, much less their behaviour, habits and manners, now that the democratic wind has begun to blow."[45] Djilas believes that the bureaucracy hates to see the bourgeoisie really weakened, since the conclusion of that process would mean that its own raison d'être would have disappeared.

Strictly speaking, it would have been naive to expect one individual to be the sole embodiment of the new social forces and to contend against society's massive reaction. Nevertheless, the Communist should be delighted if he turns out to be a tool of the dialectic, because "denial is the most creative force in history."[46] Djilas had to write his scathing short stories and articles "because like many others, I am the 'victim' of objective social processes which compel me to do so."[47]

In 1952, Djilas came to the conclusion that the Yugoslav society was a battleground of three significant forces: (1) capitalism and the bourgeoisie, (2) bureaucratism, and (3) socialism and democracy. The first two are obvious but the second represents by far the greatest danger. The third includes those forces conscious of the fact that socialism and democracy go hand in hand. Supporting them are the toiling masses, primarily the workers.[48] Clearly without their enormous physical energies, all talk about humane socialism and socialist relations is simply empty moralizing and dreaming. In other words, the efforts of workers and peasants have not been wasted: in the aftermath of World War II they have contributed to enormous change in the balance of "objective forces." Like Trotsky in the aftermath of the Russian Revolution, Djilas believed that the workers and peasants were striving to increase the "tempo" of industrial development, the productivity of labor, the economic well-being of the nation, the matter of its utilization and spread of education in the postwar period in Yugoslavia. These alterations, in his view, had very significant consequences—the primary pre-requisite for democracy and for more freedom in the cities had been created, although the villages remained relatively underdeveloped, and Yugoslavia had demonstrated its ability to solve its own internal and external problems.

These were significant achievements in Djilas' eyes:

With all that, we have a significant change in the role of the basic productive force— the working man, especially the industrial working man, (the workers, and the technical intelligensia—one part of cultural workers.) They are becoming a new, more independent force, a basic conscious factor in the further development of society and the nation's economy.[49]

Relying entirely on Marx's terminology and view of society, Djilas here utilizes Marx's doctrine that being determines consciousness, certainly a conclusion that was bound to provoke the Party bureaucracy. To some degree, it would appear that he is also rejecting Leninism for Marxism— emphasizing worker creativity and consciousness instead of the role of the Party. He made his point in October 1953: "Since socialist reality exists and is progressing, a new socialist consciousness must appear independent of officials and forums."[50]

Djilas appears to be making an extremely elementary point to the functionaries. Simply put, ordinary, common people, want to work in freedom and to perform their regular duties. The Party functionaries must learn to leave them alone and finally to stop having so many political meetings. What the Yugoslav society needs, and by implication what the Soviet Union failed to achieve under Lenin and Stalin, was to allow day-to-day freedom, which Djilas contended was the "most important objective (productive), human force."[51] Otherwise, what shall be done with the new working class?

The example cited by Djilas as evidence of the growing popular "consciousness" was the lively sense of national unity and "Yugoslavism" provoked by the leadership's crisis with Italy over Trieste in 1953.[52] It seems to me that this was a safe subject to choose at the time, although there is no way to determine whether Djilas was cooly calculating in his choice, before setting out to undermine the Party in a more direct manner. In a nation literally plagued with regional, religious and ethnic animosities, an assertion of renewed unity would find few people willing to disagree openly. Still, two components of his argument require special attention. First, it is not surprising to see Djilas link the free expression of popular sentiment with references to nature—"everywhere justice and freedom are growing, as are socialism and democracy. They all (Serbs, Montenegrins, Slovenians, Croats, Macedonians), have equally begun to love their country, its—their men, and their—its—creations, their own woods and waters, rocks and shores."[53] Obviously, socialism cannot be constructed from "woods and waters, rocks and shores," but to be fair, there is more to Djilas' argument than that. What he has in mind is that Yugoslavs are intensely proud of their political and economic achievements and most significantly they managed to stand on their own feet against both the East and West from 1941 to 1953. However, the initial association of ideas in Djilas' thought—freedom and nature must be noted.[54]

Encompassed by and revealed in all of the above was another significant aspect of Djilas' analysis—the praise of spontaneity—that in 1953-54 emerges as central in his efforts to chip away at the foundations of Party bureaucracy and particularly the monopoly of its rule. And Djilas expressed the process in very romantic and un-Leninist metaphors:

Brotherhood and Unity today is not only the accomplishment of a conscious vanguard, or a necessity of the struggle for survival or a condition for victory in the war for liberation. No, today, it is the common, everyday new life of the people. New generations breathe robustly, thinking and feeling that they are Yugoslavs ... No one preached or ordered that they do so. And yet, they do it ... The real seed was sown by Communists. But now it has taken root and grows and branches further; now it grows by itself.[55]

In this regard, the Yugoslav Communist Party has accomplished a great deal if we are to trust Djilas' assessment. Ordinarily, one would be glad when a job has been well done; but his statement implies that a goal-oriented society or organization ought to alter, and alter substantially, when some elements of the goal or plan are accomplished. Djilas seems not to realize how difficult it is to do this with any political organization that has built up a momentum of its own and has a vested interest in survival.

Nevertheless, between 1952 and his expulsion from the Communist Party of Yugoslavia in 1954, Djilas continued to broaden the range of his critique. He observed that "the conditions in which we work have changed. Our socialist economy is more or less free."[56] To Djilas, these were new forces, or "new contents," as he occasionally referred to them in the press, but they were still fragile and in fact required more legal protection by what he called "new forms."[57] In his view, it was absolutely necessary to pay more attention to these "forms."

What exactly did Djilas have in mind? By forms, Djilas seems to have meant, inclusively, laws, moral and social norms, established habits of human relationship, ways of discussion and ways of arriving at decisions. Without wanting to reduce the complexity of what Djilas was saying, one is tempted to state that he was groping for a notion of Western legal procedure or process.

Most crucial to our discussion of bureaucracy remain his notions of "forms" and methods of work "within and by the Party." He thought the old methods of "democratic centralism," by which the central committee fixed everything in advance and then handed a decision down from above, were out of date. In the article, "League or Party," published in *Borba* in January 1954, he clearly stated that the "entire Leninist form of the party and the state . . . must always and everywhere become obsolete as soon as revolutionary conditions no longer exist and democracy begins to live."[58] On a few previous occasions Djilas had pointed out that underlying these new social realities are alternatives in the economic substructure, and once again in this article he indicated that the "logic and the basis of these changes are in economic development and economic relations."[59] Throughout "League or Party," Djilas applied to the Yugoslav situation a powerful sense of historical stages: "We built our Leninist party . . . with our own forces but under the influence of Lenin's ideas and Stalin's interpretation of Leninism."[60]

Djilas reasserted on several occasions before his downfall that without these absolutely fundamental readjustments in behavior and work methods, socialism would not triumph in Yugoslavia. There simply had to be fewer meetings, less propaganda and indoctrination; but more lectures and open discussion; no privilege-producing ideological distinctions between Communists and ordinary citizens; personality must be permitted to grow and be respected for its quality and function, not its position or rank in the Party or state bureaucracy. "Life can be organized only on the basis of personal desires and complete voluntarism."[61] According to Djilas' new hopes, Communists ought to have educational and perhaps censorial duties and functions in society, but coercive authority was to be completely outlawed or abolished. In his discussion with Kardelj in 1952, Djilas naively believed that the Party or the League "would weaken, 'wither away' as a classical Marxist party."[62]

These alleged alterations in the objective situation, a definite shift in Djilas' own thinking helps to account for his critique. He did not completely abandon communism immediately—it remained an ideal, an "ultimate goal," and as late as 1956 he felt that it was the only one whose realization had been scientifically proven to be inevitable.[63] But while in prison in 1957–58, he trained his telescope on a reality closer to home. He came to argue at this time, any contemporary stage, in fact the nature of the economic world as such, could not be reduced to neat formulae. To demand that it be so was to revert to Stalinist dogmatism. By the time a state of affairs can be conclusively formulated, life has moved on and the formula has become obsolete. "Now it is necessary to build industry, educate the peasants, and develop culture, democratic authority and social relations."[64]

Djilas was deeply concerned, frequently to the point of obsession, about the tyranny of the future over the present. "For with Communism as an idea the essential thing is not what is being done but why"[65]—that is exactly the danger. Such a mode of thought practically guarantees that intention ("why") and effect ("what") will be forever discrepant. While the events and course of history will inevitably establish "the ultimate goal" of communism, elevating it as a consciously held plan of action leads one to mistake the nature and potentialities of subjectivity. As Djilas profoundly stated the matter: "Objective necessity as a goal is the basis of every superficial and self-seeking empiricism and, in our circumstances is one of the substantive sources of bureaucratism."[66] For Djilas, the consequences usher in the possible—the bureaucracy. He explains: "The sole purpose of this separation of ideals and 'ultimate goals' from immediate ones, as well as the gradual transformation of one into the other, is this: the bureaucracy."[67]

Djilas' proposed modifications follow logically. First, men must be acutely aware of the real nature of objectivity and give it its due. Otherwise, nothing will happen immediately except it be achieved through objective developments in which human will and action are only a part, one element in the process independent of human will and action.[68] In addition, all forms that express the latter must be recognized as transitory. In the second place, Djilas substitutes what we might call goals of the middle and incremental change. He posits that should communism ever develop, it will do so only after an innumerable series of concrete tasks are accomplished which provide liberties and freedom for all Yugoslavs from all forms of present Party domination. These tasks would liberate human toil and help to create a fuller form: of democracy. As it is quite evident, Djilas has not yet broken completely with "politics as idea-realization,"[69] but his reedited or revised version was not likely to arouse the enthusiasm and single-minded devotion of any Communist Party bureaucrat.

As it has been previously pointed out, Djilas in 1948–50, viewed bureaucracy as a "caste" because, while it did not own the means of production, it did command a monopoly over control and management. Since the socialist economy is so much more extensive than capitalist economy, the power and functions of the bureaucracy are thereby expanded; and as we shall see, privileges based on functions are an extremely significant characteristic of the social caste.

Although there has been no alteration from 1954 to 1957 in the legally expressed status of the Yugoslav Communist Party bureaucracy, Djilas in *The New Class* (1957) arrived at the conclusion that it had become the owner of the national wealth. "As defined by Roman law, property constitutes the use, enjoyment, and disposition of material goods. The Communist political bureaucracy uses, enjoys, and disposes of nationalized property."[70] "Ownership, he continues is nothing other than the right of profit and control. If one defines class benefits by this right, the Communist states have seen, in the final analysis, the origin of a new form of ownership or of a new ruling and exploiting class."[71]

The novelty lies in the fact that ownership is collective: no one member of the elite owns any particular piece of property, and it is precisely this which deludes it into thinking that it is not a possessing class at all. But ownership is the most important characteristic of the new class, even in the absence of stocks and bonds. As he commented, "to be an owner or a joint owner in the communist system means that one enters the ranks of the ruling political bureaucracy and nothing else."[72]

From a close study of Djilas' conclusions and definitions of bureaucracy, it is quickly evident that he has preferred to emphasize aspects of Party control and power, even though he is ostensibly describing ownership. The one alteration, and especially "the right of profit and control," is not extremely enlightening, since socialist profits are revealed in privileges that enable the bureaucracy to improve its own standard of living in preference to others— "a larger income in material goods and privileges than society should normally grant for such functions."[73] Djilas presents nothing new in this respect. Otherwise, ownership becomes an exclusive right "to distribute the national income, to set wages, direct economic development, and dispose of nationalized and other property"[74]—all of which is central control and management.

Djilas' whole argument about ownership, as well as his view of how an ordinary man sees the Communist functionary is not very convincing. Of a socialized economy, one might argue that everybody owns everything or that nobody owns anything; and perhaps both statements, judicially speaking, might be correct but largely irrelevant. By definition, a nationalized economy is one that has been removed from private hands and has been made a department of the state. According to most analysts, the only significant question then becomes, who controls the state economy. Djilas' arguments would have made a lot more sense had he maintained his initial position, claiming merely that the bureaucracy in the Soviet Union and Yugoslavia has unrestrained control over the economic life and well-being of these countries. He could not stop at this point, however, because of his ideologically imposed task of demonstrating that the new elite was a new class. One way to show that the elite constituted a class was to prove that it owned property; to achieve this end, he utilized Roman law.

In addition, the elite had to be set on firmer footing than mere oligarchic exclusiveness; it also had to be illustrated that the elite was rooted in economic exploitation of "objective" historical developments. Therefore, Djilas finally arrived at the critical position that bureaucratic monopolism was a new "relation of production," and one key expression of relations of production was, in Marxist thought, property.[75]

Underlying Djilas' interpretation of the rise of this new elite to power were two key elements in the communist theory of the state. One is that of the state alone and the other is the theory of the "withering away" of the state. Lenin referred to the state as the organ of tyranny when he wrote in The State and Revolution: "The state is a club."[76] Djilas confirmed in The New Class the need for revolutionaries to use state authority once in power. Only after his expulsion from the Party in 1954 did he claim that Marx and Lenin were unreasonable and perhaps naive to think otherwise. With increasingly complex forms of life, the need for state bureaucracy would inevitably appear after all revolutions.

How could Marx and Lenin make such errors? After 1917 in the Soviet Union and after 1945 in Yugoslavia, progression in the direction of state power and the expansion of the new class bureaucracy simply was required in order to govern. While the functions of the state continually increased, Stalin, for instance, was faced in the 1920s and 1930s with the unenviable problem of explaining such growth or concealing it. According to Djilas, his solution was rather simple: "Stalin thought that the state would disappear by having all the citizenry rise to the state's level and take charge of its affairs."[77]

The individual in the Soviet and Yugoslav states remained nothing more than a functionary. In some ways, all persons were functionaries, distinguished only by the amount of pay and by the number of privileges they enjoyed. Said Djilas: "By means of collectivization, even the peasant gradually becomes a member of the general bureaucratic society."[78]

Djilas' position on the functional role of the Soviet and Yugoslav bureaucracy is extremely important. Crucial to his explanation is the directing and managing force of the state and the manner in which it has assumed a multitude of new functions. What exactly are the functions of a state economy? How are functions used to "create the conditions for socialism?" What forms of industrialization does the state use to take the country out of economic backwardness?

Djilas claimed in 1954 that industrialization already had been substantially accomplished in both the Soviet Union and Yugoslavia, at least to a degree sufficient to make authoritarian rule unnecessary. "Having achieved industrialization, the new class can do nothing more than strengthen its hold on power and pillage the people. It ceases to create. Its spiritual heritage is overtaken by darkness."[79] Further, he insisted that with the disappearance of most of the raison d'être for the new class, the elite inevitably became more concerned about the protection of its own vested interests than about the type and "tempo" of the industrialization process, which if properly understood could really benefit the entire Soviet and Yugoslav population. Djilas opposed Trotsky's industrialization plan and claimed that Trotsky's "tempo" strategy of "full speed ahead" was cruel and inhuman.

Djilas is not entirely clear as to when this shift occurred, when industrialization came to be subordinated to subjective class interests. On certain occasions he referred to the industrialization process and to Trotsky's tempo plan as a mere trick:

Whenever Communists come to power, their assault on private ownership creates the illusion that their measures are primarily directed against the ownership classes for the benefit of the working class. Subsequent events prove that their measures were not taken for this purpose but in order to establish their own ownership. This must manifest itself predominantly as ideological rather than class discimination. If this were not true, if they really strove for actual ownership by the working masses, then class discrimination actually would have prevailed.[80]

Otherwise the new class and its paramount interests of power appear to have established total control, especially with Stalin's ruthless and complete victory over all his "Oppositionists," including Trotsky, although in Djilas' view, Lenin does bear an indirect responsibility, as the architect of "a party of the Bolshevik type."[81] Lenin was also responsible for insisting that the Party should keep its central role in government and economy, a nearly impossible task.

Here Djilas developed an interesting periodization of Soviet history, clearly arguing for revolutionary, dogmatic and nondogmatic stages.[82] These periods correspond roughly to the eras of Lenin, Stalin and the "collective leadership," although elements of each easily can be discovered in all stages. However:

During the development, from the first to the third phase, the quintessence of Communist—power—evolved from being the means and became an end in itself. Actually power was always more or less the end, but Communist leaders, thinking that through power as a means they would attain the ideal goal, did not believe it to be an end in itself. Precisely because power served as a means for the Utopian transformation of society, it could not avoid becoming an end in itself and the most important aim of Communism. Power was able to appear as a means in the first and second phases. It can no longer be concealed that in the third phase power is actually the aim and essence of Communism.[83]

Djilas further implied that Stalin was genuinely concerned with the industrialization process for reasons other than his own personal power. He also suggested that industrialization of the Soviet Union presently had been accomplished. This leaves the impression that Khruschev's and Brezhnev's industrialization "tempos" were indeed somewhat less harsh.[84]

Djilas' theory also implies a shift in the meaning of ideology. Ideology can be conceived as either: (1) the consciousness of an epoch—what a culture thinks of itself; or (2) the "false consciousness" of men unaware of their true role, distorting the reality they purport to describe and leading them to clothe their ambitions and roles in ideological costumes.[85] Djilas indicates that the movement from the first stage of Soviet history to the third manifests an alteration from the first to the second conception of ideology.

Whatever the precise dating of Djilas' three stages, the underlying progression demonstrates an economic orientation determined more and more by the power and ideological requirements of the owning bureaucracy, accentuating those branches of industry that fortify its internal and external position, rather than those which raise the external position and rather than those which raise the standard of living.

On the other hand, we have already seen that Trotsky would argue differently. His industrial and economic blueprint pointed to heavy industries by the development of which the consumer would become the chief beneficiary.[86] Though collective property was a first imperative for breaking the stranglehold of foreign and domestic capital, "now they continue to strengthen this form—without considering whether or not it is in the interest of the national economy and of further industrialization—for their own sake, for an exclusive Communist class aim."[87] A prime example, according to Djilas, of "strengthening this form" and of ideological planning was the collectivization of Soviet agriculture under Stalin. Remarked Djilas:

Stalin said, on the eve of the collectivization, that the question of "who will do what to whom" had been raised, even though the Soviet government was not meeting serious opposition from a politically and economically disunited peasantry. The new class felt insecure as long as there were any other owners except itself. This was the direct reason for the attack on peasantry. However there was a second reason: the peasants could be dangerous to the new class in an unstable situation. The new class had to therefore subordinate the peasantry itself economically and administratively; this was done through the kolkhozes and machine-tractor stations which required an increase proportionate to the size of the new class in the villages themselves. As a result, bureaucracy mushroomed in the villages too . . . The collectivization of peasant holdings, which was economically unjustified, was unavoidable if the new class was to be securely installed in its power and its ownership.[88]

The combination of political and economic power and ultimately domination over the state economy provided the new class oligarchy with the illusion of success: it created an impression that communism was working—at least for the new class itself. And this apparent success seems also to prove the correctness of the ideology. Communist leaders like himself, Djilas asserted, through "experience—the success of the revolution under 'un-favorable conditions'—confirmed and strengthened their illusion that they knew the laws of social development."[89] Ideology then proved to be not just a system of thought but a significant means to effect pragmatic action upon the world.

Because, Djilas asserted, Communists claim that they alone know the laws which govern society, they have arrived at an oversimplified and un-scientific ideology and conclusion, which nevertheless justifies the new class's power and its exclusive right to shape and direct society and its ac-tivities. To Djilas, this had become the major mistake of the Party bu-reaucracy.

Marxism, then, is inherently exclusive, since it purports to be a universal method, a proposition all Communists are obliged to accept. The so-called "further development of Marxism" in practice fortifies the new class, because the oligarchy has a monopoly over the correct interpretation which protects its dominance over science and society. Again, though, it is the cen-tral ingredient of power which, when combined with an all- encompassing philosophy, proves lethal: "It pushes its adherents into the position which makes it impossible for them to hold any other viewpoint. If this were not connected with specific forms of government and ownership, the mon-strous methods of oppression and destruction of the human mind could not be explained by the view itself."[90] A Communist bureaucratic regime, because of its complete power, can assure that everybody adheres to its ideology. At one point it was industrialization, which society could endure since it had to alleviate its backwardness. But then the guiding conception came to be the maintenance of the obvious privileges of the new class charged with conducting the affairs of the whole society:

The wonderful human characteristics of an isolated movement are slowly trans-formed into the intolerant and Pharisaical morals of a privileged caste. Thus politick-ing and servility replace the former straightforwardness of the revolution. The world has seen few heros who were as ready to sacrifice everything, including life, for others and for an idea, for the good of the people, having not been killed or pushed aside, they became self-centered cowards without ideas or comrades, willing to renounce everything—honor, name, truth, and morals—in order to keep their place in the rul-ing class and the hierarchical circle. The world has seen few heros as ready to sacrifice and suffer as the Communists were on the eve of and during the revolution. It has probably never seen such characterless wretches and stupid defenders of arid for-mulas as they become after attaining power.[91]

Djilas was to a great extent blinded by the spectacle of a new class in an os-tensibly classless society. Interestingly he did not offer a thoroughgoing Marxist, class analysis, according to which all elements of the "superstruc-ture" merely embody "new class" interests. He saw those interests, rather, as largely subjective, ideological manipulation of the economy. Nevertheless,

he appeared to be asserting that there are holdovers from earlier periods
when other interests were dominant. Distorted industrialization remains industrialization of some sort.

We can discern two implications here: First, Djilas was concerned to carve
out an area of autonomy for the state, in order to place it beyond the
perimeters of class direction. As he pointed out in 1957–58 in *The
New Class:*

the parties create generalizations, ostensibly scientific conclusions and theories, and
proclaim half-truths as truths. The fact that force and violence are basic characteristics of every state authority, or the fact that individual social and political forces em-
ploy the machinery of the state, particularly in armed clashes, cannot be denied.
However, experience shows that state machinery is necessary to society, or the nation, for still another reason—for the development and uniting of its various
functions. Communist theory, as well as that of Lenin, ignores this aspect.[92]

Djilas' second point followed from the first. Not every individual in the
Party of government branches was a member of the new class; function
remained essential in defining one's relationship to it. According to Djilas,
"since administration is unavoidable in society, necessary administrative
functions may be coexistent with parasitic functions in the same person."[93]

Consistent with Djilas' argument is the view that there is a condition of la-
tent conflict between the state administration and the new class oligarchy,
which would be impossible if the former were not in some measure
independent:

They are able to control the organs of force, that is, the police and the party, which in
turn control the entire state machine and its functions. The opposition of the organs
of functionaries of the state to the "irrationalities" of the party and police, that is, of
the politicking functionaries, is really the opposition of society carried over into the
state machine. It is an expression of dissatisfaction because of society's objective aspirations and needs.[94]

Clearly the state is not reduced to an organ of oppression; rather, it has been
subordinated to the organs of tyranny. Djilas has come to despise the Party
bureaucracy even more than the state bureaucracy.

Djilas' historical analysis of the new class also provided significant insights into the sociological foundations of Marxism, which did not originate
beyond time and space but was in fact a definite product of its own period.
And Djilas commented on the origins and influences of Marxism on
numerous occasions:

Marx's ideas were influenced by the scientific atmosphere of his time, by his own
leanings toward science, and by his revolutionary aspiration to give to the working-
class movement a more or less scientific basis. His disciples were influenced by a dif-

ferent environment and by different motives when they converted his views into dogma. If the political needs of the working-class movement in Europe had not demanded a new ideology complete in itself, the philosophy that calls itself Marxist, the dialectical materialism, would have been forgotten—dismissed as something not particularly profound or even original, though Marx's economic and social studies are of the highest scientific and literary rank.[95]

In Europe, Marx's theories and ideas were taken over by two significant groups, the Social Democrats and the Communists; but both of these organizational elements were only partially correct in citing Marx as their prime source of ideas and plans. The Social Democrats and Communists were also interested in defending their own personal practices which had arisen out of the social and economic circumstances already dramatically different from those of Marx. Pragmatic and intellectual developments went hand in hand until a major schism erupted in the European socialist movement in the 1890s.[96] As Djilas later explained, these changes in the political and social conditions in the Eastern European countries failed to develop, and as a result, Communist theorists interpreted reality from their own point of view. "Lenin in Russia and Bernstein in Germany are the two extremes through which the different changes, social and economic, and the different 'realities' of the working-class movements found expression."[97] What made Marxism appealing in both instances was not its presumed scientific element but power in certain sociopolitical groups. According to his way of thinking, "as a science, Marxist philosophy was not important, since it was based mainly on Hegelian and materialistic ideas." But, as the "ideology of the new, oppressed classes and especially of political movements, it marked an epoch, first in Europe, and later in Russia and Asia, providing the basis for a new political movement and a new social system."[98] Even in the Western Europe of their origins, many Marxist theories and concepts, particularly the increasing economic impoverishment of the working class, were being falsified. In the most advanced capitalist nations, like England and France, industrial development in fact led to an improvement in the living standards of the workers and improved social conditions generally. Why then should Marx's ideas have had such profound effect, produced such enthusiasm in Eastern Europe? With this question, I think one is carried to the heart of Djilas' critique.

What he in effect contended is that Communist bureaucratic forms won out in the struggle among various programs of modernization and industrialization.[99] These all assume that man can comprehend and control his environment, but the desire for such control leads to a marked centralization and bureaucratization of policymaking in all spheres of human endeavor, most dramatically in the economic. In this regard, the group of policies presently considered as Communist took shape only with the inauguration of the First Five Year Plan in 1928 in the Soviet Union. This is the date that foreshadowed the victory of the new class under Stalin, whose crucial program was the intensified "tempo" of industrialization. As we have already observed, Djilas differed with Trotsky on this significant issue. What is important is that Marxism proved most "applicable" in Russia and Yugoslavia and for that matter in other underdeveloped nations, but it became thereby not a program of humane distribution but one of economic growth. In this respect, Adam Ulam has argued in *The Unfinished Revolution* that "the Marxist system receives its historical significance from its ability to combine anarchism—the most violent protest against industrialism—which an intense cult of technology and a conviction of the historical necessity and blessings of industrialism."[100] Although definitions of anarchism in Russian and Eastern European history vary, Ulam here defines it in very general terms as a "feeling underlying the various forms of social protest during the Industrial Revolution."[101] In his view, anarchism is the "legacy of an agrarian society to its industrial successor. It embodies the clash of peasant values with the reality of industrial life."[102] But since Marxism also looks to the ever greater development of the forces of production, it "offers everything in the way of social protest that anarchism does, and more. By embracing it, one does not swim against the current of social development, but with it."[103]

Like Trotsky, Djilas emphasized the social and economic backwardness of Russia. The country found itself in a very serious historical dilemma; it either had to industrialize rapidly or give up all pretense of active participation on the stage of history and run the risk of becoming a captive of the developed world powers. Indigenous capital, however, and the class and parties representing it, were too weak to solve the problem. Hence the need for their revolutionary overthrow. Incidentally, it is interesting here that Djilas utilizes a very dubious "historical law" in his critique:

The reason for this is that there is an immutable law—that each human society and all individuals participating in it strive to increase and perfect production—No society or nation allows production to lag to such an extent that its existence is threatened. To lag means to die. People never die willingly; they are ready to undergo any sacrifice to overcome the difficulties which stand in the way of their economic production and their existence. The environment and the material and intellectual level determine the method, forces, and means that will be used to bring about the development and expansion of production—under any ideological banner or social force—does not depend on individuals; because they wish to survive, societies and nations find the leaders and ideas which, at a given moment, are best suited to that which they must and wish to attain.[104]

According to Djilas then, industrialization was an objective necessity. The special advantage of a disciplined and organized Communist party was not that it radically opposed the status quo; other parties also did so. But the Communists were the most ardent and consistent advocates of an industrial transformation. No other party was willing to go to this extent or to propose and demand such sacrifices from the entire nation.

On the theoretical and abstract level, Djilas' critique of the industrialization process is a monument to the fact that Communist revolutions contradict the schema created by Marx and his later followers. It did not turn out to be true that—"No social order ever disappears before all the productive forces for which there was room in it have been developed; and new, higher relations of production never appear before the material conditions of their existence have matured in the womb of the old society."[105] This generalization may have some validity for certain revolutions in the past, but the communist revolutions of the twentieth century occurred not because capitalism was "over developed" but because it was not developed enough.[106] Presumably, if left alone, Russia could have gone through a conventional capitalist stage; but the existing capitalist social structures were insufficient to carry through the rapid industrialization that circumstances demanded.

The question of power, therefore, was only a bare beginning. The creation of the economic preconditions of socialism was imperative. According to Djilas, "in history, it is not important who implements a process, it is only important that the process be implemented."[107] This task fell to the new class.

NOTES

1. Milovan Djilas, "Klasa ili kasta," *Borba*, (April 6, 1950), pp. 2-3. This important article can also be found in *Classe ou Caste, Questions Actuelles du Socialism*, No. 12, juin-juillet, 1952), pp. 26-32.

2. Djilas, "Perversion of Character of the People's Committee and Authority," *Komunist*, (*The Communist*), I, (October 1946), p. 19.

3. Ibid., p. 21.

4. Ibid., p. 22.

5. Ibid., p. 19.

6. Ibid., p. 21.

7. Djilas, "Naša revolucija je jedna od vrlo retkih koja je ostala verna samoj sebi time što je osigurava neprestano razvijanje demokratije," *Borba*, (July 14, 1953), p. 1.

8. Interview with John Morgan of the British Broadcasting Corporation (BBC), London, (December 13, 1973), p. 29.

9. He admits and comments on his behavior in his *Conversations with Stalin*, (New York, 1962), pp. 68-72.

10. Djilas, *Lenin on Relations between Socialist States*, (New York, 1950). Originally in *Komunist*, (September, 1949).

11. Ibid., pp. 7-11.

12. "Govor druga Milovana Djilasa na velikom predizborom mitingu u Titogradu," 13 March 1950, p. 2. Note that the "heartlessness" of bureaucracy is one of his persistent themes. This will eventually evolve into a major concern for the relations between ends and means and for the "importance of form."

13. Djilas, On the New Roads of Socialism, (Belgrade, 1950), p. 17. [Originally in Borba, "Na novim putevima socijalizma," (March 19, 1950), pp. 3-4].

14. Ibid., p. 9.

15. Ibid., pp. 12-18.

16. Djilas, "Klasa ili kasta," p. 2. Most of Djilas' remarks in this early period (1950-53) are directly applied to the Soviet Union, but occasionally he indicates their relevance to the Yugoslav situation "because the same objective bureaucratic tendencies are found and will continue to be so for a long time in our own reality." "Diskusija izmedju Stanovnika, Kristla i Djilasa," loc. cit., p. 82.

17. Ibid., p. 2.

18. "Diskusija izmedju . . . Djilasa," loc. cit., p. 86.

19. Ibid., p. 91.

20. Ibid., p. 88. This statement is equivalent to Trotsky's partly "bourgeois character of the state," in The Revolution Betrayed, (New York, April 6, 1950), p. 255.

21. Djilas, "Klasa ili kasta," Borba, p. 2.

22. Djilas, "Diskusija izmedju . . . Djilasa," Klasa ili kasta April 6, 1950, p. 90.

23. Ibid., p. 89.

24. See note 23 above.

25. Djilas, On the New Roads of Socialism, pp. 10-20.

26. Djilas, "Diskusija izmedju . . . Djilasa," Klasa ili kasta, p. 91.

27. Ibid., p. 90.

28. See note 27 above.

29. Djilas, "Klasa ili kasta," Borba, (April 6, 1950), p. 4.

30. Djilas, On the New Roads of Socialism, p. 20.

31. Djilas, "Diskusija izmedju . . . Djilasa," Klasa ili kasta, p. 88.

32. Ibid., p. 88.

33. See note 32 above.

34. Djilas, On the New Roads of Socialism, pp. 33-34.

35. Djilas, On the New Roads of Socialism, pp. 33-34.

36. Djilas, "Diskusija izmedju . . . Djilasa," Klasa ili kasta, p. 82.

37. For only one perspective of the modernization process see, Cyril Black, The Dynamics of Modernization, (Princeton, 1961).

38. Djilas, On the New Roads of Socialism, p. 19.

39. Ibid., pp. 14-15.

40. See Djilas, The Unperfect Society, (New York, 1969), p. 221.

41. Djilas, "Glavna snaga socijalizma," Borba, (May 3, 1952), p. 2.

42. Djilas, "New Ideas," in Anatomy of a Moral, (New York, 1959), pp. 117-119. Originally in Borba, (January 1-3, 1954).

43. Ibid.,. p. 88.

44. Ibid.,. p. 89.

45. Djilas, "Subjective Forces," Anatomy of a Moral, p. 107.

46. Djilas, "Reply, *Anatomy of a Moral,* p. 101.

47. Ibid.,. p. 103.

48. Djilas, "New Contents," *Anatomy of a Moral,* p. 36.

49. Djilas, "Objektivne snage," *Borba,* (December 29, 1953), p. 3.

50. Djilas, "Subjective Forces," *Anatomy of a Moral,* p. 106.

51. Djilas, "Objektivne snage," *Borba,* (December 29, 1953), p. 3. (This article was omitted from the *Anatomy of a Moral* collection.)

52. Djilas in my estimation magnifies the conflict considerably: "this misunderstanding (of Yugoslav esprit) has been expressed in the bureaucratic form by the Cominform since 1948, and now in a bourgeois manner in the "Trieste crisis." "Jugoslavija," *Borba,* (October 18, 1953), p. 3. (This article is omitted from *Anatomy of a Moral.*)

53. Ibid., p. 3.

54. See note 53 above.

55. See note 53 above. Popular unity is also important in view of the fact that one bureaucratic feature is centrifugal localism. For additional information on this issue, see Jovan Djordjević, "Local Self-Government in Yugoslavia," *American Slavic and East European Review* 12, No. 2, (April, 1953), pp. 188-200.

56. Djilas, "League or Party," *Anatomy of a Moral,* pp. 133-134.

57. Ibid., p. 135.

58. Ibid., p. 141.

59. Ibid., pp. 141-142.

60. Ibid.,. p. 140.

61. Ibid., p. 136.

62. Ibid., p. 137. Edvard Kardelj was the first to mention the "withering away of the Party," but significantly it was not discussed at all at the Sixth Conference of the Communist Party of Yugoslavia in 1952.

63. Djilas, "Ideal," *Anatomy of a Moral,* p. 84.

64. Djilas, "Without a Conclusion," *Anatomy of a Moral,* pp. 73-74.

65. Djilas, *Conversations with Stalin,* (New York, 1962), p. 58.

66. Djilas, *Anatomy of a Moral,* p. 76.

67. Djilas, "Is There a Goal," *Anatomy of a Moral,* p. 77.

68. Ibid.,. p. 54.

69. Ibid.,. p. 55.

70. Djilas, *The New Class,* (New York, 1957), p. 44.

71. Ibid., p. 35.

72. Ibid., p. 61.

73. Ibid., p. 44.

74. Ibid., pp. 44-45.

75. Marx, of course, says that property is a legal expression, but Djilas does not bother with that point here. For a philosophical explanation see, Eric Fromm, *Marx's Concept of Man,* (New York, 1961), pp. 58-69.

76. V.I. Lenin, *The State and Revolution,* (New York, 1971), p. 22.

77. Djilas, *The New Class,* p. 87.

78. Ibid., p. 97.

79. Ibid., p. 69.

80. Ibid., pp. 145-46.

81. Ibid., p. 84.

82. Ibid., p. 48.

83. Ibid., pp. 168-69.

84. This is not a theory of only Soviet history. The fate of Yugoslav Communism was to unify these three phases in the single personality of Tito, along with national and personal characteristics. Djilas, *The New Class*, pp. 53-57.

85. On the views of ideology and ideological transformation, see Leon Gersković, *O Socijalistickoj demokraciji*, (Belgrade, 1953), pp. 15-34; Dušan Nedeljković, *Nasa filosofija u borbi za socijalizam*, (Belgrade, 1952); and Ivan Avakumović, *History of the Communist Party of Yugoslavia*, (Aberdeen, 1964).

86. For an analysis of Trotsky on this point, see Richard Day, *Leon Trotsky and the Politics of Economic Isolation*, (New York, 1973), pp. 14-26. Also see, Alec Nove, "New Light on Trotsky's Economic Views," *Slavic Review*, (Spring, 1981), pp. 84-97.

87. Djilas, *The New Class*, p. 105.

88. Ibid., pp. 56-57.

89. Ibid., p. 21.

90. Ibid., p. 124.

91. Ibid., p. 155.

92. Ibid., pp. 84-85.

93. Ibid., p. 40.

94. Ibid.,., pp. 87-88.

95. Ibid.,. p. 5.

96. Carl Schorske, *German Social Democracy 1905-1917*, (Cambridge, Massachusetts, 1955).

97. Djilas, *The New Class*, p. 9.

98. Ibid., p. 6.

99. In his words, "Communism is the most rational and intoxicating ideology for those who want to skip over centuries of slavery and backwardness and to bypass reality itself." *Conversations with Stalin*, p. 59.

100. Adam B. Ulam, *The Unfinished Revolution*, (New York, 1960), pp. 107-133.

101. Ulam, "The Historical Role of Marxism," in *The New Face of Soviet Totalitarianism*, (Cambridge, Massachusetts, 1963), p. 17.

102. Ibid., p. 18.

103. Ibid., p. 23.

104. Djilas, *The New Class*, pp. 11-12.

105. Ibid., p. 19.

106. Ibid., p. 41.

107. Ibid.,. p. 41.

We may even say that the more conspicuously a bureaucracy is distinguished by its zeal, by its sense of duty, and by its devotion, the more also will it show itself to be petty, narrow, rigid and illiberal.

Robert Michels, *Political Parties*

7

The Significance of
Communist Bureaucracy

What kind of conclusions can we come to about Trotsky's and Djilas' critique of Soviet and Yugoslav bureaucracy? What are the merits and demerits
of their analysis? In 1932, in his autobiography, Trotsky referred to a conversation he once had with Lenin a decade earlier in which the subject of
"bureaucratic development" was discussed.[1] In Trotsky's opinion, Lenin
was not only concerned but in fact was deeply disturbed by the growth of
"bureaucratic elements."[2] Lenin agreed, if we are to believe Trotsky, that the
bureaucracy had infested not only state institutions but the party as well and
that he offered to form a "bloc" with Trotsky against the bureaucracy in
general, and against the Orgburo in particular.[3] At the time of this discussion
in 1922, it was extremely difficult to believe that bureaucratism could have
been eliminated without reverting to conditions of civil war, and anarchy,
nor could the ideas of doing so have appealed to Lenin, much less to
Trotsky. The more extreme the economic measures adopted and the popular resistance to them, the more concentrated in fewer and fewer hands did
political power have to become. The more systematic and planned the
politics, the more did the implementation and supervision have to be entrusted to a technical and administrative elite. Bureaucratization may
therefore be viewed as the direct function, on the one hand, of underdevelopment and economic impoverishment and, on the other, of the pre-
ponderant and domineering role which the state had to assume, especially
since private enterprise was to be abolished.[4]

In addition, it should be pointed out that aside from the specific Russian
conditions between 1917 and 1940, which necessarily encouraged bureau-

cratic growth, the central economic objective of Lenin's and Stalin's Russia was industrialization. This process itself required the formation of bureaucratic bodies and procedures. In the light of the West European experience in the nineteenth century, no one in Russia could be unaware of the fact that the modern industrial state could not function without large, formal, and impersonal bureaucratic institutions. If this were so in capitalist economies, where the state supposedly resisted large-scale intervention, how much more so would it be the case in a communist economy where the state took upon itself to control and direct the whole industrial sector? Neither Lenin, who in his *State and Revolution* had greatly underestimated the complexities of economic administration, not Trotsky, who though he did not underestimate them often evaded the implications of the problem, could resolve the contradiction between economic objectives and socialist ideals.[5]

As much as Trotsky would prefer to argue otherwise, the Stalinist regime in the twenties and thirties represented only in part the rule of bureaucracy. In fact, the bureaucracy was subject to and often decimated by a dictator and an institution which stood largely outside the formal, bureaucratic framework. Stalin and the secret police leaned on the bureaucracy but were not so dependent on it as Trotsky would like us to believe. Together, Stalin and the secret police contributed those elements which altered the Soviet regime into one of "totalitarianism," utilizing this term in its descriptive, not emotional sense. Trotsky recognized the peculiar nature of modern totalitarian dictatorships[6] by making the distinction between the bureaucratic apparatus, the source of Thermidor for him, and the political one, Bonapartism. Although based on enormous bureaucratic edifices, modern dictatorships can not be identified and explained solely by this phenomenon.

Yet here again Trotsky refused to go beyond Stalin in order to explore the origins of Soviet totalitarianism. Throughout his career in the twenties and thirties, he not only defended Lenin's dictatorship as far more democratic and enlightened than that of Stalin but he also claimed that if Bolshevism, as opposed to Stalinism, had won out in 1924 totalitarianism would not have come into being.[7] Consequently, he regarded such factors as a "Leninist" party—its internal freedom of expression, its open-mindedness on party issues, as well as its dedication to collective government—as Leninist features completely alien to Stalin's dictatorship. One need not deny that differences existed between Lenin's regime and that of Stalin, or that a dictator other than Stalin might have been less fanatical in his pursuit of absolute power, in order to maintain that the two systems of government were of the same pedigree. Though their progeny differed, the difference was one of degree, not of kind. Neither need one dismiss the relevance of Trotsky's claim, that the "degeneration" of Bolshevism was a consequence of the failure of the "world revolution" to materialize, in order to argue that the overall developments in the Soviet Union had a momentum of their own. In spite of his many brilliant insights about Stalin's totalitarianism,

Trotsky's final misunderstanding of it was similar to his misunderstanding of the bureaucracy—he could not, or would not, see that it was rooted not only in the conditions of the Russian Revolution but in the very aspirations of the latter.

From an institutional point of view, the issue is not whether Lenin was or was not more enlightened, or even more tolerant, than Stalin; the issue is the relationship between politics and society—and so it is of great significance that under Lenin too the one-party system was the cornerstone of political legitimacy and action.[8] Totalitarianism, whether of the left or of the right, is not sufficiently defined or explained by having recourse to its institutional aspects alone. Its uniqueness lies in two additional areas—the politicization of all spheres of individual and social life and the total economic mobilization and control of Soviet society. These features grew simultaneously out of the critical nature of the socioeconomic problems and out of the revolutionary manner in which they were to be solved by the Bolshevik Party coming to power. For this latter purpose Marxism had to be transformed into a mass ideology having two essential functions—providing a system of beliefs and therefore solutions to problems, and acting as a mobilizing force. As a result there emerged the tradition of ideological legitimization and exclusivity so that, while the ideology could be adjusted or adapted to specific needs in practice, it always remained the criterion for pronouncing upon the legitimacy of private and public behavior.[9]

The fanaticism usually associated with Soviet ideology under Stalin should not lead to the conclusion that the Stalinist regime was without any social rationale, or that it was always "dysfunctional" from the point of view of the ultimate goal of Soviet society. In so far as Stalin was determined to carry out a social and economic revolution (and collectivization surely constitutes such a revolution) total regimentation was a prerequisite, given the socioeconomic conditions, the unreliability of spontaneous support and, in fact, the real and anticipated popular resistance. The show trials, the purges and the accompanying terror had a significant purpose. They affirmed Stalin's legitimacy as a dictator, discouraged oppositional groups, and demonstrated potential and actual power to the population. Trials, purges and terror also prevented peripheral political focuses of power from forming in the party, the army and the bureaucracy. The terror against the population established and maintained an "atomized," a powerless mass society. This did not exclude the phenomenon of "Stakhanovism" or, as Trotsky sometimes overemphasized, a system of favoritism and privileges for the bureaucrats. The general tendency was towards underplaying social differences and antagonisms and not merely for reasons of Marxist dogma. As Trotsky pointed out, the 1936 Stalinist constitution, declaring that the Soviet Union was then a socialist society, had the purpose of establishing at least the semblance of unity and homogeneity.

Stalin's purges cannot be explained rationally alone. His reign of terror was also extremely counterproductive—producing instability and fear of his cadres; economic mismanagement and anarchy; large-scale obliteration of army officers, administrative personnel and, not to mention, the humanistic intelligentsia.[10] But the function of totalitarianism cannot be dismissed when evaluating the nature of Stalin's goals or achievements. This is certainly not to justify Stalinism or Soviet totalitarianism but to see both in their historical context of underdevelopment, Bolshevism and bureaucratism.

The fact that Trotsky, though pointing out some of these issues, did not bring them to a full conclusion, may explain the source of many of his unsatisfactory interpretations of Stalinism—his failure to comprehend Stalinism as part of a larger historical continuum stretching back before the Revolution, not merely to 1924. Consider, for example, Trotsky's obsession with Stalinism as a reincarnation of the French Thermidor—following, supposedly, upon the "Jacobin" phase of Lenin. It is clear that if Lenin was a "Jacobin" it was not in the sense in which Trotsky portrayed him—as a revolutionary concerned above all with ideological principles, even purity—but rather in the sense of a professional, elitist revolutionary prepared to exercise political power in a pragmatic, concrete fashion. Lenin wanted to bring about radical change, but without undue concern for ideological or theoretical implications. As one historian has argued, this was Lenin's greatest strength.[11] But was Stalin any less "Jacobin"? After all, it was Stalin who carried out a program of fundamental, revolutionary change in the socio-economic structure of the Soviet Union. How was it possible, then, when comparing Stalin's with Lenin's regime, to assert that the former constituted a period of retrenchment, stabilization and conservatism, those features which Trotsky identified with Thermidor? That he should make this assertion shows how Trotsky's determination to place Stalin outside the Bolshevik tradition could lead to absurdity.

Trotsky's ideas concerning the nature of Soviet bureaucracy and the character of Stalin led to similar results. He believed that every bureaucracy is prepared to pursue only such policies as best conserve order and stability; and since Stalin had built his empire on the shoulders of the bureaucracy instead of the revolutionary party, his reign had to be conservative or even reactionary. This obviously underestimated the extent to which a bureaucracy, in the conditions of Soviet society, could be mobilized for, and could see its interests bound up with, radical change leading to rationalized, modern, and efficient economic arrangements, whether or not these were eventually achieved.[12] But Trotsky also underestimated the political, non-bureaucratic mentality of Stalin. Though establishing and building his power through an organizational framework, he was not himself a prisoner of the organization.[13] Trotsky partly recognized this by identifying Stalin's rule as Bonapartist in character; yet the image of Stalin as embodying the bureaucratic and thus nonrevolutionary personality persisted in his analysis. And this, in turn, led him to underestimate the extent to which Stalin remained independent of the bureaucracy, utilizing it but ruling through less formal, more personal instruments of power. The Thermidorian analogy was out of place, and Trotsky's uneasy modifications of it were a reflection of the difficulties of adapting Soviet reality to the French model.

There was much that was out of place also in Trotsky's obsession with the Soviet Union as a workers' state, albeit a "degenerated" one. To make this claim involved a concession that Stalin did not altogether mark a break with the Russian Revolution; conversely, however, it revealed again Trotsky's illusion about the Revolution, namely that it had in fact created a workers' state. Those of Trotsky's followers who in the late 1930s began to propound the "bureaucratic collectivist" thesis reevaluated their earlier political positions by looking for the source of Stalinism, not in Stalin, but in Bolshevism and in the relationship between the state and the modern economy. Whatever the validity of this thesis, it had the merit of having escaped the pitfall of thinking in terms of fixed Marxist social categories.[14] It cannot be said that Trotsky avoided this pitfall; he made too much of the formal fact that the means of production in the Soviet Union were nationalized and too little of the substantial fact that they were under the direct influence and total control of the political leadership.

Djilas, by comparison with Trotsky, came to far more sweeping and in a sense radical conclusions. Whereas in *The New Class* he had detailed his denunciation of Yugoslav and Soviet bureaucracy, in *The Unperfect Society,* published in 1969, he went beyond *The New Class* and denounced Leninism, Marxism-Leninism and, to a considerable extent, Marxism itself. The wheel had come full circle.

From this point of view, *The Unperfect Society* was ambivalent. Sometimes it reads like the meditations of a statesman considering the social, political and economic problems of the future of his country. But it also reads, more often than not, like the final valedictory of Djilas the politician, free at long last to go back to his first loves: culture, literature, philosophy—in a way like Lukacs. "As for myself," he wrote, "however much I may secretly crave power, I hope with all my heart that this cup will pass from me and that I shall remain safely ensconced in the original toil-worn innocence of my ideas."[15] The style of *The Unperfect Society* itself, constantly shifting from the ground of the discussion of the merits and demerits of Marxism and of socialist ownership to that of his own bitter personal experiences, makes it sometimes difficult to follow. In some ways even more so than *The New Class* and the ironical *Conversations with Stalin,* the book reads as if it had been written in jail. Were these the actual effects of the long years of prison life or of the mental imprisonment from which he attempted so hard to escape? But however one regards it, *The Unperfect Society*, along with *The New Class*, remains significant for all students of communist and socialist bureaucracy.

It has been indicated in this study that Djilas seriously modified his conception of bureaucracy. He has concluded that politics are the key instruments for realizing some such "ultimate goal" as communism. But indifference to means currently employed makes one careless about the high price extracted, a process which guarantees that the consequences will be other than the goal intended. There is apparently something about brute reality that does not lend itself to sudden and comprehensive aspects of progress. "The human being under Communism, as in all situations at all times in human history, has proved too intractable and quite unfit for any ideal models, particularly those that seek to restrict his boundaries and prescribe his destiny."[16] This being the case, what one should take seriously is the quality of the means; the choice of one policy over another is in effect a choice of one set of means over another.[17]

Joined together with this significant doubt concerning politics is Djilas' analysis of what in the modern society is the key organizational weapon for realizing ideas, the bureaucracy. Bureaucratic structure can be considered one of the means that deeply disturbs Djilas. The bureaucracy functions as an instrument that can be used by varied interests, economic and political. Bureaucracy, a technically superior rationalization of means to ends, must of necessity involve some conception of efficiency, a value often emphasized exclusively. But it includes, or ought to include, considerations broader than that—after all, there are human beings impinged upon, the bureaucrats themselves and those on whom they do their work. Exclusively to bureaucratize individuals is to compartmentalize and diminish their existence, overlooking many values that are nonrationalizable, even nonlogical, but nevertheless part of their psychological baggage. If modern industrial man's social life has suffered atomization, then he cries out for sources of solidarity and integration, which the bureaucratic world cannot provide because these are not values that efficiency-minded organization espoused or attempted to institutionalize either in the Soviet Union or Yugoslavia.[18] Therefore, Djilas has quite correctly sensed that the politics he has known in Yugoslavia is divisive. Politics that is exclusively rationalized and goal oriented, even in a nonbureaucratic form such as interclan rivalries, is lacking precisely in the values of community. Thus Djilas is prepared to abandon much of that kind of politics and that sort of organization even if their human deficiencies have come through default rather than conscious omission. What he used to call "socialist social relations" have value here and now, beyond the technical task of realizing communism most efficiently.[19]

An apparently paradoxical case could also be made, I believe, that Djilas is not rejecting the rationalization process but in fact is arguing that there is not enough. Otherwise stated, he is criticizing the new class bureaucracies in both the Soviet Union and Yugoslavia for not being fully developed and depersonalized bureaucracies whose chief talent is to eliminate love, hate, and all other emotional elements from official business. For Djilas, the bureaucracy appropriates the lion's share of the articles of consumption to its own members and utilizes the state to implement laws to protect itself. If the main goal of communist bureaucracy is the "honor of privilege,"[20] then the privileged new class bureaucrats are not very good administrators. They distribute the goals and products of the state as if the property belonged to them—indeed they make up the "new ownership class"—which then means that a clear distinction between official activity and the sphere of private life which characterizes bureaucracies has not been realized.

NOTES

1. Leon Trotsky, *My Life*, (New York, 1970), pp. 215-216. Also, see his *The Real Situation in Russia*, (New York, 1928), pp. 301-303.

2. Trotsky claimed that Lenin said: "Yes, our bureaucratism is something monstrous." Ibid., p. 215.

3. Ibid., p. 216.

4. Whatever the merits of a capitalist as against a nationalized (socialist/communist) economy there is no doubt that the role of the bureaucracy is much stronger in the former. For an interesting discussion of this issue, see Daniel Bell, "The Post-Industrial Society: The Evolution of an Idea," *Survey*, (Spring, 1971), pp. 139-42.

5. For another view of this problem, see Barrington Moore, Jr., *Soviet Politics: The Dilemma of Power*, (New York, 1965).

6. There are numerous books dealing with the nature of totalitarianism. See, especially, Hannah Arendt, *The Origins of Totalitarianism*, (New York, 1958); Eric Fromm, *The Fear of Freedom*, (London, 1942); Leonard Schapiro, *Totalitarianism*, (London, 1970); and Raymond Aron, *Democracy and Totalitarianism*, (New York, 1968).

7. Trotsky, *Stalinism and Bolshevism*, p. 18.

8. For an account of how Lenin abolished all opposition and established the one-system government from 1917 to 1922, see Leonard Schapiro, *The Origins of Communist Autocracy*, (New York, 1960), pp. 36-73.

9. Nathan Leites, *A Study of Bolshevism*, (Glencoe, 1953), pp. 23-25.

10. On the treatment of the intelligentsia see, Nadezhda Mandelstam, *Hope against Hope*, (New York, 1970).

11. David Shub, *Lenin: A Biography*, (New York, Doubleday 1948), pp. 366-74.

12. Barrington Moore, Jr., *Soviet Politics: The Dilemma of Power*, p. 78.

13. Adam Ulam, *Stalin: The Man and His Era*, (New York, Basic Books 1974), p. 46.

14. For a Marxist view that the Soviet Union represents a system of state capitalism, see Raya Dunayevskaya, *Marxism and Freedom*, (New York 1958).

15. Milovan Djilas, *The Unperfect Society*, (New York, 1969), p. 176.

16. Ibid., p. 18.

17. Ibid., p. 283.

18. On this issue see, Daniel Bell, "The Post-Industrial Society," *Survey*, (Spring, 1971), pp. 140-43.

19. Max Weber, *The Theory of Economic and Social Organizations*, (New York, 1947), pp. 215-16.

20. Ibid., p. 254.

Selected Bibliography

The bibliography is arranged as follows: (I) Theories of Bureaucracy; (II) Works by Leon Trotsky; (III) General works on Trotsky and the Soviet Union; (IV) Works by Milovan Djilas; and (V) General works on Djilas and Yugoslavia.

I. Theories of Bureaucracy

This is an extremely selective bibliography. I am well aware that extensive literature exists on many aspects of the bureaucratic phenomenon. I have attempted to utilize the studies most relevant to my analysis of Trotsky and Djilas.

Afanasev, V.G., *Nauchnoe Upravlenie Obshchestvom*. Moscow: Politzdat, 1968.

Albrow, Martin, *Bureaucracy*. London: Oxford University Press, 1970.

Armstrong, John A., *The Soviet Bureaucratic Elite: A Case Study of Ukrainian Apparatus*. New York: Frederick A. Praeger, 1959.

Azreal, Jeremy R., *Managerial Power and Soviet Politics*. Cambridge, Massachusetts: Harvard University Press, 1966.

Bachrach, Peter, *The Theory of Democratic Elitism: A Critique*. Boston: Little, Brown, 1967.

Barghoorn, Frederick C., *Politics in the USSR: A Country Study*. Boston: Little, Brown, 1966.

Beck, Carl, "Party Control and Bureaucratization in Czechoslavakia," *Journal of Politics*, Vol. 23, (May, 1961), pp. 279-94.

Bell, Daniel, *The Coming of Post-Industrial Society: A Venture in Social Forecasting*. New York: Basic Books, 1973.

Bendix, Reinhard, "Socialism and the Theory of Bureaucracy," *The Canadian Journal of Economics and Politics*, Vol. 16, (1950), pp. 501-14.

Blau, Peter M., and Meyer, M.W., *Bureaucracy in Modern Society*. New York: Random House, 1971.

Brzezinski, Z., and Huntington, Samuel P., *Political Power USA/USSR*. New York: Viking, 1964.

Burnham, James, *The Managerial Revolution*. New York: John Day, 1941.

Churchward, L.C., "Bureaucracy—USA:USSR," *Coexistence*, Vol. 5, (1968), pp. 202-225.

Crozier, Michel, *The Bureaucratic Phenomenon*. Chicago: University of Chicago Press, 1964.

Delaney, William, "The Development and Decline of Patrimonial and Bureaucratic Administration," *Administrative Science Quarterly*, 7, (March, 1963), pp. 453-472.

Deutscher, Isaac, "Roots of Bureaucracy," *Canadian Slavic Studies*, No. 3, (Fall, 1969), pp. 453-472.

Diamant, Alfred, "The Bureaucratic Model: Max Weber Rejected, Rediscovered, Resurrected," in Heady, Ferrel, and Stokes, Sybil L., eds., *Papers in Comparative Administration*. Ann Arbor: University of Michigan Press, 1962, pp. 59-96.

Downs, Anthony, *Inside Bureaucracy*. Brown: Little, Brown, 1967.

Eisenstadt, S.N., "Political Struggle in Bureaucratic Societies," *World Politics*, Vol. 9, (October, 1956), pp. 15-36.

Fainsod, Merle, *How Russia is Ruled*. Cambridge, Massachusetts: Harvard University Press, 1953.

Galbraith, John Kenneth, *The New Industrial State*. Boston: Houghton Mifflin, 1967.

Gerth, H.H., and Mills, C. Wright, *From Max Weber: Essays in Sociology*. New York: Oxford University Press, 1946.

Gogol, Nikolai, *The Governor Inspector*. Translated by D.J. Campbell, London: Sylvan Press, 1947.

Gouldner, Alvin, "The Metaphysical Pathos and the Theory of Bureaucracy," in Etzioni, Amitai, ed., *Complex Organizations*. New York: Holt, Rinehart, 1961.

Gramsci, Antonio, *The Modern Prince and Other Writings*. New York: International Publishers, 1959.

Gramsci, Antonio, *Selections from the Prison Notebooks of Antonio Gramsci*. New York: International Publishers, 1971.

Kafka, Franz, *The Castle*. New York: Random House, 1974.

Merton, Robert K., *Social Theory and Social Structure*. New York: The Free Press, 1968.

Merton, Robert K., ed., *Reader in Bureaucracy*. New York: The Free Press, 1952.

Meyer, Alfred G., *The Soviet Political System*. New York: Random House, 1965.

Michels, Robert, *Political Parties: A Sociological Study of the Oligarchic Tendencies of Modern Democracy*. New York: The Free Press, 1962.

Mills, C. Wright, *The Power Elite*. New York: McGraw-Hill, 1939.

Mommsen, Wolfgang J., *The Age of Bureaucracy: Perspectives on the Political Sociology of Max Weber*. New York: Harper & Row, 1974.

Moore, Barrington Jr., *Social Origins of Dictatorship and Democracy: Lord and Pea-*

sant in the Making of the Modern World. Boston: Beacon Press, 1966.

Moore, Barrington Jr., *Soviet Politics: The Dilemma of Power: The Role of Ideas in Social Change.* New York: Harper & Row, 1965.

Morstein, Marx F., "Bureaucracy and Dictatorship," *Review of Politics*, No. 3, (1941), pp. 110-117.

Mosca, Gaetano, *The Ruling Class.* Translated by Hannah D. Kahn, New York: McGraw-Hill, 1939.

Nove, Alec, "Is There a Ruling Class in the USSR?", *Soviet Studies*, No. 27, (October, 1975), pp. 615-638.

Orlovsky, Daniel T., "Recent Studies on the Russian Bureaucracy," *Russian Review*, No. 35, (October, 1976), pp. 448-467.

Rigby, T.H., *Communist Party Membership in the USSR, 1917-1967.* Princeton: Princeton University Press, 1968.

Rigby, T.H., "Traditional, Market and Organization Societies and the USSR," *World Politics*, No. 16, (July, 1964), pp. 539-557.

Rizzi, Bruno, *La Bureaucratisation du Monde.* Paris: Pons, 1939.

Rosenberg, Hans, *Bureaucracy, Aristocracy and Autocracy: The Prussian Experience, 1660-1815.* Cambridge, Massachusetts: Harvard University Press, 1958.

Shachtman, Max, *The Bureaucratic Revolution: The Rise of the Stalinist State.* New York: Donald Press, 1962.

Sullivan, John, *The Dead Hand of Bureaucracy.* Indianapolis: Bobbs-Merrill, 1940.

Warnotte, Daniel, "Bureaucratie et le fonctoinaire," *Revue de l' Institut de Sociologie*, No. 17, (1937), pp. 219-260.

Weber, Max, *The Theory of Economic and Social Organization.* Translated by A.M. Henderson and T. Parsons, New York: Oxford University Press, 1947.

Wittfogel, Karl, *Oriental Despotism.* New Haven: Yale University Press, 1957.

II. Works by Leon Trotsky

Trotsky was an extremely prolific writer and revolutionary. One frequently wonders how he had the time to write so much and also possess the energy to make a revolution. Most of Trotsky's works are now available. For an excellent bibliography of his publications, consult Louis Sinclair, *Leon Trotsky: A Bibliography*, Stanford: Hoover Institution Press, 1972.

Main Sources

Biulleten Oppozitsii. This is Trotsky's most important political journal between 1930 and 1940. It contains numerous articles, speeches and critiques.

Sochieneniia, Volumes II-XV. The Soviet Publishing House (Gosizdat) intended to publish twenty-three volumes of Trotsky's works in the early twenties but after his expulsion from the Party in 1927, Stalin suspended the publications. As a result, only twelve volumes were completed.

The Trotsky Archives. (Houghton Library, Harvard University). A gold mine of information containing thousands of articles, pamphlets, notes, correspondence and other materials from 1917 to 1940. A bibliographical guide to all of these works is now available. See Guide to the Papers of Leon Trotsky and Related Collections in the Harvard College Library.

Individual works consulted

1905. New York: Random House, 1972.

The Basic Writings of Leon Trotsky. Edited by Irving Howe, New York: Random House, 1963.

The Case of Leon Trotsky. New York: Harper & Brothers, 1938.

The Challenge of the Left Opposition. Edited with an introduction by Naomi Allen. New York: Pathfinder Press, 1975.

Diary in Exile. 1935, translated by Elena Zradnaia, London: Oxford University Press, 1959.

The Essential Trotsky. London: G. Allen & Unwin, 1963.

Fascism, What It Is, How to Fight It; A Compilation. New York: Pioneer Publishers, 1944.

The First Five Years of the Communist International. 2 volumes, 2d ed., New York: International Publishers, 1972.

The History of the Russian Revolution. Translated by Max Eastman, single volume, Ann Arbor: University of Michigan Press, 1960.

I Stake My Life! New York: Pioneer Publishers, 1937.

In Defence of Marxism. New York: Pioneer Publishers, 1942.

Leon Trotsky on the Jewish Question. New York: Pathfinder Press, 1970.

Leon Trotsky Speaks. New York: Pathfinder Press, 1972.

Lessons of October. New York: Pioneer Publishers, 1937.

Literature and Revolution. London: Russell & Russell, 1957.

Military Writings. New York: Pathfinder Press, 1969.

My Life. 2d ed., New York: Pathfinder Press, 1970.

Novyi Kurs. Moscow, 1923. Also translated into English: *The Struggle for the New Course.* Ann Arbor: University of Michigan Press, 1965.

O Lenine: Materiali dla Biografa. Moscow: Progress Publishers, 1924. Also translated into English: *On Lenin: Notes Towards a Biography.* New York: Capricon Books, 1971.

Our Revolution. New York: Henry Holt, 1918.

The Permanent Revolution. New York: Merit Publishers, 1969.

Piat let Kominterna. Moscow: Progress Publishers, 1924.

Problems of the Chinese Revolution. 3d ed. New York: Paragon Book Reprint Corp., 1966.

The Real Situation in Russia. New York: Harcourt, Brace & Company, 1928.

The Revolution Betrayed. 5th ed., New York: Pathfinder Press, 1972.

The Soviet Union and the Fourth International, The Class Nature of the Soviet State. New York: Communist League of America, 1934.

The Spanish Revolution, 1931-1939. New York: Pathfinder Press, 1973.

Stalin: An Appraisal of the Man and His Influences. Edited and translated by Charles

Malamuth, New York: Harper & Row, 1946.

The Stalin School of Falsification. 2d ed., New York: Pioneer Publishers, 1962.

Stalinism and Bolshevism; Concerning the Historical and Theoretical Roots of the Fourth International. New York: Pioneer Publishers, 1937.

The Struggle Against Fascism in Germany. New York: Pathfinder Press, 1971.

Tasks Before the Twelfth Congress of the Russian Communist Party. London: New Park Publications, 1975.

Terrorism and Communism; A Reply to Karl Kautsky. 2d ed. Ann Arbor: University of Michigan Press, 1972.

Their Morals and Ours. New York: Pioneer Publishers, 1942.

The Third International After Lenin. New York: Pioneer Publishers, 1972.

The Trotsky Papers, 1917-1922. Vol. I, 1917-1919, Vol. II, 1920-1922; edited by Jan M. Meijer, The Hague: Mouton, 1971.

Voina i Revoliutsiia. 2 vols, 2d ed., Moscow-Petrograd: Progress Publishers, 1923.

What Hitler Wants. New York: John Day Co., 1933.

What Next? Vital Questions for the German Proletariat. New York: Pioneer Publishers, 1932.

Whither England? New York: International Publishers, 1925.

Whither France? New York: Pioneer Publishers, 1936.

Whither Russia? Towards Capitalism or Socialism. New York: International Publishers, 1926.

Writings of Leon Trotsky (1929-40). New York: Pathfinder Press, 1975.

III. General Works on Trotsky and the Soviet Union

Avrich, Paul, *Kronstadt 1921.* Princeton: Princeton University Press, 1970.

Berlin, Isaiah, *Karl Marx: His Life and Environment.* 3d ed., London: Oxford University Press, 1963.

Black, Cyril E., *The Dynamics of Modernization: A Study in Comparative History.* New York: Harper & Row, 1966.

Cannon, James, *The History of American Trotskyism.* New York: Pioneer Publishers, 1944.

Carmichael, Joel, *Trotsky: An Appreciation of His Life.* New York: St. Martin's Press, 1975.

Carr, E.H., *A History of Soviet Russia.* 14 Volumes: Vol. 1-3, *The Bolshevik Revolution, 1917-1923;* Vol. 4, *The Interregnum, 1923-1924;* Vol. 5-8, *Socialism in One Country, 1924-1926;* Vol. 9-14 (9-10 with R.W. Davies), *Foundations of a Planned Economy, 1926-1929.* London: The Macmillan Company, 1951-1978.

Ciliga, Anton, *The Kronstadt Revolt.* London: Freedom Press, 1942.

Ciliga, Anton, *Au pays du Grand Mensonge.* Paris: Gallimard, 1937.

Cohen, Stephen F., *Bukharin and the Bolshevik Revolution.* New York: Alfred A. Knopf, 1973.

Daniels, R.V., *The Conscience of the Revolution: Communist Opposition in the Soviet Union.* New York: Simon & Schuster, 1969.

Day, Richard B., *Leon Trotsky and the Politics of Economic Isolation.* Cambridge, England: Cambridge University Press, 1973.

Deutscher, Isaac, *The Prophet Armed: Trotsky: 1879-1921.* New York: Vintage Books, 1965.

Deutscher, Isaac, *The Prophet Unarmed: Trotsky: 1921-1929.* New York: Vintage Books, 1959.

Deutscher, Isaac, *The Prophet Outcast: Trotsky: 1929-1940.* New York: Vintage Books, 1963.

Dunayevskaya, Raya, *Marxism and Freedom.* New York: Bookman Associates, 1958.

Eastman, Max, *Leon Trotsky: The Portrait of a Youth.* New York: Greenberg, Inc., 1925.

Eastman, Max, *Since Lenin Died.* London: The Labor Publishing Company Ltd., 1925.

Erlich, Alexander, *The Soviet Industrialization Debate, 1924-1928.* Cambridge, Massachusetts: Harvard University Press, 1960.

Fainsod, Merle, *How Russia is Ruled.* Cambridge, Massachusetts: Harvard University Press, 1963.

Fainsod, Merle, *Smolensk under Soviet Rule.* Cambridge, Massachusetts, Harvard University Press, 1958.

Gleason, Abbott, *Young Russia.* New York: The Viking Press, 1980.

Goldman, Emma, *Trotsky Protests Too Much.* New York: Schoken Books, 1968.

Hilferding, Rudolf, "State Capitalism or Totalitarian State Economy," *Modern Review,* (June, 1947), pp. 266-271.

Howe, Irving, *Trotsky.* New York: Viking Press, 1978.

Hunt, Carew, R.N., *The Theory and Practice of Communism.* Harmondsworth: Penguin, 1963.

Kautsky, Karl, *Terrorism and Communism.* New York: The Rand School Press, 1946.

Keep, John L.H., *The Russian Revolution.* New York: W.W. Norton, 1976.

Krasso, Nicholas, ed., *Trotsky: The Great Debate Renewed.* St. Louis: New Critics Press, 1972.

Lane, David, *The End of Inequality? Stratification under State Socialism.* Harmondswoth: Weidenfeld and Nicholson, 1971.

Lenin, V.I., *Polnoe Sobranie Sochinenii.* 5th ed., Moscow: Progress Publishers, 1958-1965.

Lenin, V.I., *Selected Works,* 3 vol., Moscow: Progress Publishers, 1963.

Lichtheim, George, "Reflections on Trotsky," in his *The Concept of Ideology.* New York: Frederick A. Praeger, 1967, pp. 204-224.

Lunacharsky, A.V., *Revolutionary Silhouettes.* Translated and edited by Michael Glenney, London: Penguin Press, 1969.

Luxemberg, Rosa, *The Russian Revolution.* Ann Arbor: University of Michigan Press, 1965.

MacIntyre, Alasdair, "Trotsky in Exile," *Encounter,* (December, 1963), pp. 73-78.

Malraux, Andre, "Leon Trotsky," in Trotsky, *Writings, 1933-1934.* New York: Pathfinder Press, 1972, pp. 331-338.

Marx, Karl, *The German Ideology.* New York: International Publishers, 1970.

Marx, Karl, *The 18th Brumaire of Louis Bonaparte*. New York: International Publishers, 1969.

Marx, Karl, *Civil War in France*. New York: International Publishers, 1969.

Marx, Karl, *Early Writings*. Edited by T. B. Bottomore, London: G. Allen & Unwin, 1963.

Mavrakis, Kostas, *On Trotskyism: Problems of Theory and History*. Boston: Routledge & Paul, 1976.

Meyer, Alfred G., *Leninism*. London: Oxford University Press, 1957.

Molyneux, John, *Leon Trotsky's Theory of Revolution*. New York: St. Martin's Press, 1981.

Nedava, Joseph, *Trotsky and the Jews*. Philadelphia: Jewish Publication Society of America, 1972.

Nove, Alec, *Political Economy and Soviet Socialism*. London: G. Allen & Unwin, 1979.

Nove, Alec, *Was Stalin Really Necessary?* New York: Frederick A. Preager, 1964.

Olgin, Moissaye, J., *Trotskyism: Counter-Revolution in Disguise*. New York: Workers' Library Publisher, 1935.

Plamenatz, John, "Trotskyism," in Chapt. 12 of his *German Marxism and Russian Communism*. New York: Longmans, Green & Company, 1954.

Preobrazhensky, Evgenii, *The New Economics*. Translated by Brian Pearce, Oxford: Clarendon Press, 1965.

Procacci, Giuliano, "Trotsky's View of the Critical Years 1929-1936," in *Science and Society*. (Winter, 1963), pp. 62-69.

Sanchez Salazar, Leandro A., *Murder in Mexico; The Assassination of Leon Trotsky*. London: Secker & Warburg, 1950.

Schapiro, Leonard. *The Communist Party of the Soviet Union*. New York: Random House, 1971.

Schapiro, Leonard. *The Russian Revolution of 1917: The Origins of Modern Communism*. New York: Basic Books, 1984.

Serge, Victor, *Vie et mort de Trotsky*. Paris: Amiot, Dumont, 1951.

Serge, Victor, *Memoirs of a Revolutionary: 1901-1941*. Translated by Peter Sedgewick, New York: Oxford University Press, 1967.

Shachtman, Max, *The Bureaucratic Revolution: The Rise of the Stalinist State*. New York: Donald Press, 1962.

Shachtman, Max, "The Crisis of the American Party—An Open Letter to Trotsky" and "The USSR and the War," *New International*, (March, 1960).

Shachtman, Max, "1939: Whither Russia?" *Survey*, (April, 1962), pp. 96-108.

Smith, Irving H., ed., *Trotsky*. Englewood Cliffs: Prentice-Hall, 1973.

Souvarine, Boris, *Stalin*. London: Longmans, Green, 1939.

Stalin, Joseph, *Works*. Moscow: Foreign Languages Publishing House, 1953.

Stalin Joseph, *On Opposition*. Peking: Foreign Language Press, 1974.

Tucker, Robert C., *Philosophy and Myth in Karl Marx*. 2d ed., London: Cambridge University Press, 1972.

Tucker, Robert C., *The Soviet Political Mind*. New York: Frederick A. Praeger, 1963.

Tucker, Robert C., *Stalin as Revolutionary 1879-1929: A Study in History and Personality*. New York: W. W. Norton, 1974.

Tucker, Robert C., *Stalinism: Essays in Interpretation.* New York: W. W. Norton, 1977.

Ulam, Adam, *The Bolsheviks.* New York: Collier Books, 1968.

Ulam, Adam, *Russia's Failed Revolutions.* New York: Basic Books, 1981.

Ulam, Adam, *The Unfinished Revolution.* New York: Random House, 1960.

van Heijenoort, Jean, *With Trotsky in Exile: From Prinkipo to Coyoacan.* Cambridge, Massachusetts: Harvard University Press, 1978.

Venkataramani, M.S., "Leon Trotsky's Adventure in American Radical Politics, 1935-1937," *International Review of Social History, Part I, IX,* (1964), pp. 1-46.

Wilson, Edmund, *To the Finland Station.* New York: Harcourt, Brace & Jovanovich, 1971.

Wolfe, Bertram, D., *Three Who Made a Revolution.* New York: Dell Publication Company, 1964.

Wolfenstein, Victor, E., *The Revolutionary Personality: Lenin, Trotsky and Gandhi.* Princeton: Princeton University Press, 1967.

Wyndham, Francis, *Trotsky: A Documentary.* New York: Frederick A. Praeger, 1972.

Ziv, G. A., *Trotsky: Kharakteristika po Lichnym Vospominaniam.* New York: Pioneer Publishers, 1921.

IV. Works by Milovan Djilas

Anatomy of a Moral: The Political Essays of Milovan Djilas. New York: Frederick A. Praeger, 1959.

Borba za socijalizam u Jugoslaviji i peti kongres KPJ. Zagreb, 1948.

Clanci 1941-1946. Belgrade: Kultura, 1947.

Conversations with Stalin. New York: Harcourt, Brace & World, 1962.

Govor u političkom komitetu organizacije ujedinjenih nacija. Zagreb, 1949.

Is Stalin Turning a Circle? New York: National Committee for a Free Europe, 1952.

"Klasa ili kasta," *Svedočanstva.* April, 1950.

Land Without Justice. New York: Harcourt, Brace and World, 1958.

"Lenin on the Relations Between Socialist Countries," *Komunist,* September, 1949.

The Leper and Other Stories. New York: Harcourt, Brace & World, 1964.

Memoir of a Revolutionary. New York: Harcourt, Brace & Jovanovich, 1973.

Montenegro. New York: Harcourt, Brace & World, 1963.

The New Class: An Analysis of the Communist System. New York: Frederick A. Praeger, 1957.

O Današnjim zadacima partije. Belgrade, 1946.

On the New Roads of Socialism. Belgrade, 1950.

Parts of a Lifetime. New York: Harcourt, Brace, Jovanovich, 1972.

Razmišljanja o raznim pitanjim. Zagreb, 1951.

"The Storm in Eastern Europe," *The New Leader.* New York, XXXIV, No. 47, (November 19, 1956), pp. 3-6.

Savremene teme. Belgrade, 1950.
Tito: The Story from Inside. New York: Harcourt, Brace, Jovanovich, 1980.
Tridesetogodišnjica oktobarske revolucije. Zagreb, 1947.
Under the Colors. New York: Harcourt, Brace & World, 1962.
The Unperfect Society: Beyond the New Class. New York: Harcourt, Brace &
World, 1969.
Wartime. New York: Harcourt, Brace, Jovanovich, 1977.

Periodicals and Newspapers

The following newspapers and periodicals were consulted for the research
on Milovan Djilas:

Borba (Belgrade and Zagreb).
Ekonomski Pregled (Zagreb).
Jugoslovenski Istorijski Časopis (Belgrade).
Komunist (Belgrade). Title changed in 1953 to *Nasa Stvarnost.*
Naprijed (Zagreb).
Narodna Država (Belgrade).
Naša Reč (Belgrade).
Nova Misao (Belgrade).
Politika (Belgrade).
Praxis (Zagreb).
Putevi Revolucije (Zagreb).
Službeni List (Belgrade).
Socialist Thought and Practice (Belgrade).
Vjesnik (Zagreb).
Yugoslav Survey (Belgrade).

V. General Works on Djilas and Yugoslavia

Armstrong, Hamilton Fish, *Tito and Goliath.* New York: Macmillan, 1951.
Auty, Phyllis, *Tito, A Biography* Harmondsworth, England: Pelican, 1974.
Auty, Phyllis, *Yugoslavia.* London: Thames & Hudson, 1965.
Banac, Ivo, *The National Question in Yugoslavia.* Ithaca: Cornell University
Press, 1984.
Bass, Robert, ed., *The Soviet-Yugoslav Controversy, 1948- 1958.* New York: Prospect
Books, 1959.
Beneš, Vaclav L., Byrnes, Robert F., and Spulber, Nicholas, eds., *The Second Soviet-
Yugoslav Dispute: Full Text of Main Documents.* Bloomington, Indiana University
Press, 1959.
Bičanić, Rudolf, *Economic Policy in Socialist Yugoslavia.* Cambridge, England: Cam-
bridge University Press, 1973.

Burks, R. V., "Yugoslavia: Has Tito Gone Bourgeois?" *East Europe*, Vol. 14, No. 8 (August, 1965), pp. 2-14.

Bushkoff, Leonard, "Marxism, Communism and the Revolutionary Tradition in the Balkans: 1878-1914: An Analysis and Interpretation," *East European Quarterly*, Vol. I, No. 4 (January, 1968), pp. 371-400.

Campbell, John, *Tito's Separate Road*. New York: Harper & Row, 1967.

Ciliga, Anton, *La Yougoslavie sous la menace interieure et exterieure*. Paris, Plon, 1951.

Clissold, Stephen, *Djilas, the Progress of a Revolutionary*. Middlesex: Maurice Temple Smith, 1983.

Clissold, Stephen, *Whirlwind: An Account of Marshall Tito's Rise to Power*. London: Cresset Press, 1949.

Cripp, R. C., *National Communism—Influence of the Yugoslav Example*. Santa Barbara: University of California Press, 1959.

Dalmas, L., *Le Communisme Youglslavie depuis la rupture avec Moscou*. Paris: Plon, 1950.

Deakin, F. W., *The Embattled Mountain*. London: Oxford University Press, 1971.

Dedijer, Vladimir, *Stalin's Last Battle*. New York: Grosset & Dunlap, 1971.

Dedijer, Vladimir, *Tito*. New York: Simon & Schuster, 1953.

Dedijer, Vladimir, *With Tito through the War*. London: Alexander Hamilton, 1951.

Djordjević, J., *La Yougoslavie, Democratie Socialiste*. Paris: Plon, 1959.

Doder, Duško, *The Yugoslavs*. New York: Random House, 1978.

Drashković, S. M., *Tito, Moscow's Trojan Horse*. Chicago: University of Chicago Press, 1957.

Farrell, R. B., *Yugoslavia and the Soviet Union, 1948-1956: An Analysis with Documents*. Hamden, Connecticut: Shoe String Little Press, 1956.

Fisher, Jack C., *Yugoslavia: A Multinational Empire*. San Francisco: Chandler Publishing, 1960.

Halperin, E., *The Triumphant Heretic: Tito's Struggle against Stalin.* London: Heinemann, 1958.

Hammond, T. T., *Yugoslavia between East and West*. New York: Random House, 1954.

Hoffman, George and Neal F., *Yugoslavia and the New Communism*. New York: Twentieth Century Fund, 1962.

Hoptner, J. B., *Yugoslavia in Crisis, 1934-1941*. New York: Columbia University Press, 1962.

Horvat, Branko, *An Essay on Yugoslav Society*. New York: International Arts & Sciences Press, 1969.

Horvat, Branko, *Towards a Theory of a Planned Market Economy*. White Plains: International Arts & Sciences Press, 1969.

Johnson, Ross A., *The Transformation of Communist Ideology: The Yugoslav Case*. Cambridge, Massachusetts: MIT Press, 1972.

Johnson, Ross A., *Yugoslavia: In the Twilight of Tito*. London: Sage Publications, 1974.

Kennan, George F., *Memoirs, 1925-1950*. Boston: Little, Brown, 1967.

Korbel, Josef, *Tito's Communism*. Denver: University of Denver Press, 1951.

Lendvai, Paul, *Eagles and Cobwebs*. New York: Anchor Books, 1969.

Leonard, Wolfgang, *Three Faces of Marxism; The Political Concepts of Soviet Ideology, Maoism and Humanist Marxism*. Translated by Ewald Osers. New York: Holt, Rinehart & Winston, 1974.

Lukacz, Georg, *History and Class Consciousness: Studies in Marxist Dialectics*. Translated by Rodney Livingstone, London: Oxford University Press, 1974.

Lukacz, Georg, *Marxism and Human Liberation: Essays on History, Culture and Revolution*. New York: Dell Publishing Company, 1973.

Marcuse, Herbert, *One Dimensional Man*. Boston: Little, Brown, 1964.

Marković, Dragan, and Krzanac, Savo, *Liberalizam od Djilasa do danas*. Belgrade: Sloboda, 1978.

Marković, Mihailo, *The Contemporary Marx: Essays on Humanist Communism*. London: Oxford University Press, 1974.

McClellan, Woodford D., *Svetozar Marković and the Origins of Balkan Socialism*. Princeton: Princeton University Press, 1964.

McVicker, Charles P., *Titoism, Pattern for International Communism*. New York: St. Martin's Press, 1957.

Mihajlov, Mihajlo, *An Historic Proposal*. New York: Farrar, Strauss & Giroux, 1966.

Parsons, Howard, *Humanistic Philosophy in Contemporary Poland and Yugoslavia*. New York: The American Institute for Marxist Studies, 1966.

Petrović, Gajo, *Marx in the Mid-Twentieth Century*. New York: Anchor Books, 1967.

Ristić, Dragisa, *Yugoslavia's Revolution of 1941*. Stanford: Hoover Institution Publications, 1966.

Roberts, Henry L., *Eastern Europe: Politics, Revolution and Diplomacy*. New York: Alfred A. Knopf, 1970.

Roberts, Walter, *Tito, Mihailović and the Allies, 1941- 1945*. New Brunswick: Rutgers University Press, 1973.

Royal Institute of International Affair, *The Soviet-Yugoslav Dispute*. London, 1948.

Rothschild, Joseph, *East Central Europe Between the Two Wars*. Seattle: University of Washington Press, 1974.

Rusinow, Dennison, *The Yugoslav Experiment 1948-1974*. Berkeley: University of California Press, 1978.

Schopflin, George, "The Ideology of Croatian Nationalism," *Survey*, Vol. 19, No. 1 (Winter, 1973), pp. 123-146.

Seton-Watson, Hugh, *Eastern Europe Between the Wars*. 3d ed. New York: Harper & Row, 1962.

Seton-Watson, Hugh, *The Eastern European Revolution*. London: Methuen, 1950.

Shils, Edward, "The Intellectuals and the Powers: Some Perspectives for Comparative Analysis," in *On Intellectuals: Theoretical Studies—Case Studies*, pp. 27-52. Edited by Phillip Rieff, New York: Dodd Mead & Company, 1969.

Shoup, Paul, *Communism and the Yugoslav National Question*. New York: Columbia University Press, 1968.

Shoup, Paul, "The National Question in Yugoslavia," *Problems of Communism*,

Vol. XXI, (January-February, 1972), pp. 18-29.

Stojanović, Svetozar, *Between Ideals and Reality.* New York: Oxford University Press, 1973.

Sulzberger, C.L., *Paradise Regained: Memoir of a Rebel..* Praeger Publishers, 1989.

Tomasevich, Jozo, *Peasants, Politics and Economic Change in Yugoslavia.* Stanford: Stanford University Press, 1955.

Tomasevich, Jozo, *The Chetniks.* Stanford: Stanford University Press, 1975.

Ulam, Adam, *Titoism and the Cominform.* Cambridge, Massachusetts: Harvard University Press, 1952.

Vucinich, Wayne, ed., *Contemporary Yugoslavia.* Berkeley: University of California Press, 1969.

White, L., *Balkan Caesar: Tito versus Stalin.* Cambridge, England: Cambridge University Press, 1956.

Wilson, D., *Tito's Yugoslavia.* Cambridge, England: Cambridge University Press, 1980.

Wolff, Robert Lee, *The Balkans in Our Time.* Cambridge, Massachusetts: Harvard University Press, 1956.

Zalar, C., *Yugoslav Communism: A Critical Study.* Washington, D.C.: U.S. Government Printing Office, 1961.

Zaninovich, George M., *The Development of Socialist Yugoslavia.* Baltimore: Johns Hopkins Press, 1968.

Zilliacus, K., *Tito of Yugoslavia.* London: Michael Joseph, 1952.

Zukin, Sharon, *Beyond Marx and Tito.* Cambridge, England: Cambridge University Press, 1975.

Other Yugoslav Sources

Bakarić, Vladimir, *Društvene klase nacija i socializam.* Zagreb, 1976.

Bakarić, Vladimir, *Aktuelni problemi sadašnje etape revolucije.* Zagreb, 1967.

Bilandžić, Dušan, *Historija socijalističke federativne republike Jugoslavije.* Zagreb: Glavni procezi, 1978.

Bilandžić, Dušan, *Ideji i praksa društvenog razvoja Jugoslavije 1945-1973.* Belgrade: Komunist, 1973.

Bilandžić, Dušan, *Borba za samoupravni socijalizam u Jugoslaviji 1945-1959.* Zagreb: Rad, 1969.

Čulinović, Ferdo, *Razvitak narodne vlasti.* Zagreb: Glas rada, 1946.

Čulinović, Ferdo, *Razvitak Jugoslavenskog federalizma.* Zagreb: Skolska knjiga, 1953.

Damjanović, Pero, *Tito pred temama istorije.* Belgrade, 1977.

Dedijer, Vladimir, *The Beloved Land.* London: MacGibbon and Kee, 1961.

Dedijer, Vladimir, *Izgubljena bitka J. V. Staljina.* Sarajevo, 1969.

Dedijer, Vladimir, *Josip Broz Tito, Prilozi za biografiju.* Belgrade, 1953.

Dordević, Toma, *Birokratija i samoupravljenje.* Belgrade, 1966.

Dragomanović, Vladimir, *Obeležja komunističke partije Sovetskog Saveza danas.* Belgrade, 1953.

Društveno upravljenje u Jogoslaviji: Zbornik članka i govora 1950-1960. Zagreb, 1960.

Gersković, Leon, *Dokumenti o razvoj narodne vlasti.* Belgrade: Kultura, 1948.

Gersković, Leon, *Društveno ekonomsko uredenje Jugoslavije.* Belgrade: Kultura, 1958.

Gersković, Leon, *Historija narodne vlasti.* Belgrade: Kultura, 1950-1955.

Horvat, Branko, *Ogled o Jugoslavenskom društvu.* Zagreb: Mladost 1969.

Jelić, Ivan, *Jugoslavenska socijalistička revolucija: 1941-1945.* Zagreb: Skolska kniiga, 1979.

Jelić, Ivan, *Komunistička partija Hrvatske 1937-1945.* Zagreb, 1972.

Kardelj, Edvard, *Borba KPJ za novu Jugoslaviju; Inforacioni referat na savjetovanju komunističkih partija u Poljskog.* Bel-grade, 1948.

Kardelj, Edvard, *Borba za priznanje nezavisnost nove Jugoslavije, 1944-1957.* Belgrade: Radnička štampa, 1980.

Kardelj, Edvard, *The Communist Party of Yugoslavia in the Struggle for New Yugoslavia, for People's Authority and for Socialism* (report to the Fifth CPY Congress). Belgrade, 1948.

Kardelj, Edvard, *Pravci: Razvoja političkog sistema socijalističkog samoupravljanja.* Belgrade: Izdavački centar "Komunist," 1977.

Kardelj, Edvard, *Problemi nase socijalističke izgradnje.* Belgrade, 1960.

Kardelj, Edvard, *Snaga narodnih masa.* Zagreb, 1945.

Kardelj, Edvard, *Socialist Democracy.* Belgrade: Federation of Yugoslav Jurists Associations, 1952.

Kardelj, Edvard, *Speech Held at the General Assembly of the United Nations Organization.* (September 19, 1948), Belgrade, 1948.

Kidrić, Boris, *O novom finansiskim i planskom sistemu.* Belgrade, 1951.

Kidrić, Boris, *Privredni problemi FNRJ.* Zagreb, 1948.

Law on the Five Year Plan for the Development of the National Economy of the Federal People's Republic of Yugoslavia in the Period from 1947-1951; With Speeches from Josip Broz Tito, Andrija Hebrang, Boris Kidrić. Belgrade, 1947.

Lukić, Radomir, *Teorija države i prava.* Belgrade: Savremena administracija, 1976.

Micunović, Veljko, *Moscow Diary.* Translated by David Floyd. New York: Doubleday & Company, 1980.

Milatinović, Mile, *Slucaj Andrije Hebranga.* Belgrade: Prosveta, 1952.

Morača, Pero, ed., *Pregled posleratnog razvitka Jugoslavije 1945-1965.* Belgrade: Zavod za izdavanje udžbenika socijalističke republike Srbije, 1966.

Narodna skupština FNRJ. Stenografske beleške, 1941-1954. Belgrade, 1952.

Nedeljković, Dušan, *Naša filosofija u borbi za socijalizam.* Belgrade, 1952.

O kontrarevolucionarnoj i klevetničkoj kampanji protiv socijalističke Jugoslavije. Two vol., Belgrade, 1950.

O neistinim i nepravednim optužbama protiv naše partije i naše zemlje. Belgrade, 1948.

Pašić, Najdan, *Savremena država.* Belgrade: Bigz, 1976.

Pijade, Moša, *About the Legend that the Yugoslav Uprising Owed Its Existence to Soviet Assistance.* London, 1950.

Pijade, Moša, *Izabrani govori i clanci, 1941-1947.* Zagreb, 1950.

Ranković, Aleksandar, *Izabrani govori i članci, 1941-1945.* Zagreb, 1951.

Savez komunista Jugoslavije, odluke v kongresa komunističke partije Jugoslavije. Zagreb, 1948.

Savez komunista Jugoslavije, program i statut komunističke partije Jugoslavije. Belgrade, 1948.

Savez komunista Jugoslavije, Centralni komitet. *Istorijski arbiv komunistic kkke partije Jugoslavije.* Belgrade, 1949-1952.

Stojanović, V., ed., *Birokratija i tehnologija.* Belgrade: Sedma sila, 1966.

Tito, Josip Broz, *Dela.* Belgrade, 1947.

Tito, Josip Broz, *Govori i članci.* Zagreb, Belgrade, 1960.

Tudjman, Franjo, *Okupacija i revolucija.* Zagreb: Institut za historiju radničkog pokreta, 1963.

Vranicki, Predrag, *Historija marksizma.* Zagreb, 1961.

Vukmanović-Tempo, Svetozar, *Revolucija koja tece, memoari.* Two vol., Belgrade, 1971.

Zbornik dokumenata i podataka o narodno-oslobodilačkem ratu Jugoslovenskih naroda. Belgrade: Prosveta, 1949-1965.

Ziherl, Boris, *Članci i razprave.* Belgrade: Kultura, 1948.

Index

About the Author

Michael M. Lustig received his B.A. in History and Political Science at York University (Canada) and M.A. and Ph.D. in Soviet and Eastern European studies at Brown University. He teaches at Boston University and is a fellow at the Russian Research Center, Harvard University.